Perfect Gentleman

Volume II

The Life and Letters of George Washington Custis Lee

Bernice-Marie Yates

xulon
PRESS

Table of Contents

George Washington Custis Lee, 1867
Private Collection

Chapter One

In His Father's Footsteps

*A*s the Lee family started to reunite in Richmond after the tragic events of the past four years, it was abundantly clear that Arlington was most likely lost forever and their rented home in Richmond would not remain acceptable as their permanent residence.

Several weeks following the surrender, General Lee's activities were limited to those of leisure. Typically, he would sit alone in quiet contemplation in the back parlor, take naps or gaze out onto the small enclosed garden at the rear of Mr. John Stewart's house on Franklin Street. Frequently in the evenings, he would take walks with one of his children and visit with friends. His conversation revolved around establishing a quite life in the country, perhaps to purchase a farm. Yet, inasmuch as Generals Robert E. Lee and George Washington Custis Lee retained the status of Prisoners of War their immediate situation required them to remain in Richmond until the circumstance was resolved well enough for the family to depart the city.

Finally, in June a letter arrived offering the use of a small four-room cottage owned by Mrs. Elizabeth Randolph Preston Cocke, a distant relative to Robert E. Lee. Although Mrs. Cocke and General Lee were related from the Robert "King" Carter line of descendants, they were not acquainted. Nevertheless, their attachment was deep. Mrs. Cocke had four sons who served the Confederacy. Her son, Lieutenant William Cocke was assigned to the 18th Virginia under General George Pickett. On the third day in Gettysburg at the "Bloody Angle," Lieutenant Cocke met his destiny. The reality of his fate was too much for Mrs. Cocke to accept. She hoped in vain that he was among the prisoners. As fate would have it, his remains were place in an unmarked mass Confederate grave in Gettysburg. Without a doubt, her gesture to the Lee family was a great magnanimous gift, a breathe of spring air for the entire Lee family but most especially for General Lee himself. On behalf of his family, R. E. Lee accepted Mrs. Cocke's invitation.

However, before they could leave the city, General Lee and Custis needed to inform the proper officials that they were planning to vacate the city permanently. General Lee wrote the following note to Lieutenant Colonel Albert Ordway, Provost Marshall, Department of Virginia on June 21, 1865:

Colonel: I propose establishing my family next week in Cumberland County, Virginia near Cartersville, on the James River canal. On announcing my intention to General Patrick, when he was on duty in Richmond, he stated that no passport for the purpose was necessary. Should there have been any change in the orders of the Department rendering passports necessary, I request that I may be furnished with them. My son, G. W. Custis Lee, a paroled prisoner with myself, will accompany me. Very respectfully your obedient servant.[1]

Shortly after the note was sent and word received of its approval, Custis mounted Traveller and rode ahead to prepare for his family's arrival. On June 28th, General and Mrs. Lee along with daughters Mildred and Agnes, boarded a packet-boat at sunset and started their journey up the James River then along the Kanawha Canal. They arrived near the Pemberton landing at dawn the following morning. Here they were greeted by Custis and Edmund Cocke, a veteran of the Army of Northern Virginia. From this point they traversed to Cartersville and then finally to "Oakland," the Cocke family plantation located about two miles from the stoic structure they were to reside at for the next several months. The Lees enjoyed their week-long visit at Oakland with the exception of Custis, who became ill with a reoccurring bout of dysentery. He remained at the plantation until the attack subsided.

But R. E. Lee was anxious to move into their temporary residence. The structure was a simple design not uncommon to the area and popularized by the tobacco growing gentry. The building was constructed by Thomas C. Brown in 1841 on 442 acres of a successful farm. Brown named the house and property "Cottage Hill." In early October, 1859, Thomas L. P. Cocke purchased the estate. Upon the suggestion of his mother, the romantic and poetic name of "Derwent" was given to the acreage.[2]

In his book *Derwent: Robert E. Lee's Sanctuary*, Joseph H. Crute, Jr provides a description of the interior of the structure as well as the use of each room.

It was a two story frame house of four rooms over an English basement with a gabled roof between well-proportioned chimneys and a shed-like room off the first floor. Mrs. Cocke had provided furniture from Oakland to make it as pleasant and comfortable as possible. From a small front porch with four slender columns, the Lees entered the front door, of "Cross and Bible" style, into a central hall that extended to the rear of the house. The flooring throughout the house is of six-inch rift pine, the woodwork in the four main rooms and upper hall is identical with that of the main hall. On the left of the front door stood the staircase with a utilitarian balustrade. The room on the left caught the eye of General and Mrs. Lee, as it contained a pent closet having the unusual feature of ornamental doors. The framing of this closet was especially noticeable because of its lines of fluting and the carvings at the top and bottom between the lines. This room became their "family room," it served as the bedroom of General and Mrs. Lee (suffering from arthritis, Mrs. Lee could not negotiate steps), Agnes and Mildred often visited their mother here, and the General used the closet shelves for his books, letters and valuable papers. It was probably in this room that Lee wrote many of his letters.

The room on the right of the hall was the parlor. It has one door that opens to a side porch and another to the she-like room. Under the main stairway in the hall is a flight of steps to the basement dining room. This room has a large closet that kept the glass and chinaware; the ceiling is of exposed timbers; and there is a door to the back yard where a path led to the detached kitchen. Opposite the dining room, a battened door opens into a storeroom. Upstairs the two rooms, excluding a small trunk room, were the bedrooms of Custis and the two girls. All the main rooms have windows on the north and the south, giving cross ventilation, and all have fireplaces.[3]

There were two other structures on the property, a barn which housed Traveller and an unused farm office.

Shortly after the Lees were settled into Derwent, R. E. Lee wrote to his son, Rob, about the residence and his uncertain state of affairs as a prisoner of war status:

> I enclose a letter from Mr. Spillman in reference to Romancoke. The only way in which I know a little con be given to the place is by a deed signed by me as Executor of your Grandfather's will & by yourself as Legator. But the estate is still encumbered by the Conditions of the Will. As soon as the Courts are in operation & I am restored to civil right (if I shall be), I desire to settle up the Estate & deliver over all the property to the owners—They can then dispose of it as they think proper. I have informed Mr. S. his letter was referred to you. We are all well, and established in a comfortable but small house, in a grove of oaks, belonging to Mr. Thomas Cocke. It contains four rooms, and there is a house in the yard which when fitted up will give us another. Only your mother, Agnes and Mildred are with me. Custis, who has had a return of his attack of dysentery is at Mrs. Cocke's house, about two miles off—is convalescent, I hope. I have been nowhere as yet. The weather has been excessively hot, but this morning there is an agreeable change, with some rain. The country here is poor but healthy, and we are at a long distance from you all. I can do nothing until I learn what decision in my case is made in Washington. All unite with me in much love.[4]

Although the Lee family had taken refuge at Derwent far from
the harried life in Richmond, both father and son now needed to
obtain gainful employment to support the family. Notwithstanding
Custis' current health problems which delayed him joining the
family at Derwent, he wrote from Oakland on July 11th to General
Francis H. Smith in reference to a teaching position at the Virginia
Military Institute:

> My Father, Genl. Lee, informs me that you have
> kindly offered to apply for my appointment as Professor
> or instructor at the Military Institute, if I will accept the
> position.
> I will be very glad to accept any position at the Va.
> Mil. Institute for which I am qualified; but think it proper
> to state that I am among those <u>excepted</u> by President
> Johnson in his "Amnesty Proclamation," [this proclama-
> tion granted former Confederates in the army holding the
> rank of Colonel or lower and men in the Confederate navy
> with a rank of lieutenant or lower the opportunity to apply
> for a pardon. Thousands were grant these pardons.] and
> can not, of course, say what action will be taken in my
> case and that of others in the same class, excluded from
> the general "Amnesty and Pardon." I expect to remain near
> Cartersville for a month or two, and any communication
> left for me there, or with Mr. James H. Cocke, corner of
> Clay and 11th Sts., Richmond, Va. will reach me.[5]

Though improved, Custis lingered at Oakland a little longer. On
July 22, General Lee wrote to his youngest son, Rob, "Custis, I am
told is better. He is still at Mrs. Cocke's—."[6] Custis arrived at
Derwent shortly thereafter.

Still dubious about the treason indictment pending against
Generals Robert E. Lee, G. W. C. Lee and other high ranking military officers, as well as Jefferson Davis, the Honorable Revered
Johnson offered his professional services to Lee when his case
became relevant. Fortunately, General U. S. Grant insisted that the
federal government honor the paroles he issued to the officers and

soldiers of the Army of Northern Virginia. Therefore, no further action against these men should have been warranted. In part, Grant's letter to Lee specifically addressed his situation:

...In my opinion the officers and men paroled at Appomattox Court House, and since, upon the same terms given to Lee, cannot be tried for treason so long as they observe the terms of their parole. This is my understanding...I will state further that the terms granted by me met with the hearty approval of the President at the time, and of the country generally. The action of Judge Underwood, in Norfolk, has already had an injurious effect, and I would ask that he be ordered to quash all indictments found against paroled prisoners of war, and to desist form further prosecution of them. This opinion, I am informed, is substantially the same as that entertained by the Government. I have forwarded your application for amnesty and pardon to the President with the following endorsement thereon:

Respectfully forwarded through the Secretary of War to the President, with the earnest recommendation that this application of Gen. R. E. Lee for amnesty and pardon may be granted him. The oath of allegiance required by recent order of the President to accompany applications does not accompany this for the reason, as I am informed by General Ord, the order requiring it had not reached Richmond when this was forwarded.[7]

General Lee replied to Mr. Johnson's proposal in a letter dated July 27, 1865:

I very much regret that I did not see you on your recent visit to Richmond, that I might have thanked you for the interest you have shown in my behalf, and your great kindness in offering me your professional services in the indictment which I now understand is pending against me. I am very glad, however, that you had an opportunity of reading a copy of General Grant's letter of the 20th inst. to me, which I left with Mr. MacFarland for that purpose, and also that he might show it to other officers on the Army of Northern Virginia in my condition. I did not wish to give it greater publicity without the assent of General Grant, supposing that, if he desired it made public, he would take steps to have it done. Should he consent to your request to have it published, I, of course, have no objection. But should he not, I request that you only use it in the manner I have above indicated. Again offering you my warmest thanks for you sympathy and consideration for my welfare, I am, with great respect, Your obedient servant.[8]

Thanks to Grant's letter, the indictment against Lee was completely quelled, yet he would die "a prisoner of war on parole." President Andrew Johnson never acknowledged his application for amnesty. His American citizenship was not restored until July 22, 1975 by President Gerald R. Ford. The Senate Joint Resolution 23 was signed into law by President Ford at Arlington House on August 5, 1975. Within his remarks, he said "I am very pleased to sign Senate Joint Resolution 23, restoring posthumously the long overdue, full rights of citizenship to General Robert E. Lee. This legislation corrects a 110-year oversight of American history. It is significant that it is signed at this place."[9]

Custis finally arrived at Derwent prior to the end of July. Moreover, his prisoner of war status was still dubious. Yet like his father, he wished to start a new life and be of "service to my home state of Virginia." On August 18th from Derwent he wrote to General Smith of the Virginia Military Institute:

I have just recd. from Belmead your note of the 14th inst. for which and your other kindnesses, believe me to be truly grateful.

I am very sorry that I did not meet you at Belmead during your last visit there, as you requested: but I was away from home when your note arrived, and only got there after dinner of the day you left Belmead for the North. I set out for Belmead that same evening; but, as you know, arrived too late to meet you. I did not understand that you would leave Belmead so soon or I would have been there earlier.

As I have said before, I will gladly accept any position at the Va. Mil. Inst. for which I am qualified, if the U.S. authorities will permit me so to do: but what action, if any, they intend to take against me and others in my condition I cannot say. As they will not be able to make anything out of me in the shape of money or property, they may not think it worth their while to trouble me.

As to my capabilities as an instructor, I believe I am best prepared to teach:

> Civil & Mil. Engineering
> Pure Mathematics
> Nat. Philosophy

in the order in which I mentioned them. I have also a pretty good elementary knowledge of the other branches usually taught in this country.

If my appointment to the Institute will cause any trouble, I, of course, would not wish to be recommended for the position. With best wishes for the success of the Institution of which you have been so long the head, and for the well being of yourself and family, I remain very respectfully and truly,

G. W. C. Lee

P. S. From what I know, and have heard, I believe Alfred Rives has the best education on the subject of Engineering of any man of his age in the State. He has also had a large share of practical experience.[10]

Custis anxiously awaited a reply from V.M.I. as to the teaching position. Yet in the meantime, he tried to have a normal life. His father wrote to Robert Jr., "Custis is paying a visit to his friend, Captain Watkins, in Powhatten. He came up for him last Saturday, and bore him off. He has got quite well now, and I hope will continue so."[11]

In early August General Lee received a visit from Judge John W. Brockenbrough, the rector of Washington College in Lexington, Virginia. To Lee's astonishment Brockenbrough was sent by the Board of Trustee of the educational facility to offer him the post of president of the college. Lee was reluctant about taking the position for several reasons. He said, "The proper education of youth requires not only great ability, but I fear more strength that I now possess, for I do not feel able to undergo the labor of conducting classes in regular courses of instruction. I could not, therefore, undertake more than general administration and supervision of the institution." [12] The Board of Trustees carefully considered Lee's letter and they were quite willing to acquiesce to his terms. Lee's letter of acceptance was addressed to Judge Brockenbrough, "I received yesterday your letter of the 31st cult. transmitting certain resolutions of the Board of Trustees of Washington College, passed at their meeting that day; and will, if not prevented, attend the session of the Board called on the 20th inst., and enter upon the duties of the Presidency of the institution in compliance with the wishes of the Board."[13] Lee's qualifying statement, "...if not prevented" relates to his prisoner of war status. He alluded to this situation as one of the conditions for refusing the post in his original letter to Brockenbrough, "Being excluded from the terms of amnesty in the proclamation of the President of the U.S. of the 29th May last, and an object of censure to a portion of the Country, I have thought if probable that my occupation of the position of President might draw upon the College a feeling of hostility; and I should, therefore, cause injury to an Institution which it would be my highest desire to advance."[14]

Accepting the position as President of Washington College was welcomed relief for General Lee. He and his family finally had a place to settle down and renew their lives in the quiet of a small town. The only question remaining was, were would Custis settle?

Unfortunately by mid-August, Custis' health wavered once more, perhaps due to the anxiety over his uncertain future. He thought about possibly settling in Mexico but he "could not bear the idea of leaving the Old State."[15] Finally, he decided to stay in Virginia after his appointment to the Virginia Military Institute was confirmed at the end of the summer. During the several weeks of the interim period, the Superintendent of V. M. I. Francis H. Smith had corresponded with Scott Shipp about the appointments and activities proposed for the Institute:

...I have been hard at work since my return getting my plans arranged. I shall make recitation rooms of the Hospital & cabins erected—covert the gas house into chemical laboratory & Drawing Academy & can readily get board &c. in Lexington for cadets. Gen. Custis Lee has consented to serve as Prof. of N. & Ex. Phil & Col. Gilham leaves for New York next week to lay in a full stock of chemicals & c. We are resolved to give efficiency to this Dept. Hardin has been here, but has not yet determined to put in his fortune with us. I vexed him a little by telling him he was anxious to join in, but was coquetting like some of our spring belles. I am daily receiving letters from old cadets & am encouraged.

Still I am alive to greatness of the work before us, & if we will only all labor as we can, success will be earned. Col. Preston, Massive & Gilham are cordially enlisted.

The greatest piece of news is, that W. College has prevailed upon Gen. R. E. Lee to take the Pres. of the College. This he does because he has no other present means of support & he accepts upon condition that he shall not teach. As an honorary appt. it is all well—is a good stroke of the College, may do it substantial bene-fit—& will certainly liberalize it. This makes it the more necessary that our work be one of vigor—while I will say to you that high is my admiration of the father as a General & gentleman—the son is the better man for the Professorship. I am determined to give the go-by for the present to the question of uniform & drills &c. until the military are withdrawn from the state. I want to have no collision with them. I will preserve the military organiza-tion & be ready to take up arms when civil liberty is restored. I send one of my printed copies of the appeal.

Do bring with you a large pile of Green backs to_____the work. Do what you can in Missouri to get funds & to give currency to our work. My wife and family join me in kind regards. Colstons house can be had for 6000 in gold. My advice to you is to build; buy a lot for the purpose.[16]

As revealed in General Smith's letter, he was happy that Custis agreed to join the faculty and that R. E. Lee would bring a breath of new life to Washington College. Yet with all of his grand plans and determination to rebuild the Institute, the practical aspect of housing students and staff was a dilemma. Housing was at a premium in Lexington and the Lees would have another temporary residency problem after their departure from Derwent.

During the war most of the buildings at the Institute were destroyed with the exception of the superintendent's house and the porter's lodge. It was decided that Custis would have a room in the superintendent's house. "The rooms of the superintendent's house, so far as they could be spared, were used for recitation rooms, and two of the professors, General Lee [Professor of Civil and Military Engineering and Applied Mechanics] and Colonel Shipp, [Commandant of Cadets, and Instructor of Infantry, Cavalry and Artillery Tactics, and Professor of Military History and Strategy] were quartered, the one in the Treasurer's office, and the other in the Superintendent's office, while their classes were taught in these rooms."[17]

The beginning of September found Custis still ailing with his reoccurring bouts of dysentery, as his father mentions in a letter to his nephew, Fitz Lee: "We are are all here as usual. Agnes has recovered from her attack, though still thin and feeble. Custis is with us but not well and your Aunt about as you last saw her...I have had a comparative quiet summer, but will have to commence soon to make my bread."[18]

On September 15 the Lees set out from Derwent permanently. Robert E. Lee departed for Lexington while the other members of the family including Custis removed to Oakland once again. General Lee's journey took four days. He traveled alone in the hot, humid late summer weather. He stopped the first night at Bremo, the family home of Dr. and Mrs. Cocke located in Fluvanna County.

The design of the Bremo estate was strongly influenced by Thomas Jefferson's neoclassical preferences. Jefferson, a close friend of the original owner suggested ideas which were incorporated into the structure but the overall design was dominated by the owner's personality. The entrance portico was similar to that at Monticello but the grand pillars were Tuscan opposed to the elegant Doric columns of Monticello. This minor alteration was imposed to satisfy the stoic taste of the original owner, General John Hartwell Cocke of Revolutionary War fame. The sight of this grand domicile must have reminded Lee of the loss of Arlington, along with the knowledge that their lives would never return to a more refined era.

The next day Lee moved onto Reverend Philip Slaughter's Stony Point home. By mid-afternoon on the third day, Lee had arrived at an old inn named Mountain House near Rockfish Gap. The next morning astride Traveller, he continued on his way through Waynesboro and Greenville finally reaching Lexington by midafternoon on September 18.[19] General Lee immediately obtained a room at the local hotel. This room would remain as his home until suitable housing on the campus was available for the entire family.

Custis tarried at Oakland until the second week in October. However, he did communicate with General Francis H. Smith on October 2nd:

> I have rec'd your favor of the 21st ult., accompanying the official notification of my appointment to the chair of Engr. at the Va. Mil. Institute. I have also rec'd your letter of the 6th ult. with the accompanying pamphlets— "Special Report of the Supt. of the VMI on Scientific Education in Europe," and "Report of the Board of Visitors of the VMI," for which and your continued kindness to myself, please accept again my grateful thanks.
>
> I am very sorry that I did not get your letter in time to meet you in Lynchburg as you desired, but I hope to be in Lexington this week, which I hope will give time for what is necessary, as I see by the newspapers, that the Institute

does not commence its exercises until the 16th inst.

I did not mean to say in my note to you that I was unwilling to teach Nat. & Ex. Phil., but that I thought I was better qualified to teach other courses. I graduated No. 1 at West Point in Nat. Phil., but having paid little attention to it since that time, I thought I might be somewhat behind hand. I am willing to undertake any branch that you think I am capable of teaching, and if I do not equal the expectations formed of my ability, I can of course resign and make way for some one better suited for the position. I have given more attention to Mil. Engr. and have had more experience in it that in any other branch. The question of salary is of no consequence, so that I can live, as I have lost everything by the war. My chief desire is to be useful and so something for my native state.

I write in great haste to catch an opportunity, and will give you my views more fully when I see you. Again thanking you for your kindness to me, I am most respectfully yes. truly [20]

The next day R. E. Lee wrote to Mrs. Lee from Lexington:

...General Smith informs me that the Mil. Institute will commence its exercises on the 16th, Inst. & that Custis was unanimously elected to chair the Civil Engr. Dep.— I am living at the Lexington Hotel & he must come there, if he comes up...All inquire kindly after you & hope you will be comfortable. Give much love to Custis & the girls & kind remembrances to all at Oakland.[21]

Custis arrived promptly at Lexington and joined his father at the hotel. The day before Custis began his tenure at the Virginia Military Institute, his father took the opportunity to write to Mrs. Lee about the various activities and arrangements in town, "...The exercises of the VMI Institute commence on Monday (tomorrow) but few cadets have yet reached here. Custis is very well & quiet." At the conclusion of his letter which was completed on the 11th, he remarked that neither he or Custis could accompany friends to the Natural Bridge [of Virginia] and that "Custis & I will be left alone."[22]

On October 16th Custis formally accepted his position as Professor of Military and Civil Engineering and Applied Mechanics, in compliance with General Francis H. Smith's letter of September 21, 1865. His duties under this position were outlined in the Annual Report of Superintendent, June, 1866:

> Instruction has been given to the first class, by daily recitations of one and a half hours, in civil and military engineering, with problems in stone cutting. Facilities for the usual illustrations have been wanting, by the destruction of our models and library. These we hope to replace, from time to time. In addition to these duties, General Lee has had the exclusive charge of the first and second classes in chemistry during the absence of the professor.[23]

A few days after accepting the professorship at the Virginia Military Institute, he wrote to his friend, Alfred Landon Rives in Albemarle County seeking his advice and opinion on the course of study and textbooks he should utilize under his tutelage:

> As you may have heard, possibly, I have been appointed Professor of Civil and Mil. Eng. at the Va. Mil. Institute, and being desirous, as well to be usefully employed, as to earn my bread, I have accepted the position, tho' with much diffidence as to my ability to properly to perform the duties of Prof. My reading has been mainly directed to Mil.
>
> Engineering, tho' I have had some little experience and knowledge in the civil branch of the science. I think that more attention should be paid at this school to civil that to Mil. Engineering, and I would be very glad to have your advice as to the proper course to be carried out here in both branches. I have thought that it might be well to carry the class through Mekam's *Field Fortification and Permanent Works* (they are the best textbooks on the subject the I know of) without taking up too much time with either,

leaving as much time as possible to civil Engineering—For the want of better, I had proposed to commence with Mahan's civil Engr. [a United States Military Academy textbook written by Professor Dennis Hart Mahan, Custis' former professor at the Academy, West Point, New York] to give a general idea of the principal subjects, tho' I would be glad to substitute for any of the books mentioned better ones if you can suggest them. It is of course desirable to have English textbooks, or rather textbooks in English, if they can be procured, as I do not think that the young men I have are very familiar with French, tho' I suppose they could make out with the French if I read their course to them every day. Most if not all of the books with which I am familiar are so voluminous that they can not well be used in an elementary course such as must be taught here, and they usually relate to only one subject. I am anxious to obtain a good work on railroad engineering, as this branch will be the one most often followed as a profession by the young men of the State.

Please give me your ideas on the subject in general and as much in detail as your time and inclination will permit. Any information, advice &c. will be most thankfully rec'd. Have you any of the *Permanent Fortifications* that you had printed during the War? Where can they be obtained? I wish for the interests of the State you could have been induced to accept this position instead of myself. But so long as I am here, I must do my best; and I will always be ready to resign in favor of yourself or other more competent person.

I do not think the prospects for the Institute are particularly bright at present, alto' Genl. Smith and the others of the old faculty seem to be very hopeful. We must try to deserve success, at any rate, and then if we fail, we will not have ourselves to blame. What has become of our friend Genl. St. John? What do you propose for yourself in future, provided the "Best Govt. in the world" will let you do anything? [24]

*George Washington
Custis Lee, 1865
Private Collection*

*Faculty of the Virginia Military Institute,
1865 1. Francis H. Smith, 9. Scott Shipp,
11. W. B. Blair, 14. G. W. C. Lee
Virginia Military Institute Archives*

*George Washington
Custis Lee, 1867
Private Collection*

*George Washington
Custis Lee, 1868
Virginia Military
Institute Archives*

Lee Chapel on the campus of Washington and
Lee University, Lexington, Virginia
Photograph by Author

Rives responded to Custis' letter with advice and suggestions but he did not accept the offer of the teaching position Custis had procured at VMI.

Both father and son were settling into their new academic positions by the end of October. In a letter written to Mrs. Lee who was still at Oakland, the General reported on Custis and their various activities, "Custis has a bad cold, but is otherwise well. He has a room now at the Institute but takes his meals at the Hotel with me. We rode down last Saturday to the Natural Bridge together & enjoyed the Scene very much. The scenery along our whole ride was beautiful & there is grandeur as well as beauty in the scenery at the bridge. One of its great beauties is the entire absence of all work of man."[25] Only two days later Lee wrote to his youngest daughter, Mildred, "Your brother too is wild for want of admonition. Col. Blair is now his "fidus Achatis," [Faithful Refuge] as he is almost as grey as your Papa, & wears the Same uniform, all grey he is sometimes taken for him by the young girls, who consider your brother the most attentive of sons, & giving good promise of making a desirable husband. He will find himself married some of these days before he knows it. You had better be near him."[26]

By early November Mrs. Lee, Agnes, Mildred and Rob had relocated at Bremo. General Lee wrote to his wife about the conditions of the President's House at Washington College, "The whole week has been unfavorable for work, yet still some progress has been made in the repairs. I have had the plasters freshening the walls & I hope this week they will finish. Then the painters, then the servers & then if the furniture arrives we shall soon be ready...Custis & I am as usual, grave & melancholy, we sympathize with each other in silence."[27]

Once Mrs. Lee was settled in at Bremo, Agnes took her leave and departed for Richmond to participate in the wedding of Sally Magee Warwick. Seeking her father's approval to attend the ceremony, Agnes sought his advice. From Lexington, he replied to her letter in a tongue in cheek manner:

> It is very hard for you to apply to me to advise you to go away from me...But in order to help you to make up your mind, if it will promote your pleasure and Sally's happiness, I will say go. You may inform Sally from me however, that no preparations are necessary, and if they were no one could help her. She has just got to wade through it as if it was an attack of measles or anything else—naturally. As she would not marry Custis, she may marry whom she chooses. I shall wish her every happiness, just the same, for she knows nobody loves her as much as I do. I do not think, upon reflections, she will consider it right to refuse my son and take away my daughter. She need not tell me whom she is going to marry. I suppose it is some cross old widower, with a dozen children. She will not be satisfied at her sacrifice with less, and I should think that would be cross sufficient.[28]

General Lee's fun-loving letter was actually not based in reality, since Agnes arrived in Lexington shortly after Sally's wedding and Custis was long over the fictitious disappointment of a jilted suitor. Nevertheless, R. E. Lee took pleasure in mildly teasing his children.

He also encourages Agnes to entreat her mother to come to Lexington where she could reside with him at the hotel, "She can come to the hotel where I am, and stay until the house is ready. There is no difficulty in that, and she can be very comfortable. My rooms are up on the 3rd floor and her meals can be sent to her."[29] Mrs. Lee finally arrived in Lexington on December 2, 1865 with Mildred, Agnes and Captain Rob. Shortly thereafter the family settled into the newly renovated President's House at Washington College.

Even before General Lee departed from Derwent, he was contemplating writing a book on the campaigns of the Army of Northern Virginia as a commendation to the officers and men of the army. Prior to the activities surrounding the entire Lee family's arrival in Lexington, Custis wrote to William Washington, a former professor of painting and drawing at the Virginia Military Institute, then located in Washington, D.C. with reference to this proposed manuscript:

> I am very glad to have your note of the 23rd inst., which is the first intelligence I have had of you since I last saw you. My father desires me to send his best thanks for the interest taken in his behalf by yourself and Mr. Shillington, and say that he will not forget the kind advice and offer, if he shall be able to prepare the book to which you refer.
>
> He is very desirous of writing the history of the Campaigns of the Army of N. Va., as a tribute to the valor and devotion of its officers and men, and is collecting information, which may be made use of by others, if not by himself. As yet, he has not written a line, and I can not say when he will be able to commence.
>
> I trust you are doing well in Washington, and that you are as comfortable in mind as the times will admit of; and with our best wishes for you, I am [30]

As fate would have it the proposed manuscript never materialized into a book, although General Lee continued to collect data for that purpose. It is equally unfortunate that Custis never pursued this project after his father's demise or in fact wrote his own memoirs.

Reprising the theme he established in an earlier letter to Agnes, R. E. Lee once again takes to teasing her by writing, "My Worrying Little Agnes." He continues to playfully criticize about the loss of

Miss Sally as a daughter-in-law, "Sally is going to marry a widower. I think I ought to know, as she refused my son, and I do not wish to know his name. I wonder if she knows how many children he has." Then, in a vain attempt to make it appear as if Custis still cared for Miss Warwick, he writes "Custis is promenading the floor..." Finally, he closes by stating, "I miss you very much and hope this is the last wedding you will attend."[31]

After the wedding transpired, Agnes traveled to Norfolk to visit friends. In a letter to her written in late January, Lee was still seeking sympathy by stating, "Mildred is active and cheerful and Custis and I as silent as our wont." [32] Agnes finally arrived in Lexington in the spring of 1866.

At this point Custis was in the process of obtaining the best textbooks and other data he could pertaining to the curriculum he was teaching at V. M. I. He had received a letter from Colonel Alfred Landon Rives suggesting a number of books which might be useful. Now, Custis was taking his time in replying to Rives' letter.

> Your very kind and acceptable letter, in answer to mine on the subject of engineering in general, was received a long time ago; but may things have concurred to prevent my writing in reply, or rather continuation of the subject; among the principal of which was the desire to avoid troubling you about my affairs, at least until I had made every effort to procure the works you mentioned.
>
> I found that the habit here was to commence the course of engineering with the military branch of the science; and as I am more familiar with the part of the subject than the other and found that I had preserved some few valuable works in relation to it and was tolerably conversant with the general results arrived at in our late struggle, I got along quite well. I trust, in that part of the course. Finding too that my notions in regard to it correspond with yours, I went on with more confidence in the work.
>
> Now I am on the course of civil engineering and alto' I have had some five or six years practical experience in certain branches of the general art, and have read a

moderate amount in relation to it, I feel the want of a more extended knowledge, and intend adding to my library, and to my information, too. I hope, as means and opportunity [the remainder of the letter is missing] [33]

Not long after the Lee family permanently settled in Lexington, General Lee was daily besieged with massive correspondence from many people for a variety of reasons. Along with the duties of developing an engineering curriculum, Custis served as his father's personal secretary and frequently wrote responses to these letters as his father dictated the responses. One such letter he received was from Captain William Parker Snow of Nyack, New York. Snow's request of General Lee was to review a manuscript he wrote entitled *Biographical Sketches of Southern Generals* for any additions or corrections. Custis wrote the reply for his father:

I have received your letter of the 3rd inst.; and thank you for the friendly sentiments you express. I have only been able to give your "Biographical Sketches of Southern Generals" a hasty perusal, and can now reference them to the general impression left upon my mind at the time, than to any particular facts. I thought upon the whole, they were generally truthful; and where I discovered errors, that they were due to the difficulty of attaining the truth under the circumstances by which you were surrounded; and which could hereafter, if thought desirable, be readily corrected. I cordially concur in your wish that peace my be restored to the country, and hope it may be established on such a basis as to give permanent satisfaction to the people. Wishing you all health and prosperity, I am with great respect yr. Obd. sev.[34]

The winter quickly became spring. R. E. Lee was happy to report that "Custis & Fitzhugh are both here & so are Agnes and Mildred." Rob was away at Pamunkey and he did not mention the whereabouts of his daughter, Mary. [35] He seemed happy in his situation. A few days later in a letter to Rob he states that "We are only tolerable well. Agnes is pretty sick and Custis is under the weather."[36]

Custis continued to communicate with Alfred Landon Rives on engineering matters:

> I have just rec'd your note of the 29th ult. and write to beg you not to trouble yourself about the notes in regard to *Mercy's Method of Arches*. I can well understand how you have not the time to devote to such matters, and it was entirely on the supposition that the subject was already prepared, that I allowed myself to ask for it.
>
> I can do very well without the notes you have kindly set to work upon, for this season; and by the next, expect to have a good collection of books, from which I can get all that is requisite.
>
> If you should ever take up the subject of arches in the course of your engineering operations, I will be glad to have your conclusions on that as well as other subjects; always provided that you will not be bothered in the sending then to me. So please do not trouble yourself with the subject now.
>
> I am sorry that your "rewards" begin to slacken; but hope that it is only the calm before the heavy shower of greenbacks.
>
> I am very much obliged to you for the book you propose sending, and will accept it with pleasure.
>
> I should like very much to accept your invitation, this summer; but can hardly now say what is to become of me. I suppose it is hardly possible to induce you to turn your steps in this direction but should business or pleasure bring you this way, I need not assure you how glad we will be to see you.
>
> My father is in so immediate want of the maps; but should you at anytime have any to spare of those received, he will be glad to have them. He desires to be kindly remembered to your father and self, in which I beg leave to join.[37]

In mid-June the students of both Washington College and the Virginia Military Institute were taking their final exams of the academic year. General Lee had taken Mrs. Lee to the nearby Rockbridge Baths in order that she may have the benefit of the waters to relieve her pain. This treatment gave her temporary relief. However, she had an minor accident and of course the fall only added to her discomfort.

General Lee and Custis were both busy with exams at this point and he was forced to communicate by letters with the absent Mrs. Lee. His notes were of common interest to her; mostly containing news about family and friends, "I shall endeavor to go to the Baths Monday, and hope during the week you may be able to determine whether it would be more advantageous for you to remain there or go further, as I shall have to return here as soon as I can. I can accomplish nothing while absent. Custis has determined to accompany Mr. Harrison to the White Sulpher Monday, and the girls seem indifferent about leaving home."[38] Mr. George Harrison, to whom R. E. Lee refers, was a cousin to the Lees and owned the last cottage on Baltimore Row at White Sulpher Springs resort. Harrison frequently invited the Lees to join his family at "Old White" now named "Greenbrier" in the West Virginia hills about sixty miles from Lexington for the summer. Eight days later Lee reported from Rockbridge Baths to his youngest son, "Custis has gone to the White Sulpher, but expects to be in Richmond on August 6th to meet Fitzhugh, with the view of going to the Warrenton White Sulpher Springs in North Carolina, to witness the erection of a monument over dear Annie, which the kind people of that country have prepared for the purpose. My attendance on your mother, which is necessary, prevents my being present."[39]

By August 2nd Custis had returned to Lexington. He found his father occupied with builders, so he "shook hands [with his father], got his dinner, and left for the Institute." Then Lee added, "So I do not know where his is from or where he will go next." [40] As Lee indicated in an earlier letter, Custis and Fitzhugh were planning to attend the memorial service for their sister Annie. They did attend the ceremony but did not linger at the Springs in North Carolina. Before August 18, Custis had returned to the Cartersville near "Oakland."

Custis had formed a close relationship with the Cocke family immediately following the war. He actually remained longer at Oakland than he did with his own family at Derwent. He had formed a male bond with the Cocke sons and had a brief flirtation with Phoebe Alexander Preston Cocke, daughter of the Elizabeth Randolph Preston Cocke, the matriarch of the Cocke family.

From Oakland, Custis continued his personal correspondences with various people. The following letter to Colonel Adam Badeau, Military Secretary at the Headquarters Armies of the United States, Washington City, D.C. was an acknowledgement of a request to extend William Henry Fitzhugh Lee's parole so that he might attend the memorial service in North Carolina. However, as Custis explains, he was unaware that his brother Fitzhugh had received the extension prior to his request.

> I was absent from Lexington when your letter of the 26th ult.arrived; and as I have been traveling ever since, until now; have not before had the opportunity of making an acknowledgement.
>
> I did not know when I wrote that my brother had received an extension of his parole which would enable him to visit North Carolina; and as he was at the time residing in New Kent Co., I applied for an extension for him that he might receive it in time.
>
> Thank you for your attention in this matter, I as very respectfully, [41]

Custis lingered on with the Cockes until his duty to the Virginia Military Institute forced him to return to Lexington. His father reported to Annette Carter that "Custis is in Cumberland at Mrs. Cocke's & I presume will not return before the 10 Pro. when his duties will begin. Fitzhugh & Robert are so distant, with no P.O. nearer to them than Richmond that we rarely hear of them"[42] Nevertheless, Fitzhugh wanted to be informed of all of the family gossip, especially about Custis.

Unbeknown to Fitzhugh, Custis had promptly returned to the Virginia Military Institute when he wrote to his sister Agnes, "I can't hear a word from Custis—What has become of him? Does Miss Phoebe still hold him in Cumberland? When I asked Rob to guess who was to be married & told him he would never think of the right person—He at once said that Custis was the man."[43] Obviously Custis was not "the man" since he did not marry "Miss Phoebe."

Everyone was now going about their routines as the autumn arrived. Rob recalled in his book, *Recollections and Letters of General Lee,* an event which created humor in the household.

> A young friend who was a cadet at the Virginia Military Institute called on my sisters one evening, and remarked, just for something to say: "Do you know this is the first civilian's house I have entered in Lexington." My father was in the room in his gray Confederate coat, shorn of the buttons; also my two brothers, Custis and Fitzhugh, both of whom had been generals in the Confederate Army; so there was quite a laugh over the term "civilian." [44]

Through the course of procuring gainful employment, Custis sent out resumes in several directions aside from Virginia. He inquired in Maryland, the Carolinas and Georgia. When the professorship at the Virginia Military Institute arose he was anxious for the position for more than one reason. Firstly, he would be doing a useful service to Virginia, secondly he would have gainful employment in a teaching position he was highly qualified for, although his modesty prevented in for admitting this fact, and lastly he was near his family. Then, late in the fall of 1866, he was offered the Presidency of the Maryland Agricultural College. This query offered two difficulties: his commitment to the Virginia Military Institute, and the responsibility to his family. Both obligations required serious deliberation.

On December 15, 1866, James T. Earle of the Maryland Agricultural College wrote a letter to General Francis H. Smith of the Virginia Military Institute informing him of the College's intent of acquiring George Washington Custis Lee as their next president.

> You will have learned from the papers, that Gen. Custis Lee has been elected to the Presidency of the

Maryland Agricultural College, and that we desire to secure his services. One chief difficulty in effecting our object, will be, we know, the moral obligation under which Gen. Lee will feel to fulfill his engagement with you Institution; and you will do us the justice to believe that we would not consent to procure him at the cost of disregarding it.

But a professorship in any Institution, Gen., is much easier to fill that its Presidency; and if not asking too much, we would be under great obligations for your assistance in the heavier and more responsible task of procuring a President for our College in the person of Gen. Lee. We of Maryland will appreciate this act of temporary detriment for our good: for we would not willingly on any way be instrumental in detracting for the value and efficiency of the Institution over which you preside with so much ability and usefulness. On the contrary, our sons of Maryland are now being educated by you; and we know of no Institution to which we would prefer to see them sent. But we desire to place Gen. Lee in a position, where he can not only educate our own sons, but where in the spirit of reciprocation we may have its in our power to make some return in educating your sons, who may desire the advantages in their studies of blending the Acts of Peace with those of War.

We feel greatly obliged, and that you will be entitled to, and will receive the thanks of all true Marylanders, if you can, consistently with your obligations to the Military Institute, give is your influence in securing the services of Gen. Lee.[45]

The college was chartered in 1856 and constructed on a tract of land consisting of 420 acres of the Riverdale Plantation owned Charles Benedict Calvert. In 1864 the college obtained federal financial aid by means of the Morrill Land Grant Act, therefore assuring that the facility would instruct course in agriculture, mechanical arts and military tactics. However, due to the war and the college's proximity to Washington, D. C., the enrollment nearly ceased and the college was forced to declaring bankruptcy by the end of 1865. Notwithstanding, early in the following year the Maryland legislature appropriated funds to develop the college into a full state institution.[46] Their success depended upon the inducement of students to enroll in the college. The board of trustees needed a college president who was young and knowledgeable with a name that would attract collegians. George Washington Custis Lee met their qualifications and they did everything in their power to entreat Lee to accept the position.

General Smith of the Virginia Military Institute responded immediately to Mr. Earle's letter:

> Gen. Pendleton has placed in my hands your letter of the 15th inst. and has also communicated to me the substance of the papers transmitted through him to Gen. G. W. C. Lee.
>
> You are doubtless aware of the prostrate condition in which this institution was left by the war. Its buildings, library and apparatus were burned; five of its faculty and one hundred and twenty-five of its alumni were killed in battle and it was under such circumstances that the Board of Visitors met in Sept. 1865 to reorganize the Institution. Gen. G. W. C. Lee was then called to the chair made vacant by the death of Major Gen. [Robert Emmett] Rodes. I cannot tell you how essential his services were to us then-and how important they are to us now. We are just beginning to develop the Department of Applied Mechanics, for which Gen. Lee's qualifications _____for him, and I should be doing violence to truth and duty, should I fail to express to you, that it is the unanimous wish of the Board of Visitors and Faculty of the Institution that Gen. Lee will still continue to give to this important state school, the benefit of this labors, in the work of restoring it to its former condition of usefulness.
>
> With this distinct statement of the _____condition of the case, I have said to Gen. Lee, that I had no desire,

and did not feel at liberty, to oppose my barrier to his accepting any appointment elsewhere by which his personal interests or his usefulness might be promoted. I should sincerely regret the loss of his services and I should congratulate you, if you should be so fortunate as to secure his services for the Agricultural College of Maryland.[47]

About the same time as the Maryland position came through, he had received an offer for a professorship from a college in Georgia as well. He was trying to decide what he wanted to do about his future, as the family was gathering in Lexington for the Holidays.

In the autumn, Mildred decided to visit the Lee cousins in Maryland. The Goldsboroughs lived on the east shore of the peninsula near Easton at their family estate named "Ashby." From this place she traveled to many locations and was away for several months. She was not able to come to Lexington for Christmas. In a letter from her father dated December 21, 1866, he relates his concerns for her and causally mentions, "Traveller and Custis are both well, and pursue their usual dignified gait and habits, and are not led away by the frivolous entertainments of lectures and concerts."[48] Custis remained until the end of his life both ultraconservative personally and professionally.

Perhaps overly cautious and not wanting to offend either the Trustees of the Maryland Agricultural College or the Board of Visitors at the Virginia Military Institute, he took his time in deciding whether to accept the position offered him in Maryland. Nearly a month after he received the nomination from Mr. Earle, he finally responded with his answer:

Your letter of the 15th ult., giving the information of my election to the Presidency of the Maryland Agricultural College, was received towards the close of last month; and I very much regret that circumstances beyond my control should have occurred to prevent a reply until now. I hope, however, that this delay, so much longer than was either intended or desired, will not occasion inconvenience to the Trustee or injury to the College.

From the best consideration of the subject, in my power, I have come to the conclusion, that I would not be doing right in leaving this institution at this time, and must therefore decline the position you so kindly and cordially offer.

It may be proper to state in this connection that the experience of the last eighteen months has satisfied me that I am not so well fitted for the important and responsible duties involved in the education of the young, as for more active pursuits; and I have been seriously thinking of exchanging my present avocation for one more active in which I hope to attain to greater usefulness. This would seem to be an additional reason for not accepting your desirable offer.

With the expression of my high appreciation of the honor conferred upon me by your selection, my grateful thanks for the extreme kindness with which the invitation has been given, and my best wishes for the prosperity of your College and the happiness of those connected with it, I have the honor to be...[49]

The same day Lee wrote another letter on this subject to General Francis H. Smith informing him of his decision to stay at the Virginia Military Institute for the present time, although he was bored with teaching and wanted a more challenging opportunity.

I have the honor to acknowledge the receipt of your note to me of the 21st, ult., enclosing a copy of your letter to the Hon. James T. Earle [Maryland state senator] of the same date, on the subject of my election to the Presidency of the Maryland Agricultural College.

Your letter to Mr. Earle expresses such sentiments in regard to myself as I should have expected from the uniform kindness and consideration you have shown towards me, and for which you will always have my sincere thanks; and although I believe that you have over estimated my importance to this Institution, I none the less appreciate the friendliness which has induced the error, as I conceive it to be. With my best wishes for your health and happiness [Post Scriptum] I transmit herewith a duplicate of my letter to the Hon. James T. Earle, of this date.[50]

After Lee declined the presidency of the Maryland Agricultural College, their Board of Trustees appointed Charles L. C. Minor to the position. When President Minor began the academic year in October, 1867 only eleven students were enrolled. He retained this appointment until 1868.[51]

With the Maryland Agricultural College matter behind him and his refusal of an offered professorship in Georgia as well, Custis continued his quiet life in Lexington. He desired a situation beyond the classroom. It is believed he was anxious to find employment with a civil engineering firm, but his chances and opportunities were remote due to the desperate economic circumstances in the South. He spent much of his free time communicating to friends and acquaintances on subjects of personal interest. In mid-February he recommenced his exchange of letters with Colonel Alfred Reves:

I rec'd your note of the 14th ult., some time ago, and would have replied before this time but for hearing that you had started upon your trip to the North; which I trust you found as pleasant as instructive in the investigation of new books.

Capt. Brooke gave me the little book you were kind enough to send me; and I find it very valuable, the best thing of the kind I have ever had; and independently of its merits, I esteem it most highly as a token of your remembrance and consideration. I have been wishing and attending to write to thank you for it ever since its reception. At first one thing and then another, occurred to prevent—chiefly a disabled hand and an affection of the eyes. I believe I am pretty well rid of these troubles.

I did not accept either the Georgia professorship or the position at the Maryland Agricultural College, wishing to stick to Old Virginia awhile longer; but I fear it is a luxury I can not very long afford, and I am not altogether satisfied with my present arrangement.

I am sorry to learn that your business is so dull just now, and hope it will improve with the opening of Spring. I presume poverty is the cause in Richmond as elsewhere. I heard of Capt. Macmurdo's being in Dixie, and was in hopes that he would pay us another visit, as he did last winter; but suppose he thought from what he saw when here, that there would be a poor chance of doing anything in Lexington.

I would be very glad indeed to learn the results of your investigation of books. I can only look over the catalogs, and every now and then send for a book; but am frequently disappointed in them. We have some of the standard works here, and are generally increasing our library; but slowly for the want of means.

Col. Preston Johnston has just arrived here to take a chair in Washington College. He tells me a good deal about Genl. St. John, and gives the best account of him.

I hope you will adhere to your determination not to let our correspondence drop. I am determined to do my part of it. Please present me most kindly to the members of your household & believe me to be very truly yes.[52]

This letter is revealing as to Custis' feelings at the time. On the one hand he seems to be hinting of his desire to leave teaching and acquire other employment, especially in the engineering field and in Richmond. Yet, on the other hand, he realized that asking Rives for a job was inopportune as Rives' business had fallen off and the economic situation in Virginia, as throughout the South remained desperate. Nevertheless, he wants to keep the hope alive by desiring Rives to continue their communications.

During the winter months Custis aided his father in researching the activities of the Army of Northern Virginia for his proposed manuscript. General Lee freely communicated with his sons and nephew Fitz Lee on this subject. He was anxious for details and pressed his son, Fitzhugh, "I requested Custis to write to you for a report of your operations during the winter of 1863-4 down to April 18, 1865. How are you progressing with it?" [53] Once again Custis was his father's personal secretary; perhaps he wished a respite from always being at hand and available. Nevertheless, Custis did his duty to V. M. I. and his family.

The spring quickly became early summer and the second semester at the Virginia Military Institute had come to closure. In the *Annual Report of the Superintendent* for the academic year of 1866-1867, General Smith reported on the Department of Military Engineering and Applied Mechanics, General G. W. C. Lee Professor:

> This department gave instruction to the first class in military engineering before January, a part of the time by daily recitation, of one hour each, and a part tri-weekly. The class was also taken over the course of surveying, which had been excluded by the pressure of other studies from the regular course. In January the first class was examined and passed in military engineering, and applied mechanics commenced. It was deemed best to suspend the course for the remainder of the session, after a short experiment in it. The department of practical engineering, from the want of suitable textbooks, needed by the first class for daily recitations, and the absence of Colonel Massie on account of sickness, made it indispensable to avail the service of General Lee in the department of mathematics. The first class was accordingly relieved for applied mechanics, and the time designed for this study was given to practical engineering.
>
> General Lee has, at my request, been also engaged in a topographical survey of the grounds of the institute, and by a detail of one cadet daily from the first, second, and third classes, which gave valuable practical instruction to them with the instruments, the work has been nearly completed. It is recommend the the course of surveying with the care and use of the field instruments be transferred from the

mathematical department to that of engineering, &c., to which it more appropriately belongs, and in which it can certainly be efficiently prosecuted.[54]

With their academic responsibilities completed for the recent year, the Lee family decided to take a vacation at White Sulpher Springs. The family arrived at "Old White" on July 24th; the first summer holiday for General Lee since the end of the war. The family consisting of Mrs. Lee, Agnes and Custis arrived by stage, while the General rode on horseback. The last cottage on Baltimore Row was assigned to the family. The cottage was owned by their cousin George Harrison and he was glad to offer its service to the Lees [33]

General Lee was delighted to have a respite from his university chores and as Freeman wrote, "The social impulse of the General was always strong and now, in renewed contact with long-separated friends, it asserted itself vigorously." [56] As for Custis, his mother wrote to Rob, " I rarely see Custis. He has a room over at the Hotel & I have so much company he is always afraid to come in here."[57] It appears that Custis had a reputation as an introvert. One young woman who met him said he was so "diffident" that the vein in his forehead bulged during the introduction.

However, Christiana Bond, a socialite from Baltimore had kinder words. She said Custis had a "grave, self-restrained courtesy and low musical voice."[58] During the summer of 1867, while visiting Old White Sulpher Springs, Miss Bond recorded two separate events concerning Custis directly:

> In his genial sympathy with the social pleasures of the young people it disturbed General Lee that his son, General Custis Lee, held himself aloof. He had playfully promised him as a cavalier to the youngest of his favorites, but day after day General Custis failed to appear. At last his promise was gained, and in the promenade in the long parlor he was introduced.
>
> Immediately he fell into his father's plan, and stood in constant attendance by the young girl's chair, usually silent and erect as if on guard. One morning when he had

stood a long time beside the group of girls I said, "General Custis, why do you not sit down? Gravely he answered, with a touch of his father's humor, "I am a modest man, and for a modest man to have his hands and his feet on his mind at the same time is too much; when I stand my feet are off my mind and I have only my hands to attend to."

General Custis Lee shared his father's characteristics, and there was humor in his kindness, too. One day there came a plain girl with an unassuming chaperon. They were not at home in the circle in which they found themselves, and the young lady was not of the material of which a belle is usually made. I remember yet her freckles and her dumpy little figure. But it chanced that during the war her father had done kindly service to Southern prisoners, some of whom had belonged to General Custis Lee's command. The word went forth that the girl should know the rapture of being *a belle*. General Custis took the matter in hand— the old soldiers were loyal and grateful. They thronged around her. How she danced and walked and flirted! What famous men contended for the honor of her hand! How she was encircled by a brilliant group, all bent upon doing her honor! No doubt her children proudly cherish yet the memory of the time when their quiet, plain little mother was the bell of the White! If we who were in the secret smiled, it was a sympathetic smile, for we recognized the true chivalry and gratitude which lay beneath the little comedy. And with what a beaming smile our chief looked on!

"Let us go," he said, when his hour for retiring came, "I know my son Custis; he will never fail in his duty. We may return tomorrow and find him still promenading here." [59]

Although his father was well intended toward the introduction of many young ladies, Custis no doubt resented his father's interference and insistence that he participate in the social events that the resort offered. Perhaps Custis found this extreme socializing a necessary evil while vacationing at the "White." He probably preferred the company of a good book or the intelligent conversation of educated individuals. Even though he acquiesced to his father's demands, this forced socialization was unacceptable to his demeanor. However, once he was comfortable with a stranger, he quickly accepted them into his circle and became relaxed and congenial in their presence. Miss Bond sites another example for Custis' acceptance of her:

> Strange as it seems to us now—Lexington the seat of the Washington and Lee University and of the Military Institute could only be approached by a night journey either by stage or by canal boat. Remembering the horrors of the journey by stage over roads of unspeakable roughness, I gladly undertook the return journey by canal boat to Lynchburg, under the escort of General Custis Lee. Nothing could have been more delightful that the novelty of gliding in the sunset and the moonlight through the lovely Virginia scenery. But the scene when at a late hour we went below, was a shock. The floor of the boat was literally covered with the bodies of sleeping men, and it was necessary to leap over them one by one through the length of the cabin, to arrive at the curtained space assigned to the women passengers. A sliding panel the length of the berth permitted one to rest with head and shoulders outside and thus endure what otherwise would have been an intolerable night. The sight of an occasional deer with her fawns coming down to drink in the gleaming water of the James River and the beauty of the wooded banks beguiled the tedium of the sleepless night.
>
> In the moonlight we had hours of talk on the deck, in the midst of which I said, "Is it true that your father would never use the word "Yankee," but said, "Charge those people?" "Yes," he said, "it is true; but," he said, "I did not share his feelings."
>
> Again in answer to my rather inane question, "Why did the South so suddenly give up?" General Custis said, "I can only answer for my command; for four days we

had had nothing to eat but the corn the men carried in their pockets." General Custis Lee had none of the his father's acceptance of the South's defeat and the wrecking of all his hopes. He seemed broken and disheartened, perhaps because life was still before him; while with General Robert E. Lee there was the resignation of a Christian and the calm consciousness of fulfilled duty as a soldier and a patriot.[60]

Quickly the summer was over and the renewal of the academic year had approached. It was proposed that Custis would escort his mother, sister and Mary Pendleton back to Lexington while General Lee would return at a leisurely pace astride Traveler.

Upon his return to Lexington he wrote to his son Rob, a struggling "young farmer," "The girls are as usual, and Custis is in far better health than he was before his visit to the Springs. He seems, however, not happy, and I presume other people have their troubles as well as farmers."[61] Custis was a constant concern for Lee. He wanted his all of sons to be happy, especially Custis. In spite of his serious intent, Custis was usually the brunt of his little jokes. In a letter to Annette Carter, written around the same time, he related:

...Since you left, Capt. Henderson has not been to see us, but takes long walks with Custis. What he imparts to him may be numbered among the secrets of the grave, while I talk to Traveler, & feel equally sure of his discretion...I cherish the hope of being able to get to Guided to see you all once again. You had better make up your mind to marry Custis & come & live with me always. He is so poor that you will not be tempted into any extravagance.[62]

Notwithstanding, Lee's constant search for a wife for Custis was endless, while his other son, William Henry Fitzhugh had courted the Virginia belle, Mary Tabb Bolling since the closure of the war. She was the daughter of G. W. Bolling of Petersburg. Their wedding date was set for November 28, 1867. Even though Mrs. Lee would be unable to attend the ceremony, Fitzhugh was anxious for his father to be present. Lee resisted the idea at first but after

Fitzhugh paid his parents a short visit, Lee was persuaded to attend.

Suddenly, as fate would have it, Robert E. Lee and George Washington Custis Lee were subpoenaed to appear at the Federal Circuit Court in Richmond on November 26 in order to participate in the trial of Jefferson Davis. In a letter to Fitzhugh, Lee informs him of his travel plans, "Custis says it will be inconvenient for him to leave here before the time necessary for him to reach Petersburg by the 28th, and we have arranged to commence our journey on Monday night, 25th inst., at 12 m., so as to reach Richmond Tuesday evening, remain there the 27th and so to Petersburg the 28th."[63] As it turned out, father and son reached Richmond the afternoon of November 25, with accommodations at the Exchange Hotel. W. H. F. Lee met his father and brother at the hotel. It was a bittersweet return to Richmond under these circumstances. Through the afternoon and evening, the Lees made a series of visits to various friends, including the Caskies and then to Judge Robert Oldies home, where Jefferson Davis was residing for the duration of his trial. The conversation between of Lee and Davis was lost to posterity, but Lee did remark to Mrs. Lee, " I saw Mr. Davis, he looks astonishingly well, and is quite cheerful. He inquired particularly after you all."[64]

The next day the Lees promptly appeared at the Federal courthouse. Neither Robert E. Lee or Custis Lee were summoned to speak on November 26th. Now it had become public knowledge that the elder Lee was in town, and he was besieged by a steady stream of visitors and well-wishers. Later that evening he wrote to Mrs. Lee, "No one seems to know what is to be done. [He continued the next morning, November 27] Judge Chase had not arrived yesterday, but it was thought probable he would reach here in the ten o'clock train last night. I have not heard this morning. I will present myself to the court this morning, and learn, I hope, what they wish of me."[65] At last, on the afternoon of November 27, Robert E. Lee was summoned to testify. He was questioned for two hours and then he was excused from any further testimony. Apparently Custis was not required to testify and the whole proceeding came to further delays and ultimately a *noble prosaic* [an entry on the record denoting that the prosecutor or plaintiff will proceed no further in his action or suit] was filed.

At long last, the wedding day of William Henry Fitzhugh Lee and Mary Tabb Bolling had arrived. As Fitzhugh had arranged, a special car was attached to the regular train from Richmond to deliver the wedding guests to Petersburg. The General was visibly moved by the events in Richmond and he sat quite resolute and silent for the twenty-two mile ride. Of the Lee family, the General, Mildred, Custis, Rob and cousin Fitz Lee attended while Mary and Agnes Lee stayed with their mother in Lexington. General Lee stayed with General and Mrs. William Mahon.

The morning after the wedding, General Lee wrote to Mrs. Lee, "Our son was married last night and shone in his happiness. The bride looked lovely and was, in every way, captivating. The church was crowded to its utmost capacity, and the streets thronged. Everything went off well...Mr. Davis [Jefferson] was prevented from attending by the death of Mrs. Howell [Davis' mother-in-law]...Fitzhugh Lee was one of the grooms men, Custis very composed and Rob suffering from chills...I shall remain to-day and return to Richmond to-morrow. I wish to go to Brandon Monday, but do not know that I can accomplish it."[66]

By November 30, the General, Custis, Rob and Fitz Lee had all returned to Richmond. The party remained in Richmond for one day. From Richmond the General, Custis and Rob blade farewell to Fitz Lee and they traveled onto Brandon where they stayed for one night then back to Richmond. Before the General and Custis started out for Hickory Hill, the Wickham family home, Rob said good-bye to his father and brother and returned to his home. The two remaining Lees visited at Hickory Hill on December 5 and began their return journey to Lexington December 6th, arriving there on December 7th. Father and son had been traveling and visiting at a grueling pace for about twelve days. In some ways Lexington was a welcome sight.

Upon their arrival at Lexington, R. E. Lee repaired to the president's house at Washington College and Custis immediately went his quarters at VMI. As usual, Custis took his meals with his family but he continued his residence on campus at his room adjacent to Colonel Scott Shipp's room.

The Christmas Holidays passed quietly after the whirlwind

happenings in November. The winter months were very dreary and routine. Mary and Agnes spent most of the winter in Maryland, while Mildred took full charge of the household. Everyone longed for the warm spring breezes. By the end of March, R. E. Lee was reporting to Annette Carter, "Notwithstanding the inclement spring, the fields are green, the buds are shooting forth, the violets have appeared, & the songs of the birds are added to the thankfulness of man, that winter has passed. (But it) has been a quiet winter with us...daily visits from Custis & a circle of your cousins..."[67] Lee continued by adding news of an early spring cotillion being sponsored by the Washington Literary Society of the College, "...their celebration which is generally very interesting to the young people, & all the Belles of the town will be present, prepared with bouquets to shower upon their favorites. Your cousin Custis will I know keep firmly aloof. He never permits himself to be inveigled into such frivolities, & I shall not be able to present."[68]

By the end of May, Mildred was becoming fast friends with Charlotte Haxall, the future Mrs. Robert E. Lee, Jr. and R. E. Lee was commenting to his daughter-inlaw, "Custis retains his serenity of character...and as soon as the college exercises close...I hope [it] will bring some relief to me also."[69]

The summer of 1868 proved to be an active period for the Lee family. In a letter to his son, Fitzhugh, R. E. Lee informs him of the summer plans of the family:

...I will take your mother to the Warm Springs, from the 10th to the 15th, and after trying the water there about two weeks, if not favorable, will take her over to the Hot [Hot Springs, five miles from Lexington]...I intend to go myself to White Sulpher for about a fortnight, to drink the water and will take Mildred with me. Agnes, having gone last summer, will not care to go, I presume, and can remain with her mother. Mildred has been quite sick for the past week, but is now much better, and in a week will be strong enough for the journey, I think...Custis still talks of visiting you, but I have not heard of his having fixed the day of his departure. He is quite well.[70]

By July 14th Custis was still in Lexington. Assisting his father in every way possible, he made sure his mother was comfortably install on the stage along with Mildred, and Agnes for their trip to Warm Springs. Since his father was escorting the ladies, Custis did not accompany them. They were at Warm Springs for only a few days when Mildred became seriously ill with typhoid fever. For anxious weeks Mildred suffered. Her only consolation was that she had constant attention from her sister, Agnes and her father. In early August, R. E. Lee communicated to Fitzhugh, "..Mildred is too sick to move... I cannot speak of our future movements. I fear I shall have to abandon my visit to the White."[71] Yet, by the middle of the month Mildred was on the road to recovery, but very weak. Lee had not heard from Custis since their departure from Lexington and inquired with Fitzhugh if he knew of Custis' plans. Custis lingered close to Lexington with short trips to visit friends, but none of this trips were for more than a day or two.

At the end of the month, Lee finally arrived at White Sulpher Spring with Mildred. His visit was not as pleasant as he had hoped and he remained merely a few days before returning to Hot Springs where he had left Mrs. Lee and Agnes. Mildred was weak but better and he wrote to Rob from there, " I hope she will be strong enough to return with me."[72] The unrestful summer ended with the family returning to Lexington by mid-September.

At the college, the news was not good. The enrollment at Washington College dropped by more than sixty students from the previous academic year. It was speculated that the economic situation throughout the South played a large part in this decline and Lee started the new academic year in a fiscal slump.

During the summer Custis had gained some much needed freedom from family responsibilities. In an effort to perpetuate his independence, he decided to maintain taking his meals at the Institute as he did in the summer. By mid-October, he was settled into his academic routine, as his father wrote to his brother, Fitzhugh, "We see but little of Custis. He has joined the mess at the Institute which he finds very comfortable. So that he rarely comes to our table, to breakfast now, & the rest of his time he seems to be occupied with his classes & studies."[73]

Although the days of the autumn and early winter were relatively uneventful for Custis, the family hopefully anticipated a visit from their cousin, Edward Lee Childe of Paris, France in October. The entire family enjoyed Childe's visit as well as the awaited visit of General and Mrs. William Henry Fitzhugh Lee in November. Groomed as to the ways of the Lee household, the new Mrs. W. H. F. Lee was immediately successful in obtaining approval from her father-in-law. This was a happy time for the Lee family and everyone regretted the younger Lees departure before the Holidays. Nevertheless, they looked forward to Rob's Christmas visit. This was an especially merry Holiday, as all the Lee children were present except Fitzhugh.

Robert E. Lee, Jr. wrote in his *Recollections of General Lee* of his visit, "The new house was approaching completion, and my father was much interested in the work, going there very often and discussing with the workmen their methods.

That Christmas I spent two weeks in Lexington, and many times my father took me all over the new building, explaining all the details of his plan."[74]

No sooner had the Lees arrived in Lexington in 1865, when conversation of constructing a new President's House designed specifically for Robert E. Lee began. Lee was flattered. However, he did not want special privileges. Although both General Lee and Custis had an influence in the design of the structure, the actual architect was C. W. Oltmanns. The architect strove to design a "house modest in plan but elaborate in detail."[75] The interior rooms were spacious and light with attention to every particular aspect. The marble mantelpieces were especially fine and mirrored the residents' status in the community.

According to an early unpublished biographical account on Custis Lee, the author, former Professor James Howe of Washington and Lee Univiersity stated in the 1940's, "It has been generally considered that both these buildings [the President's House and the Chapel] were planned by General Lee and constructed under his direct supervision. However, the plans for both have recently been found, and were drawn by Custis Lee, having a few pencil annotations by his father. Father and son must have spent many pleasant hours over these plans, but most of the detailed work was evidently done by the son, and the same is probably true of the supervision of construction. In this work Custis Lee was in his true element as engineer."

The floor plan was reminiscent of Arlington House in some respects, especially the second floor. Aside from the servants' quarters in the rear of the second story structure, the arrangement of bedrooms, central hall and walk-in closet or small sewing room were identical to the second story floor plan at Arlington. The only exception was the staircase, centrally located at the President's House, whereas at Arlington there were flanking staircases to accommodate the flow of traffic.

It is thought that father and son worked closely with Oltmanns in order to modify the overall plan to meet particular needs of the family. The three-sided veranda is a prime example. It was suggested that an extended porch was constructed to allow Mrs. Lee to move freely in her wheelchair. Nevertheless, there are other influences as well. It is speculated that the Lee dominance can be seen in the ventilating system, the interior chimneys and the hidden bell system for summoning servants. But the most interesting element of the entire structure is the concept of total containment under one roof. Not only are all parts the house located under one roof but the stable and carriage house are found here, also.

Robert E. Lee would reside in this house for only sixteen months before his demise, but Custis would remain there for twenty-six years prior to his retirement.

Soon, the year of 1868 had come to a close and Rob returned to his home in the "low country." Life for the Lees went on much as it had before. General Lee was enjoying unusually good health, while Custis' health wavered. Nevertheless, it led his father to comment by mid-January, "Custis, I think, looks better."[76]

General Lee did not seem concerned about his daughters not marrying but he wanted his sons to marry. In a letter to a friend, he commented on all of his children but his lengthiest notation concerns Custis & Rob, "Custis & Robert are still bachelors & I fear likely to remain so for sometime. The latter is farming in King William on the Pamunkey river & is able to make a support. He intends to improve his house this year & I hope then will get himself a good wife." [77] From the tone of the letter it appears that Lee has resigned himself that Custis will never marry. Unlike his brothers, Custis lost his inheritance in the war and this situation compounded his mind set not to marry. The fact of the matter remained that Custis had only himself to offer an imminent bride, he had no home of his own or extended financial prospects to induce any woman. This reality certainly was a cause for deep seeded bouts of occasional depression and various health problems. Obviously, this was a concern for his father. By the end of February, R. E. Lee wrote to Rob, " Custis is in better health this winter that he has been, and seems content, though his sisters look after him very closely."[78] Perhaps the reason for the improvement of health was partly due to the good news they received in mid-February.

Early in December, 1868 a division of judges were certified to the Supreme Court of the United States. With this appointment, a general amnesty was declared on December 25 immediately placing a stop action on the prosecution of any former Confederates for treason. On February 15, 1869, the indictments against General Robert E. Lee, General George Washington Custis Lee, General William Henry Fitzhugh Lee, General Fitzhugh Lee along with another fourteen generals and nineteen other people accused in the indictment was declared nolle prosequi.[79] Obviously, this news was a welcome relief to all concerned.

The solace and joy of the news about his amnesty was short lived for Custis. Lee remarked to his son Rob again, " We are all pretty well. Your mother has been troubled by a cold, but is over it I hope. The girls are well, and have as many opinions with as few acts as ever; and Custis is so-so."[80] Lee's ardent concern for Custis is replicated in every letter, especially in the letters to Rob and Fitzhugh, with comments such as "Custis is well though now static."[81]

In reality, Custis had little to be euphoric about. He was in a mundane position at V. M. I. as well as he being deprived of his birthright. Unlike his father, Custis wanted more from life but the means of obtaining his goals were stymied and out of reach due to circumstances beyond his control.

His father encouraged him to become more active and social.

But Custis preferred the association of the V. M. I. colleagues and the development of his classes. His friends at the Institute were the younger professors, like himself. Among them were Colonel Scott Shipp [later General], whose living quarters were adjacent to Custis' quarters at the Superintendent's house. Shipp remained at these quarters until his marriage in the summer of 1869. Shipp was a professor in the Department of Infantry, Cavalry and Artillery Tactics, Military History and Strategy, as well as serving as Commandant of Cadets. Along with Shipp, Custis was friendly with two other young professors: Colonel Wilfred E. Cutshaw and Captain Deas. He retained a close bond with Colonel W. B. Blair, an older colleague at the Institute, who lived off campus with his family. When his old friend William Preston Johnston accepted a professorship at Washington College, Custis immediately renewed their relationship which was fostered when they were aides-de-camp to Jefferson Davis. William Preston Johnston remained a strong and loyal friend to the younger Lee.

Custis was a dedicated educator. From the Virginia Military Institute papers, a lengthy narrative by a former cadet provides an insightful description of his teaching ability at the Institute as well as a personal attributes:

It is difficult for this writer, one of his "Old Boys" to speak of this peerless man, with possibly incurring the charge of giving too lavish praise to him. But that could not be. No one who knew General Custis Lee failed to see he was a remarkable man. But those who were in daily contact with him in the relation of pupils to teacher knew best how to appraise the qualities of mind and heart of this prince of men. There is no question that the cadets of the First Class who were his pupils—and who knew him best—revered him about every member of the Institute Faculty (and there was perhaps not one of that body who was not far above the average college professor in ability and in aptitude for teaching, as well as in personal qualities). But General Custis Lee was unique—in a class by himself. He was a most scholarly man, and (as those who were most competent to judge said) fully qualified to teach almost any course at the Institute. But engineering had always been his special field and in that department of Science we doubt if his superior, in mental equipment and ability to instruct, could have been found, at that time in America.

But we prefer to remember him as the conscientious teacher and the courtly gentleman. We hated to fail to come up to the mark he expected of us in his Class; for, if we did, we knew what would follow—a heart to heart "interview: with us after the class had been dismissed for the day. How we dreaded those little conferences! We would have been glad to have dodged them, if by simply taking the "zero" mark for complete failure, [if] we could have done it. But that was not Custis Lee's way. He realized what his duty to every member of his class was, and that if one failed to grasp any part of the day's instruction, he must endeavor to remove the difficulty. And, so he would say—"Mr._____will please remain a little while after the class is dismissed;" and then, in his modest way, he would say to the delinquent (deficient) cadet—"I want to try to make that point which has given you trouble clear to you." And then he would elucidate the whole matter.

He had the gentlest voice one ever listened to, and the sweetest smile, and he was as handsome as Adonis, and perfect in grace. He was much more reserved than his father, even. He never cared for public notice— shirked, in fact, general intercourse; but with those few who were his intimates at the Institute, General [Scott] Shipp, Colonel [Wilfred Emory] Cutshaw and Captain [William Allen] Deas, and possibly one or two others, he would freely and most delightfully converse, and he was a most charming companion.[82]

In the Annual Report of the Superintendent for the past academic year, it is evident why Custis was unable to be more social and how truly dedicated he was to the Department of Civil and Military Engineering and Applied Mechanics:

> Instruction has been given to the first class, divided into two sessions, by daily recitations, of one hour each, in Military Engineering, upon which the class was examined in January; also in daily recitations, of one hour each, for two sections in Applied Mechanics. In Civil Engineering, the class had recited daily in like order, from January to June, and will be examined on this branch of the course at the June examination.
>
> This department has been very much pressed this year, partly from the difficulty of getting suitable text books upon the important range of studies embraced in it—and partly from the fact that is was necessary to make tentative efforts so to arrange the course as to meet the wants of the academic classes. The experience of the year will doubtless lead to such an arrangement of the course as will give satisfactory solution to the difficulties referred to —and make the department most efficient for the instruction required in the academic school. In addition to the regular studies of the first class, this department has been charged with instruction in the special school of Applied Mechanics, the class reciting on every alternate night, since the 1st of February.[83]

By early summer the new President's House of Washington College was overflowing with many young ladies, all friends of the Lee girls. It became overwhelming for the Lee men and it prompted General Lee to write to his son Rob," I wish to pay you and F—a visit the week following, about July 1st. I am trying to persuade Custis to accompany me, but he has not yet responded...the house is full of young ladies...others in expectation."[84] Although General Lee would not admit that his health was declining, it was becoming obvious to those people he was closely associated with by the June commencement.

By the second week in July both Washington College and V.M.I. were closed for the summer recess. Detained by business at the college, General Lee wrote his future daughter-in-law Charlotte Taylor Haxall [Mrs. Robert E. Lee, Jr.] that "Custis who was to have accompanied me, will go down [to Pamunkey] in a day or two & I hope that he will have the pleasure of seeing you. I have begged him to look well at you & to tell me all about you."[85] General Lee finally arrived at the White House in late July after attending his brother Sidney Smith Lee's funeral, who died suddenly. Custis had already been at his brother's home for about a week when his father arrived. The change of society and location was therapeutic for Custis as his father remarked in a letter to his mother, "Custis is here, much improved."[86] But the father was not improved.

In early August, Mrs. W. H. F. Lee traveled to Petersburg to visit her family while the Lee men went on the Richmond to await her arrival. General Lee signed the register at the Exchange Hotel and word of him being in Richmond traveled fast. Visitors poured into the hotel and the gentlemen were compelled to receive the callers in the public parlors of the hotel. The next day the Lees departed Richmond for the Rockbridge Baths. The younger Mrs. Lee and her baby, Robert E. Lee III were warmly welcomed by Mrs. Lee. The young mother remained with her mother-in-law, while the General accompanied by Agnes and Mildred went onto White Sulpher Springs for a short vacation under doctor's orders.

The General and his daughters returned to Lexington in early September. Custis was already there and planning his fall semester. Both the younger Mrs. Lee and older Mrs. Lee had returned to Lexington as well. Tabb Lee and son remained in Lexington throughout the autumn. She visited several friends in the area among whom were the William Preston Johnstons. The Lees enjoyed a ten-day visit from Blanche and Edward Childe with their little dog, "Duckie."[87] After the Childes' left Lexington in mid-October, it became evident that General Lee's health was in decline. It is uncertain what precipitated the affliction but the ultimate diagnosis was an "inflammation of the heart-sac," the same condition he suffered in 1863.

By early November, Lee was active again, even though riding Traveller and carrying out his college duties sometimes left him short of breath and exhausted. Once again Custis was his confidant.

Lee told Custis he did not understand the full extent of his condition but he knew his heart was taxed and he calculated his days as numbered. Neither Custis or Lee discussed this conversation with anyone else. Yet the knowledge of his condition created periods of melancholy for Lee and anxiety for Custis.

Early in December, Lee wrote a pleasant note to Fitzhugh, joking about Custis and Rob, " Give my love to Brutus. [Rob] Tell him I hope Mrs. Taylor will retain one of her little daughters for him. She always saves the youngest of the Flock for Custis, as he is not particular as to an early day." [88] Lee retained his good humor through the Holidays.

As the Christmas Holidays approached, three of the Lee children were not in Lexington. Robert and Fitzhugh were at their own homes with Mildred visiting them alternately. Mary, Agnes and Custis were present. Always the dutiful son, Custis probably realized that this would be his father's last Christmas or maybe he thought he should be close at hand if needed. Whatever the reason he remained in Lexington.

The Lees opened the President's House on New Year's Day, 1870. Lee wrote to Mildred, "On New Year's Day the usual receptions. Many of our friends called. Many of my ancients as well as juniors were present, and all enjoyed some good Norfolk oysters...I think I am better...Custis busy with the examination of the cadets, the students preparing for theirs."[89]

Everything continued much as it had since the end of the war. General Lee communicated with his children frequently with jovial comments about Custis and girls. On Valentine's Day, he wrote to Fitzhugh, "Mildred, I hope is with you. When she gets away from her papa, she does not know what she wants to do, tell her...Custis is well and very retired: I see no alarming exhibition of attention to the ladies."[90]

Lee's physical condition had not altered over the winter. Upon the suggestion of family, friends and his doctor, Lee decided a change of climate and society would rehabilitate him. Eleanor Agnes was to accompany him on his journey. Before he informed the staff at Washington College of his decision, Lee wrote to Mildred of his intentions to visit the grave of Anne Carter Lee who died in 1862, and to continue his extended tour further south. He also gave her instructions, "You must take good care of your mother and do everything she wants. You must not shorten your trip on account of our departure. Custis will be with her every day, and Mary is still with her. The servants seem attentive."[91]

On March 22, he disclosed to the faculty his plans for a leave of absence and he immediately appointed Dr. J. L. Kirkpatrick to act in his stead.[92] Two days later Lee departed from Lexington on a journey which would be his farewell tour.

The trip on the outset was physically draining and by the time Agnes and General Lee reached Richmond the following day, he was unable to visit friends or attend to domestic matters for Mrs. Lee. In a letter to Mrs. Lee, he wrote: "I reached here Friday afternoon, and had a more comfortable journey than I expected. The night aboard the packet was very tiring, but survived it and the dust of the railroad the following day. Yesterday the doctors, Houston, McCaw and Cunningham examined me for two-hours, and I believe, contemplate returning to-day...I think I feel better that when I left Lexington, certainly stronger, but am a little feverish. Whether it is produced by the journey, or the toddies that Agnes administers, I do not know."[93]

His brief stay at the Exchange and Ballard House provided him with opportunities to entertain and visit friends, but as he told Mrs. Lee, he was afraid to go to church since "The day was unfavorable, and I should see so many of my old friends, to whom I would like to speak, that it might be injurious to me."[94] Nevertheless, General Lee continued, "I expect to continue our journey tomorrow, if nothing prevents, though I have not yet got the information I desire about the routes. Still, I will get on."[95]

Agnes and the General departed for Warrenton, North Carolina the following day. They finally reached Savannah on April 1st. From Georgia the General reported to Mrs. Lee,

I have had a tedious journey upon the whole, and have more than ever regretted that I undertook it. However, I have enjoyed meeting many friends, and the old soldiers have greeted me very cordially. My visit to dear Annie's grave was mournful, yet soothing to my feelings, and I was glad to have the opportunity of thanking the kind friends for their care of her while living and their attention to her since her death...I came off to Mr. [Andrew] Lowe's where I am now domiciled.

His house is partially dismantled and he is keeping house alone, so I have a very quiet time...[Lowe] has invited some gentlemen to meet me at dinner—General Joe Johnston, General [Alexander Robert] Lawton, General [Jeremy Francis] Gilmer, Colonel [J. L] Corley, etc. Colonel Corley [Lee's former chief quartermaster from the time when Lee took command of the Army of Northern Virginia] has stuck with me all the journey...[96]

The next day Agnes wrote home a detailed account of their activities and visits. At the end of her letter, she states, " General and Mrs. Gilmer asked especially after Custis..."[97] Prior to the war Custis had formed a close bond with Jeremy Gilmer his commanding officer. Gilmer, an experienced military engineer became a mentor to the younger Lee. At that time Custis became acquainted with Gilmer's family and continued his relationship with them long after Gilmer's death in 1883.

By the middle of the April, Lee's concerns turned toward family matters from letters he had received from Lexington. The excerpt from the following letter to Mrs. Lee primarily pertains to properties within the Lee family and especially Arlington:

I received yesterday your letters...inclosing Reverend Mr. Brantley's and daughter's [Mary Custis Lee] and Cassius Lee's. I forwarded the petition to the President, accompanying the latter to Cassius, and asked him to give it to Mr. Smith [Lee's attorney]. Hearing while passing through Richmond, of the decision of the Supreme Court referred to, I sent word to Mr. Smith that if he thought the time and occasion propitious for taking steps for the recovery of Arlington, the Mill etc., to do so, but to act quietly and discreetly. I presume the petition sent you for signature was the consequence. I do not know whether this is a propitious time or not, and should rather have had an opportunity to consult friends, but am unable to do so. Tell Custis that I wish that he would act for me, through you or others, for it is mainly on his account that I desire the restitution of the property. I see that a resolution has been introduced into Congress 'to perfect the title of the Government to Arlington and other National Cemeteries,' which I have been apprehensive of stirring, so I suppose the matter will come up anyhow. I did not sign the petition, for I did not think it necessary, and believed the more I was kept out of sight the better. We must hope for the best, speak as little and act as discreetly as possible.[98]

After writing this letter to Mrs. Lee, the General continued onto Cumberland Island by means of the St. John River spending the night at Colonel Cole's estate, near the town of Palatka then returning to Savannah. Cole was a former subordinate officer to Lee. He noted in a letter to Mrs. Lee, "We visited Cumberland Island, and Agnes decorated my father's grave with beautiful fresh flowers. I presume it is the last time I shall be able to pay to it my tribute of respect." [99]

After returning to Savannah the Lee party began their leisurely excursion north through Charleston and Wilmington, visiting friends along the way. By May 1, the Lees arrived in Norfolk. They continued their trip moving along the James River stopping at "Brandon" and then "Shirley" further north upon the river. After reaching Richmond, Agnes and the General departed for "White House" where they united with Mrs. Lee on the evening of May 8. Mildred, Mary and Custis remained in Lexington, while Rob was persuaded by his father to travel the fifteen mile from "Romancoke" to William Henry Fitzhugh's home "White House" to visit with his parents and sister. According to Mrs. Lee, the General expected to return to "Lexington somewhere about the 24th..."[100] Nevertheless, Rob escorted his father on a round of visits in the area. After returning to "White House" Lee continued onto Richmond with Agnes remaining there a few days before continuing his journey home to Lexington.

In a letter written to Mildred dated May 23rd, Lee informs her of his further plans:

...I find I shall be detained here too long to take the Wednesday's boat from Lynchburg, but, if not prevented by circumstances now not foreseen, I shall take the Friday's boat, so as to reach Lexington Saturday morning, 28th inst...Your mother proposes to leave in the boat for Bremo on the 1st proximo, spend one week there, and then continue her journey to Lexington. Agnes has not made up her mind whether she will go with me, her mother, or remain for a while. I hope to find you well, though alone. [Mary Custis Lee had departed for the west by this time] Love to Custis...[101]

A few days prior to this letter to Mildred Lee, the General wrote from "White House" to his cousin Annette Carter:

It would give me great pleasure to continue my journey to Goodwood [Carter family estate] but I cannot longer prolong my absence from Lexington. The examinations will begin next week, & I must be there if possible. But I hope to see you all this summer...I shall go to Richmond on Monday 23rd & after a consultation with my Drs. will proceed slowly to Lexington & shall be obliged to remain there till July...Cannot you be present at Commencement, the last of June? 4th Thursday? My health is much better than when I left Va. & I am quite comfortable again...Mary & Mildred are in Lexington under the charge of Custis, & I presume the latter is anxious to be relieved.[102]

Apparently the extended Southern tour did little permanent good for General Lee. He went about his regular end of the academic year schedule. He was present for the examinations and commencement and he kept up with his letter writing. In a letter to Mrs. Margaret Hunter, he declines an invitation to visit the Hunters, but rather invites them to come to him:

I am very much obliged to you for you kind invitation to visit you and I need not assure what pleasure it would give me to do so. But you know what difficulty I have leaving Lexington and must remind you of the fashion in the upper valley, which is for the young to visit the old, and not the old to the young...Mildred too was here along with Custis. My family taking advantage of my absence had dispersed. Your Cousin Mary...went to the Pamunky to visit her sons and Mary [his daughter] has gone to St. Louis with Major Henry Turner...I expect, however, your cousin M. and Agnes to return Saturday and I hope in time we shall all be reunited.[103]

Unlike his father, Custis did not request a leave of absence to accompany his father on his Southern tour. He remained on duty at the Virginia Military Institute. As was the custom, the Superintendent issued his annual report in June:

Department of Civil and Military Engineering and Applied Mechanics—General G. W. C. Lee, Professor, assisted for the first half of the year by Captain W. M. Patton. Instruction was given to the first class, divided into four sections, reciting daily one hour each, to 1st January, in Engineering Geodesy. Since the semi-annual examination, the resignation of Captain Patton imposed the duty of instruction for the whole on the professor. The class was then divided into two sections, reciting daily on Civil Engineering. The same class was also taught Military Engineering during the whole year in the same divisions, and have alternated with the class in Ordnance, Gunnery and Strategy, making the recitations in Military Engineering tri-weekly through the entire year.[104]

Custis lingered at VMI until the middle of July when he departed for a vacation. Earlier in the month his father once again departed Lexington for Baltimore to seek the medical advice of Dr. Thomas H. Buckler. While in Baltimore he stayed at the Taggart home. On the morning of July 2, Dr. Buckler visited Lee at the Taggart house where apparently he diagnosed Lee with a rheumatic condition which aggravated "the action of the heart." Buckler prescription was "guard against cold, keep out in the air, exercise, etc., as the other physicians prescribe" and finally "...try lemon juice and watch the effect." From Baltimore Lee moved onto Goodwood, the Carter estate and then to Alexandria by mid July. From Alexandria he wrote to Mrs. Lee: "Next week I shall go to Ravensworth and from there I shall proceed to Lexington." General Lee took the opportunity to speak to his attorney and cousin, who advised him on business matter and the probability of regaining Arlington from the federal government "...I have seen Mr. Smith this morning and had with him a long business talk, and will see him again after seeing Cassius. The prospect is not promising." Lee concludes his letter by saying, "I cannot fix yet the day of my return, but it will be the last week in July. I hope Custis has got off, though I shall not be able to see him."[105] Lee went to Ravensworth as he had mentioned in his letter. From there he returned to Lexington instead of visiting his sons again. He wrote from Ravensworth to Mrs. Lee, "Tell them it is too hot and that I am too painful."[106]

Through the summer Lee received many invitations for travel. Lee was obliged to decline a trip to Paris from Dr. Thomas H. Buckler, the physician he visited in Baltimore, as well as other inducements in and around Virginia. However, he did travel with Colonel [Professor] White to Hot Springs, Virginia for relief of his rheumatism. He remained there through August.

During his father's rounds of visits, Custis, too, was visiting friends. While at Hot Springs, Lee learned of Custis' visit to Edward Cocke of Oakland and his intention to return to Lexington by September 1st to resume his teaching duties at the Virginia Military Institute once again. Lee wrote to his son, Fitzhugh, "Custis will be there [Lexington] by the first, and we shall all, hope, be together again."[107]

Lee's constant concern about his family extended to the horses and cow the family owned. Still at Hot Springs, Lee wanted Custis to take charge of these animals since he did not trust the new stable attendant's ability. He wrote to Agnes, "When Custis comes, ask him to see to the horses and the cow and that they are gently treated and properly fed. I know nothing of Henry's capacity in that way. I hope to be home next week and an very anxious to get back."[108] Lee remained at Hot Springs through August returning in early

September. There was a mark decline in his physical condition and Lee tarried in Lexington near his family until the end of his life.

According to Colonel William Preston Johnston, who recorded the events of the last days of Lee's life, the consuming illness from which Lee suffered was the lingering result of a severe sore throat resulting in a rheumatic inflammation of the sac inclosing the heart he acquired in 1863. It was well known at the time of the Gettysburg campaign that Lee was ill with dysentery and other ailments. These facts lead some historians to conclude that his judgment during the campaign may have been impaired due to these maladies. However, it is doubtful that anyone at the time realized the seriousness of his condition or the degenerating results.

In his last letter to his nephew, Fitz Lee dated September 19, 1870, it is obvious that he was weak as his handwriting appears fragile and uncharacteristically slipshod, but his thought process was a clear and distinct as always. At the end of the letter he informs Fitz of family visits and a desire for he [Fitz] and Custis to preform a laudable act. "We have had a pleasant visit from Fitzhugh. He was called home the other day but left his wife & boy with us. Robert is also here. I wish you were with us my dear nephew and could gratify us in the same way that F. has—You & Custis must set out & do something creditably for yourselves." [109] Lee's shaky hand ended his letter with his usual wish for prayers and happiness.

Custis' life continued at V. M. I. in the same manner as it had since 1865. He was fully aware of this father's serious health condition. Nevertheless, he resorted to his innate habit of coolness under pressure and total resolve. He would need every ounce of strength to maintain his family through the arduous events forthcoming as well as his own preparation toward becoming the patriarch of his immediate family.

Aware that his health was dubious, Lee persevered with his presidential duties; arranging classes and locating housing for the students. Then on Wednesday, September 28, 1870, General Lee began his day like any other but by the evening his constitution would waiver and ultimately fail within days. The following is an accurate record of the final days of General Lee's life transcribed by Reverend J. William Jones, D.D.:

In the morning he was fully occupied with the correspondence and other tasks incident to his office of president of Washington College, and he declined offers of assistance for members of the faculty, whose service he sometimes availed himself. After dinner, at four o'clock, he attended a vestry-meeting of Grace (Episcopal) church. The afternoon was chilly and wet, and a steady rain had set in, which did not cease until it resulted in a great flood, the most memorable and destructive in this region for a hundred years. The church was rather cold and damp, and General Lee, during the meeting, sat in the pew with his military cape cast loosely about him. In a conversation that occupied the brief space preceding the call to order, he took part, and told with marked cheerfulness of manner and kindliness of tone some pleasant anecdotes of Bishop Meade and Chief-Justice Marshall. The meeting was protracted until after seven o'clock by a discussion touching the rebuilding of the church edifice and the increase of the rectors's salary. General Lee acted as chairman, and, after hearing all that was said, gave his own opinion, as was his wont, briefly and without argument. He closed the meeting... He seemed tired toward the close of the meeting, and, as was afterward remarked, showed an unusual flush, but at the time no apprehensions were felt.

General Lee returned to his house, and, finding his family waiting tea for him, took his place at the table, standing to say grace. The effort was vain; the lips could not utter the prayer of the heart. Finding himself unable to speak, he took his seat quietly and without agitation. His face seemed to some of the anxious group about him to wear a look of sublime resignation, and to evince a full knowledge that the hours had come when all the cares and anxieties of his crowed life were at an end. His physicians, Doctors H. S. Barton and R. L. Madison, arrived promptly, applied the usual remedies, and placed him upon the couch from which he was to rise no more.

To him henceforth the things of this world were as

nothing, and bowed with resignation to the command of the Master he had followed so long with reverence. The symptoms of his attack resembled concussion of the brain, without the attendant swoon. There was marked debility, a slightly impaired consciousness, and a tendency to doze; but no paralysis of motion or sensation, and no evidence of suffering or inflammation of the brain. His physicians treated the case as one of venous congestion, and with apparently favorable results. Yet, despite these propitious auguries drawn from his physician symptoms, in view of the great mental strain he had undergone, the gravest fears were felt that the attack was mortal. He took without objection the medicines and diet prescribed, and was strong enough to turn in bed without aid, and to sit up to take nourishment. During the earlier days of his illness, though inclined to doze, he was easily aroused, was quite conscious and observant, evidently understood whatever was said to him, and answered questions briefly but intelligently using monosyllables, as had always been his habit when sick.

When first attacked, he said to those who were removing his clothes, pointed at the same time to his rheumatic shoulder, "You hurt my arm." Although he seemed to be gradually improving until October 10th, he apparently knew from the first that the appointed hour had come when he must enter those dark gates that closing, open no more to earth. In the words of his physician, "he neither expected nor desired to recover." When General Custis Lee made some allusion to his recovery, he shook his head and pointed upward. On the Monday morning before his death, Dr. Madison, finding him looking better, tried to cheer him. "How do you feel today, General? General Lee replied slowly and distinctly: "I feel better," The doctor then said: "You must make haste and get well; Traveler has been standing so long in the stable that he needs exercise." The General made no reply, but slowly shook his head and closed his eyes.

Several times during his illness he put aside his medicine, saying, "It is no use," but yielded patiently to the wishes of his physicians or children, as if the slackened chords of being still responded to the touch of duty or affection.

On October 10th, during the afternoon, his pulse became feeble and rapid, and his breathing hurried, with other evidences of great exhaustion. About midnight he was seized with a shivering from extreme debility, and Doctor Barton felt obliged to announce the danger to the family. On October 11th, he was evidently sinking; his respiration was hurried, his pulse feeble and rapid. Though less observant, he still recognized whoever approached him, but refused to take anything unless prescribed by his physicians. It now became certain that the case was hopeless. His decline was rapid, yet gentle; and soon after nine o'clock, on the morning of October 12th, he closed his eyes and his soul passed peacefully from earth.[110]

After her husband was put to rest, Mrs. Lee wrote to a friend about his last days, "He never smiled, and rarely attempted to speak, except in his dreams, and then he wandered to those dreadful battlefields." [111] It was noted that he called upon Ambrose Powell Hill saying, "Tell Hill he must come up! and finally his last words, were an order to "Strike the tent!" This seems logical for Lee to return to the War between the States in the last moments of his life, because it is this period which made him not only a great leader, but also established his legacy.

A celestial phenomenon occurred the week of General Lee's death. Many saw it was an omen. A Scottish immigrant woman living in Lexington recorded in her diary the following passage from W. E. Aytoun's *Edinburgh After Flodden* after she observed the aurora's brilliance:

> "All night long the northern streamers
> Shot across the trembling sky:
> Fearful lights, that never beckon
> Save when kings, or heroes die."[112]

The shimmering aurora borealis illuminated the sky with its streamers of colorful light on that mid-October evening. Just like another aurora borealis that was observed eight years earlier after the great Confederate victory of the Battle of Fredericksburg. Perhaps some former Confederate soldiers might have pondered the astronomical event from Fredericksburg and superstitiously thought that it was right that the spirit of the greatest Confederate general of them all should be welcomed into heaven itself by such a display. Regardless of the emotion of the time, the general's death marked the closure of an era that would never be seen again.

There were several tributes to the General in the days prior to his funeral, scheduled for Saturday, October 15th. The day before the funeral, General Lee's remains were taken to chapel on the campus of Washington College to lay in state until the next day. Mrs. Lee had accepted the offer of the college to have his body placed in the crypt in the basement of the chapel near his office. General G. W. C. Lee, General W. H. F. Lee and Captain R. E. Lee, Jr., and other family members, along with Colonel W. H. Taylor, Colonel C. S. Venable and many others were present as they watched the flag of Virginia draped in mourning and hung at half-mast above the college.

The next day the service was simple in accordance to General Lee's wishes. As Jones recorded, "It was desired to avoid all mere pageantry and display, and that all the honors paid should accord with the simple dignity of the dead. This spirit prevailed in all proceedings and gave character to the ceremonies of the day."[113]

Aside from his family and friends, there were many former Confederate officers and enlisted men along with dignitaries of the State of Virginia, Trustees, Faculty and students of both Washington College and the Virginia Military Institute. But the most touching tribute was the symbol of the riderless horse, Traveller. In the end Robert E. Lee was placed to rest in a vault constructed of brick, lined with cement. It was double capped with white marble, and inscribed:

ROBERT EDWARD LEE
Born January 19, 1807
Died October 12, 1870

Later, a recumbent life-size sculpture of General Lee was placed directly above the crypt on the main floor of the chapel.

In the days following the funeral, the Lee family, as with any family who suffered this type of loss, had to make adjustments and decisions. Washington College offered Mrs. Lee life right to the house constructed for her and General Lee when he accepted the post at the college. Nonetheless, she refused the offer to stay there, since she felt the house should be the residency of the next college president. Yet, the next president was already living there.

Custis moved from his quarters at the Virginia Military Institute in the fall of 1869 about the time his father's health was starting to decline. He took the bedroom next to his father's bedroom on the second floor, while his sisters occupied the bedrooms across the hall and his mother had a room on the first floor. His room was large and frequently doubled as his study or private library. Located on the western exposure, the afternoon sun filled the room and provided him with natural light into the evening.

After a week of suspended classes at Washington College and V. M. I., the schools resumed their classes. This was a proper decision, as Robert E. Lee spent the last five years of his life dedicated to the pursuit of educational excellence. Custis had just resumed his duties at V. M. I. when the trustees of Washington College announced his election to succeed his father as president of the college. This immediate selection prior to the end of October, 1870 appeared by all accounts to be a superior choice.

George Washington Custis Lee not only retained the name of Lee, but that of Washington, also. He was a recognized intellectual, graduating first in his class at the United States Military Academy, and who presently held the position of Department Chairman and Professor of Military and Civil Engineering and Applied Mechanics at V. M. I.

Since the conclusion of the war, he was offered the presidencies of at least two other institutions of higher learning but declined both positions. Not only did he possess excellent qualifications, but he was familiar with his father's work and plans for the College. Having just turned thirty-eight the month before, he appeared to be a man in the prime of his life in superb health. From all indications Custis Lee was the obvious and best selection to replace his father.

At the same time the Washington College trustees announced their successor to Robert E. Lee, they proclaimed a change in the name of the facility in addition. The new name would be Washington and Lee University, honoring first Washington who financially supported the college and Lee, whose administrative skill propelled the school into the modern realm of an university.

The younger Lee was enthusiastically welcomed to the position by faculty and trustees alike. Many of the alumni added their endorsements. Yet, prior to their announcement, the trustees felt it was proper to inquire with various people as to their selection. Trustee John Echols wrote to Judge John W. Brockenbrough that he was "satisfied" and the general consensus in the state of Virginia was positive about their choice. Echols inquired with former Confederate president Jefferson Davis as to Custis Lee's abilities, to and Davis recommended him highly. However, Davis wrote to William Preston Johnston, "The only defect I found in him was his extreme diffidence in his own ability, and that leaned so much to virtue's side, that most parents would be glad to have such an example before their sons."[114]

The only apparent question regarding Custis' qualifications for the position was that he did not belong to any particular church. This point was very surprising to the trustees since his family was steeped in Episcopalian reverence. Lee took steps to quickly remedy the situation by attending confirmation classes resulting through the winter and spring of 1871 and was confirmed in June by Bishop Whittle of the Grace Episcopal Church at Lexington. His martial status had no impact, but made him the brunt of jokes over the years. His salary was the same as his father's, $1,500.00 annually, while his mother enjoyed an annuity of $3,000.00, in addition to life right to the President's house.[115]

President's House, Washington and Lee University
Photograph by Author

Newcomb Hall
Special Collections, Leyburn Library,
Washington and Lee University

G. W. C. Lee, 1870's
Private Collection

President G. W. C. Lee's Office
Special Collections, Leyburn Library,
Washington and Lee University

George Washington
Custis Lee, by Benjamin
West Clinedinst Washington
and Lee University,
Lexington, Virginia

In the meantime Custis continued with his classes at V. M. I. He maintained an active correspondence with several former Confederate colleagues, especially Colonels Walter H. Taylor and Charles Marshall.

For sometime Colonel Charles Marshall was contemplating an account of his wartime experiences and relationship with General Robert E. Lee. Now he was called upon to write a memorial volume as requested by the trustees of Washington College. Marshall had requested that Mrs. Lee and Custis write any anecdotes or perhaps a narrative, which might aid him in his research. Several weeks after his father's death, Custis responded to Marshall's request, "I write a line to say that I have received your letter of the 19th, ult., and will send what I have been collecting for you in a day or two. You must feel perfectly free to use or reject anything in my mother's narrative. I wished to copy it for you; but have so much pressing upon me just now, that there might be too much delay."[116] The next day he wrote to wrote to Colonel Walter H. Taylor concerning two points: firstly to acquire data on the campaigns in West Virginia and secondly on the Southern coast and to obtain his opinion on how to on a permanent resting place for his father's remains. [Apparently, the Virginia Legislature want his remains located in a stationary memorial in Richmond.]

You may have heard that Col. Marshall has been requested to prepare a sketch of my father's life and public service for the Memorial volume which the authorities of Washington College purpose to publish as soon as practicable, and that he has counted to do so. I have promised to give him all the assistance in my power, which will, I fear, amount to nothing more than troubling friends.

Marshall will want an outline of the operations in West Virginia and on the Southern Coast. Can you not find time to write a brief sketch of one or both of these? Or, if you can not, can you advise me to whom to apply? A brief outline will be sufficient, but the more complete the sketch the better.

I should like to have your advice as to whether it will

be but to give a formal answer to the kind offer of the Legislature, in regard to the custody and internment of my father's remains, during this session or not. My mother, who has been quite sick since you left us (She is now much better) seems indisposed to be separated from them, and indeed say that so long as she remains here, it is her wish that they remain where they now are.

I desire to do all that can be done to show our appreciation of and gratitude for, the kind action of the Legislature; and this is why I trouble you for your opinion and advice in the matter.[117]

The Christmas Holidays came and went as they had for many years but the Holidays would never be the same for the Lee family.

Custis began to conclude his classes and prepare the students for their exams. At the same time he wrote his resignation to General Francis H. Smith and the Board of Visitors of the Virginia Military Institute, dated January 2, 1871:

Having accepted the office of President of Washington College, I hereby tender the resignation of my commission as Professor of Civil and Military Engineering in the Virginia Military Institute, and ask that it may be accepted to take effect on the 31st inst., or as soon thereafter as adequate provision can be made for the instruction of my class. With my best wishes for the continued prosperity of the Institute, and the happiness of those connected with it, and my grateful acknowledgement for the uniform kindness and courtesy extended to me by all, I have the honor to be...[118]

When knowledge of Custis' resignation became publicly recognized, one former cadet from that year commented upon him resigning his position at V. M. I. to take the post of President of Washington College, "He gave up his congenial life at the Institute with the greatest of regret, but in this case, as in every other crisis in his life, Duty was the controlling factor in his decision."[119]

Nevertheless, his resignation was accepted by the Board of Visitors and the Superintendent Francis H. Smith:

> Your communication addressed to the Board of Visitors, dated January 2, 1871, tendering your resignation as Professor of Military and Civil Engineering in this institution, has been submitted to the Board, and they have instructed me to inform you that your resignation has been accepted by them, upon the terms of your letter. I am also directed by the Board of Visitors to convey to you the expressions of their profound regret at parting with as a Professor. You came to the Institute at the period of its utter prostration; you have contributed by your usefulness and prosperity, and you have given to the department, which you have filled for more than five years, a reputation which is acknowledged throughout out State and Country. The Board of Visitors fully recognize the claims of duty which so strongly present themselves in your call to the Presidency of Washington College, and it is their sincere wish that your success in this more enlarged sphere of usefulness may be commensurate with the high qualities you carry with you on entering upon this new work. Most cordially responding to the sentiment conveyed in the Orders of the Board of Visitors, I have the honor to be, very respectfully.[120]

In the letter from General Smith accepting his resignation, he included the following excerpt from the minutes of a meeting of the Academic Board of the Virginia Military Institute, dated January 27, 1871:

> The Academic Board met in regular session.
> Present all except Gen. G. W. C. Lee.
> The Faculty of the Virginia Military Institute having been notified by General G. W. Custis Lee that he had resigned the Professorship of Military and Civil Engineering and Applied Mathematics in this Institute, and

that he had accepted the Presidency of Washington College, the following minutes was entered upon the record of their proceedings:

We cordially congratulate our colleague, Gen. G. W. Custis Lee, upon his election as President of Washington and Lee University, believing that the administration of an Institution so prominent necessarily opens to one of his character and ability a wide field for usefulness and an opportunity for establishing a high and solid reputation among the educators of this State. We feel especially moved to express our sincere wishes for his success in the effort which he now proposes to make to complete an important work so auspiciously begun by his late illustrious father. We cannot, however, withhold the expression of our regret at the loss which our institution sustains by the resignation of a Professor so faithful and able. It is as a Faculty that we more nearly feel the severance with a gentleman whose peculiarly characterized, in council by wisdom, and in social life by courtesy and gentleness. Resolved, that the Superintendent cause an extract of the record, including the foregoing minutes, to be communicated to Gen. G. W. C. Lee.[121]

To these above minutes was added yet another tribute from the Virginia Military Institute, as he left his position with them to succeed his father:

Professor G.W.C. Lee was born at Arlington, Va. [actually at Fort Monroe, Virginia] He entered the U.S. Military Academy at West Point, as a cadet in June, 1850 and graduated at the head of his class in June, 1854. Promoted in the Corps of Engineers, he acquired great distinction in the various works of construction to which his duties called him, and resigned for the army in 1861 that he might tender his services to his native State, in the Civil War then opening. Appointed a Brigadier General on the staff of he President of the Confederate States, he was promoted to Major General, and was in command of a division of the forces around Richmond at the close of the War in 1865. Unanimously called to the Chair of Military and Civil Engineering and Applied Mechanics in the fall of 1865, he gave six years of earnest and effective labor to the duties of this appointment, contributing by his counsel and work to the restoration of the prosperity of the Va. Military Institute, and when he resigned in February 1871, he carried with him into his new and important duties in a neighboring sister Institution, the regards and best wishes of the Board of Visitors and Faculty of the Institute.[122]

A heavy snowstorm drifted into Lexington on February 6, 1871, the day designated for the installation of George Washington Custis Lee as the new president of Washington and Lee University. As if the weather was predicting the tenure of his presidency, this singular decision was the biggest mistake of George Washington Custis Lee's life.

When the sense of duty is taken too far, it sometimes plays a large role in destroying a person's sense of well-being by gradual wearing down their mental and physical ability to function. What appeared at first as a promising opportunity evolved into a vast waste of a brilliant mind and suffocation of man in the prime of his life from an active and independent existence.

Interestingly, the date of his inauguration was the anniversary of the birth of his old friend, Major General James Ewell Brown Stuart, it cannot be documented from certain whether or not this minor fact crossed his mind, as he entered the old chapel on the campus to a crowd of local people, faculty from both V. M. I. and the former Washington College as well as family, students and cadets. General G. W. C. Lee was escorted to his chair of honor by the Honorable J. Randolph Tucker, Professor of Law. The *Southern Collegian* described General Lee's appearance on that day, "...he came up the aisle, neatly dressed in black cloth, one could not but be struck with the resemblance, in his every feature and every movement, to his father. The same firm, unassuming military step;

the same calm, piercing eye; the same broad forehead and massive under jaw—in a word, but for the difference in age, one could have believed that the loved and familiar form of our late President was again before us."[123]

Judge John W. Brockenbrough delivered the main address. His masterful oration was one in which he cited past administrations and looked forward to the new administration,

> ...with unerring certainty to the conviction among the ranks of living men, the son of Gen. R. E. Lee was the most fit person to secure the full fruition of a policy so wisely originated and matured during the years of a nobly spent life. That conviction had riveted itself already in the public mind, and in selecting you as the President elect of this venerable Institution of Learning, we but give expression to the widely diffused general sentiment of the public heart and head. Your own ripe scholarship, well-balanced mind, your hereditary devotion to duty, your thorough moral and intellectual training, are but so many guarantees for your perfect success in accomplishing the great work committed to your hands. We rest upon those guarantees with assured confidence that, in the Providence of God, a full measure of success awaits you. We know you will earnestly seek, in the coming time, to carry our in perfect fulfillment the enlarged and beneficent scheme so wisely begun, but yet unfinished work, of your illustrious Predecessor.[124]

Lee's acceptance speech was very brief and to the point, asking for the cooperation of trustees, faculty and students:

> I cannot but be grateful, Sir, for the kind sentiments you have been pleased to express in my behalf (however little I may deserve them,) and am sincerely anxious to meet your expectations to the fullest extent. Solemnly realizing the duties and responsibilities of the position I am about to take, I ask of the Honorable Body which you represent, and of the Faculty and Students of this Institution, their promised assistance and co-operation, and earnestly praying for Divine guidance, I accept the

trust committed to my charge, and am now ready to take the required oath of office.[125]

With Lee's brief acceptance speech concluded, Judge Brockenbrough verbally administrated the oath of office to the Presidency of the Washington and Lee University to George Washington Custis Lee:

> I solemnly swear that I will faithfully discharge the duties of the office of President of Washington and Lee University, to which I have been elected by the Trustees thereof, to the best of my skill and judgment, without favor, fear, of affection. So help me God.

In swearing the oath publicly and signing the oath privately before Judge Brockenbrough, Custis Lee had made a commitment he would live to regret over and over.

Even though he was now the new president of Washington and Lee University, the duty to fulfilled his commitment to the Virginia Military Institute lingered on. After the morning ceremony concluded, Lee took his familiar stroll to the campus of the Virginia Military Institute to conclude his course of Applied Mechanics. On Friday evening, February 10, he wrote to General Francis H. Smith:

> The course of Applied Mechanics, as proposed for the 1st Class, was finished this morning; and its members were informed of the termination of my professorial relation to them. I would not thus give them up before the completion of their course of Civil Engineering, of which the course of Applied Mechanics is the most difficult part, did there not seem to be a necessary for so doing; and I have the satisfaction of leaving them in charge of one well qualified to continue their instruction.
>
> It is an agreeable duty to bear witness to the unexceptionable good conduct of the class in my intercourse with its members, and to acknowledge my obligations for the courtesy and consideration which they have uniformly

extended to me.

In leaving the Va. Mil. Institute, where I have received nothing but kindness from all connected with it, I cherish the hope that the separation will be official only, and that our personal relations will be as friendly and cordial in the future as they have been in the past. I must ask you, General, who have conveyed to me, in such gratifying terms, the acceptance of my resignation by the Board of Visitors, to express to that Honorable Body the gratitude with which I have received their kind action.

And for yourself and the other members of he Academic Board, who have judged my failings so charitably and valued what I have done so generously, please accept my heartfelt thanks and sincere assurance of esteem.[126]

Lee actually began his tenure at Washington and Lee University on Monday, February 13, 1871. These first few months were perhaps his best months at the university. He was enthusiastic about continuing his father's plans for advancing and developing the university both academically and physically. In his personal life, he continued his correspondence with Colonel Charles Marshall, giving him important data about his father war days:

I send you, by this mail some additional papers which I have recently come across, thinking they may be of use to you, vicz; Letter (copy) to Genl. early explaining his relief from command of Valley &c.

Letters of Genls. Pickett & Fitz Lee in reference to the battle of Five Forks some notes & a part of a letter, in my father's hand writing. Telegrams in reference to operations before Petersburg from Genl. Beauregard.

I have also Genl. Beauregard's reports of the battles of Bull Run, Manassas & Shiloh, in one book, which Genl. Beauregard requests shall be returned to him.

When you are writing to this place, sometime, you can let me know whether or not you wish it.

I have not been able to get the extract from Genl. Cullum's Book of the Graduates of the Military Academy.

Your friends in Washington could, I am sure, get the extract or the book itself, through Genl. Humphreys, Chief of Engineer Corps, U.S. Army. I am very glad to learn that you are getting on so well with your work. Please remember us most kindly to Mrs. Marshall, and believe me to be very truly yrs.[127]

Along with requests from friends on data pertaining to his father's war campaigns, Custis was constantly receiving letters from strangers, both North and South, for a memento of his father. It was Custis' habit to reply politely but with a curt edge to the Northerners' requests. His response to a New Yorker's request for an autograph of Robert E. Lee is an example: "In compliance with your request of the 5th inst, I enclose one of the few of my father's autographs remaining in my possession."[128]

His first annual report was thorough and professional in range and scope. He compiled the various reports from the department chairmen into a methodical analysis. A typical end of the year report from a department chairman was this one submitted by William Preston Johnston, Professor and Department Chairman of History and Literature:

I have the honor to transmit herewith a detailed report of my classes in History and Literature: also a copy of the Intermediate and Final Examinations proposed to the Class.

The number of distinctions given is in all compared to the number of students who have entered these classes. I do not attribute this to the difficulty of the Examinations, but to the want of previous training in the Students. I have sought to adapt the instruction to the young men under my charge. The Junior Class has studied, reviewed and been examined on the Whole of Smith's Greece & Siddell's Rome 250 pages of the Students' (abridged) Gibbon, 1600 or 1700 pages of reading matter. The

Senior Class in History read Hume to the reign of Charles I, and the abridged Hume to that of William III. They also studied Gnizot, and received about 100 Lectures from me on topics connected with the text, or on the History of Europe for the Fall of the Roman Empire on all of which they were examined.

The Class in Literature Studied all of Shaw's larger Manual, the best textbook accessible, for their purposes, and Read's Lectures on Literature and on the History of England. I lectured to them on topics connected with the text and on Shakespeare's plays, requiring from them a close study and understanding of Julius Caesar, Hamlet, Macbeth and Merchant of Venice. They also Studied so much of Goodrich's Lord Chatham, Lord Mansfield, and Edmund Burke and their speeches on American affairs, on all of which they were examined. I feel that it is due to the young men under my charge to say that their conduct in the Lecture Room has been marked by a visible improvement in dignity and order; and that in every point of view it has been satisfactory and pleasing to me.

My department has suffered from a want of the ordinary means of information; the College Library being more entirely barren of works in History and General Literature that in any other Department. The ordinary works of reference are also needed. When it is considered the a supply of this want would benefit every department in College, it seems reasonable that I may look for at least a moderate outlay at no distant day. [129]

In the report from the chairman in the mathematics department, W. Allen, his annual report was similar to Johnston's report: "During the past session there have been 45 students in the school of Applied Math of whom 30 have been in the Engineering classes and 15 in that of Elementary Astronomy. Their progress had in the main been satisfactory. The details are given in the accompanying report. No addition has been made during the year to the apparatus of this department...It is desirable that the collection of models and drawings of important engineering works should be enlarged as soon as justifiable." [130]

Aside from the academic reports requested by President Lee, he also wanted an accounting of the Young Men's Christian Association. This annual report was submitted by C. B. Willingham on June 12, 1871. It listed the membership of seventy-six gentlemen, the various denominations: 57-Presbyterians, 25-Episcopalians, 15-Methodists, 10-Baptists, 4-Campbellites and 1-Catholic, and the frequency of worship services, both nightly and weekly. He concluded his report by stating, "The association is in a very flourishing condition, holding its meetings monthly and has an average attendance of about 50." [131] The new president supported the organization as a moral appendage of the university.

The continual theme from all of the chairmen for instructional materials and books was consistent. New President Lee impelled the trustees to consider their requests very seriously and make necessary arrangement to acquire the desired supplies. Lee's first annual report to the Board of Trustees was methodical and comprehensive:

> I have the honor to submit the following report for the Session of 1870- 71. As my official connection with the institution commenced in February last, that part of the report only, which refers to the later half of the Session, is based upon personal observation.
>
> The exercises of the institution began on the 15th Sept. 1870. The number of students in attendance during the Session is three hundred and thirty-six (336), including four (4) Resident Masters, From:

Virginia	70	Maryland	7
Texas	39	New York	5
Kentucky	36	Illinois	3
Tennessee	25	Florida	2
Louisiana	24	Pennsylvania	2
S. Carolina	20	Ohio	1
Missouri	20	Indiana	1
Alabama	16	Iowa	1

Georgia	15	California	1
Mississippi	15	Idaho Territory	1
Arkansas	14	District of Columbia	1
W. Virginia	8	France	1
N. Carolina	7	Canada	1

They were arranged into classes in the several schools as follows:

Latin	196	Mathematics	232
Greek	127	Applied Math.	45
English & Literature	164	Nat. Philosophy	24
Modern Languages	206	Chemistry	79
History	38	Law	31
Moral Philosophy	27	Business School	19

The usual division of classes into sections of convenient size, and the provision of asst. Professors and Instructors, when necessary, were made.

It gives me much pleasure to express the opinion of the Faculty that the general conduct of the students, during the session, has been better than ever before, and that their application to study has been as good, at least, as heretofore. Two (2) left without permission; four (4) were required to withdraw; and forty (40) were allowed to withdraw on account of sickness and other sufficient causes.

Your attention is invited to the accompanying reports of the Professors for full information as to the methods of instruction, progress of the pupils and some important suggestions and recommendations.

I trust it will not be considered improper to renew the recommendation that the purchase of apparatus for the School of Natural Philosophy, Applied Mathematics, and Chemistry be annually continued as the means at the disposal of the Board will permit.

It is not deemed advisable to make any further recommendation in regard to the School of Applied Chemistry, and the important subject of Natural History, until after conference with the Professor of the former.

For the Condition and needs of the Department of Law and equity, I respectfully refer you to the report of its Professors.

The daily morning services in the Chapel have been continued this, as during the proceeding session; and you will be grateful to learn that there has been a much larger attendance of students upon there exercises that for any previous session.

The Young Men's Christian Association continues prosperous and useful. For particulars, I invite your attention to the report of its Vice President, prepared by my request.

The report of the Librarian shows the general condition of the Library. Its needs, especially in works for the use of the Professors in current instruction are urgent; and it is earnestly recommended that there be supplied by as liberal annual appropriations as possible.

With the approval of as many of the Faculty and Trustees as I have had the opportunity of consulting on the subject, I respectfully recommend the employment of an architect to prepare a general design for the University buildings, such an one as will best harmonize what has bee done with what is required. To accomplish this properly, he should come here examine the existing buildings, obtain all the information possible as to what is needed, and then study out, at his leisure, a plan for us to work to, as circumstances may permit.

I submit, herewith, for the information and action of your honorable body, so much of the proceedings of the Faculty as will be of interest. [132]

This ambitious plan of improving the academic classes as

recommended by the Faculty, and the suggested plan of hiring an architect to draw up plans for new buildings from Lee himself was all but totally rejected by the trustees who cited financial difficulties. These recommendations were in alignment with the plans R. E. Lee was advocating at the time of his death. It can only be speculated whether he would have been successful in obtaining the trustees support. This setback in the first year of Custis Lee's tenure laid the foundation for his relationship with the Trustees of Washington and Lee University and opened the door to the series of resignations which would follow in subsequent years.

The next month, Lee's professional relationship with the Virginia Military Institute became final. The Superintendent's Annual Report of 1871, stated: "Gen. G. W. C. Lee, on his resignation of his Professorship in the Virginia Military Institute, kindly tendered $2,200 held by him in the bonds of the Institute, being advances made by him from his salary as a Professor, for rebuilding the Institute for the like purposes, makes the total amount held by the Corcoran Art Gallery in the bonds of the Institute, $4,200." [133] Although his personal affiliation was strong, the professional allegiance was now broken. With this closure, he was forced to remain at Washington and Lee University or seek opportunities elsewhere. He decided to stay at the university for the present time. His decision was wholly contingent upon his family. Where could he take an incapacitated mother and three dependent sisters? He had little choice, but to stay in Lexington.

About nine months after the death of his father, Traveller, Robert E. Lee's famed war-horse died of lockjaw [tetanus.] In the book, *Cry Heart,* the author describes the story of the last days of the celebrated horse as told to him by General Lee's daughter, Mary Custis Lee:

> I was sitting on the veranda of our home in Lexington with my brother, General Custis Lee, when Traveller, always a privileged character, but of course a special pet since his master's death, came browsing around in the yard, and, seeing someone on the piazza, advanced whinnying for the lump sugar that he always

expected. I entered the house to procure him one, and when I returned with it, I found my brother examining his foot, saying, "This horse appears to be lame." A very small nail or tack was extracted, and the wound was so slight that it did not appear to even bleed.

After eating the sugar with relish and being caressed, he moved leisurely away. In the course of a day or two the hostler reported him unwell. We had no veterinarian in Lexington, but the two doctors who had attended my father during his last illness devoted themselves assiduously to the sufferings of his famous war horse.

Everything skill and devotion could be done. He was chloroformed, liquid nourishment forced down his throat, and then when he could no longer stand upright, a feather bed was laid on the stable floor to give him all the relief possible.

Our little town—indeed, the whole neighborhood—was intensely sympathetic. Not only the gentlemen of the town but the farmers around came to offer suggestions and condolences. It was all to no avail. The efforts to relieve him merely prolonged his sufferings, which, when all hope was gone, I advocated putting an end to it at once. But my brother could not bring himself to do that, though poor Traveller's groans and cries were heartrending in the extreme, and could be plainly heard in the house. I don't think any of us were able to sleep that last night, and it was really a relief when all was over.

When I went down to look at him after death, from being a powerful, well grown horse he seemed to have dwindled away to the size of a colt, and I am sure we almost felt that we had lost a member of the family. I have often heard my father state at the end of the most arduous day, with often the night thrown in, he apparently was as fresh and lively as when first mounted. He was bought for a second or spare horse; but as one after another of the more showy steeds, notably after our Confederate capital, succumbed to the fortunes of war,

> Traveller came gradually to the front and remained there,
> my father riding him not only at Appomattox but on his
> sad return to Richmond. [134]

This sad event did nothing to lift Custis' spirits. In some ways it was like losing his father again. Traveller was more than a Confederate symbol: he was a living representation of Robert E. Lee, himself.

After Traveller's death, his bones were prepared to be placed on display, but visitors wrote on the bones and conducted other abuses. Finally, it was decided to bury the remains. Today, people who visit the Lee Memorial Chapel on the lower level by the Lee crypt adjacent to the exterior of the door will note the grave of Traveller. Frequently, visitors leave small Confederate battle flags and coins.

Quickly, the summer evolved into the autumn again. The first full year of his tenure as President of Washington and Lee University was about to unfold. As the students registered for their classes, Lee stood by to welcome and direct them to the appropriate professor. This was a difficult task for a man who was not naturally outgoing. Frequently, he appeared awkward or aloof; at any rate this was not his intrinsic environment. Some of his former students from the Virginia Military Institute thought he was pressured into a position he did not desire, and was forced to acquiesce to it because of his name and the situation of his mother and sisters. The administrator's role was not a position that Lee relished. He was much more comfortable in the classroom. But even there he longed to renew his life as an engineer, doing what he truly loved. Unfortunately, this was not to be. Realizing his hopeless circumstance, he became more and more reticent.

As if to add insult to injury, the presidency of Washington and Lee University offered little stimulus to this brilliant man. The position soon became rote and mundane. It lacked the creative order of mathematics and the structural beauty of engineering. The only flicker of hope in breaking this inertia laid with the Trustees reconsidering the constructional building plans Lee proposed for the university. This refusal by the Trustees to hire an architect struck the very soul in Lee. In hiring an architect, Lee could work with him to improve the physical arrangement of the facility and therefore truly make a serious contribution. The trustees denial forced him to realize he was nothing more than a figurehead. As early as late 1871, he was considering to resign from this position. A deep languor was beginning to formulate within Lee.

During the winter of 1872, his mother encouraged him to seek a change of scene and society. She wrote to her youngest daughter, Mildred, "We have had sweet weather for a few days but now there is a deep snow again. Custis expected to have been in New Orleans by this time, indeed was all packed up, but has been detained of course he does not <u>want</u> to go & I much fear will get out of it yet hope he will find it inevitable, for it would be such a benefit to him to make a change during this inclement season."[135] He did manage to traverse to New Orleans but the thought of returning to the position in Lexington brought about distress. He developed a pattern of steady absences from the campus until he submitted his first resignation in 1874.

After his return from New Orleans, he occupied himself with personal correspondence from his office. Utilizing the Washington and Lee University letterhead, he communicated with various people throughout his long tenure at the institution.

Many of the letters he received and responded to were from former military men who were writing manuscripts on the recent war. Colonel Charles C. Jones of New York requested a considerable amount of information from Lee which responded to in kind:

> Yours of the 29th ult. received. Col. Johnston tells me that he has sent you his fathers' autograph by mail. I have no Field Returns; but Col. Walter Taylor, Norfolk, Va., may be able to put you in the way of getting one. Do you wish the autograph letter of my father for the hand writing simply, or do you wish it to publish in your work? A letter suitable to the one subject might not do for the other.[136]

Lee used every opportunity to help Jones in his queries, but to no avail. Eleven days later Lee wrote to Jones again:

My mother has been looking over my father's letters to find one to answer your purpose, but so far without success. Those in other respects proper for publication are of such a private nature that my mother would rather not have them made public, and the few in our possession not of a strictly private character are not in other respects suited for publication. If we can find one, however, altogether appropriate, I will send it to you.

To the best of my knowledge, my father was never a Major General in the Confederate service. He was made full Genl. as you state. I can not give the dates of his respective commissions, nor do I know the precise time of his assuming command of the armies of the Confederacy. It was in the Spring of 1865, not long before the evacuation of Richmond and Petersburg. Col. Walter Taylor of Norfolk, Va. would probably remember the date, and might recollect, also, the dates of his commissions. Col. Charles Marshall of Baltimore, Md. would, also, probably be able to give you the dates wanted.

Regretting that my answers are so unsatisfactory, I remain[137]

Finally, the spring semester had come to a close and G. W. C. Lee was signing his name to many graduation diplomas, Distinguished Proficiency and Proficiency certificates. The tedium of this duty was overwhelming, but necessary.

During the summer he continued his correspondences to the many inquiries from friends and strangers alike. Helping those who were trying their hand at writing on the war. Frequently, he was compelled to ask former military acquaintances for their aid. In a letter, dated July 19, 1872, he thanked Reverend J. William Jones for his assistance:

I have just received your of the 18th inst. and and am very much obliged to you for what you have done in reference to a second edition of Genl. Early's address.

I am very sorry that you have been suffering from a

boil—I know from painful experience how troublesome such an affliction is. The proofs of Dr. Palmer's address were received last Monday, I think, and returned without delay. I suppose we shall have our copies here in the course of a week or ten days from this time, and when they arrive, a number of them will be forwarded to you.[138]

Aside from all of these inquiries for data pertaining to his father, part of Lee's duties was to correspond with parents, former students, and prospective students. In response to a parental inquiry in regard to the gentleman's son, Lee wrote:

In reply to your note of the 4th inst, I have to state that it appears from our Records that Mr. Thomas Hugh Somerville was a student at this institution for four sessions, and the his course of studies and progress were as follows;

1st Session- Senior English, Senior French, Intermediate Latin, and Junior Mathematics. In the first two he was passed as Proficient.

2nd Session- Senior Latin, Intermediate Mathematics, Junior German, and Chemistry. In the last he was passed as Proficient; and in Mathematics and German, although he passed his examinations, as he did not continue there studied and take the Senior course in them, he could no be declared Proficient.

3rd Session—Moral Philosophy, and Junior Law. In the first he was passed as Distinguished Proficient.

4th Session—Senior Law. In this he was graduated in June last, receiving the Degree of Bachelor of Law. Your son has, probably, in his possession his Diploma, and the several Certificates of Proficiency and Distinguished Proficiency, to which he is entitled.

It gives me pleasure to add that, during his whole stay here, he was a faithful and diligent student, and that his general conduct was unexceptionable.[139]

Lee's life continued in the same prosaic manner through the beginning of 1873. He continued with personal correspondence which generally referred to knowledge pertaining to his father or the war. These inquiries were to provide data useful for others who were attempting to publish their own books. It is difficult to determine why Custis Lee never attempted to write about his father's activities during and after the war, as his brother Robert and cousin Fitzhugh did in subsequent years. Nevertheless, he answered each letter in a gentlemanly manner, if not in a informational manner:

I received same days ago your very kind letter of the 11th inst., and the accompanying Memorial [for Robert E. Lee] of the Hon. Wm. Kelly who has been for some time known to me by reputation, although I have never had the pleasure of a personal acquaintance with him.

I have read the Memorial with the gratification due both to its exalted subject and author, and wish to have it preserved in the library of this institution for the instruction and guidance of the young men now here, and of those who may come hereafter.

Col. Marshall has several times enlarged the scope of his proposed work, which has had the effect of delaying its publication; and I can not venture to express an opinion as to when it will be ready for issue. I shall be glad to have the opportunity of sending you a copy as soon as it makes its appearance.

As you have made such friendly mention of my father— for which, and your kindness to myself, I can not sufficiently thank you—I take the liberty of sending you, herewith, a copy of an address, delivered at this place by Genl. Early more than a year ago, which is said to be accurate as to facts, and which may perhaps be of interest and value historically, if in no other respect.

Again expressing my gratitude for your kind attention, sentiments, and acts, I remain, with best wishes for your happiness...[140]

In the spring there arose an issue which Lee took a special interest. Apparently, a confusion over collecting donations for the former Grace Church [the Robert E. Lee Memorial Episcopal Church] and the Lee sarcophagus became an issue and the old dilemma "to reestablish more definitely the denominational quality of Washington and Lee" university sprang forth again.[141]

The situation came to the forefront when a letter from Dr. William N. Pendleton expressing concern over the issue of the school remaining nonsectarian, as General Robert E. Lee wished, at the time when he accepted the appointment to the presidency in 1865. Now in 1873, the trustees desired to make the school a singular denomination. Dr. Pendleton took this position extremely seriously and reiterated his opinion privately in a letter to President Custis Lee and publicly to the newspapers and religious journals. The controversy continued for many years with no true resolution to the question during Lee's tenure at the university.[142] Lee, although interested, continued his father's stance on the position and declined to become more personally involved. It was not until the administration of Custis Lee's predecessor, William Lyne Wilson, that the issue became practically obsolete and forgotten.

During this debate, Lee's old medical problems became predominate. Coupled with the chronic inertia over his bleak professional situation, Lee's rheumatism and arthritis began to incapacitate him. Years after his retirement, Judge W. H. Tayloe commented in his recollections of Custis Lee, "One hardly knows what to say of General Custis; he did not wish to succeed his father. He was very retiring. Students saw little of him save as passing to and fro. One year I was of the Faculty as Professor of History and then I saw something of him." [143]

Judge Tayloe later recalled other occasions he was in Lee's company:

> I saw him on business. I asked credit for tuition. The faculty referred the matter to him. I had the interview. It was brief. I told him that I would have to go home if I could not get the credit; which was granted. Ten years elapsed before I was able to pay. But I made up the delay

in a later gift of Liberty Bonds.[144]

Tayloe continued his recollections by describing a dinner engagement he had at the Lee's residence:

...I dined with him upon invitation. I was asked to dinner in connection with William S. Graves, brother of C. S. Graves, I forget the year. I remember it was the year of Middlemarch. Fine dinner. He was a fine host. Polite and affable. A negro boy waited on table. I was struck with the fact that the boy walked on the toes of his shoes to be noiseless.[145]

Finally, Tayloe remembered meeting Mary Custis Lee during his vacation in the early summer of 1873 before she left for Europe:

...I was visiting Miss Lizzie Kirkpatrick one night and there met Miss Mary Lee and Miss Stiles. Miss Mary said "I have a visitor Miss Snowden of Alexandria, we wish to go to the top of the College for the view. I trust you can come over tomorrow evening and escort us." Of course I did so; and thus began an acquaintance that I greatly enjoyed. My visits were frequent. I saw much of Mrs. Lee, Miss Mary and Miss Agnes; Miss Mildred was not at home. I never saw General Custis in his home. Mrs. Lee was confined to her chair. Miss Agnes died that year.

The atmosphere was fine; reminding me of the atmosphere Millet created in The Angelus. [This fine painting depicts two peasants in the midst of their angelus, a prayer which twice a day gave cadence to rural life. The work was from the Barbizon School of Art and was quite important to the artist, Jean-Francois Millet. The solemn ceremony created in this painting portrays the figures in a state of reverence both perpetual and unalterable.] Gone forever; we never again will enjoy such atmosphere.[146]

Evidently, this was the manner in which Judge Tayloe desired to remember the Lee women more than sixty-five years later.
Custis traveled to Bremo and Oakland in July of that summer.

He felt comfortable in the company of the Harrison and Cocke families. At one time both family and friends thought Custis may marry either Belle Harrison or Phoebe Cocke, but this was not to be. Nevertheless, he remained friends with the families until the end of their lives. When he returned to Lexington, he continued his correspondence with Colonel Charles Marshall:

> I have been wishing to write to you for some time; but, besides an attack of rheumatism which has made it difficult for me to write, I have been hoping to have an opportunity of seeing you some where this Summer, which would be more pleasant and satisfactory.
>
> I was very sorry to learn the other day that you had been quite sick; but at the same time very glad to learn that you were then much better; and I hope that, if not, already quite well, you soon will be. Can you not at some leisure moment drop me a line to inform me of your movements this Summer—for the next month or six weeks—so that if possible, I may make my arrangements to meet you.
>
> My mother returned here last week, and expects to remain for the rest of the year, at least.
>
> If Mrs. Marshall and yourself will make us a visit, we shall be very glad to welcome you to our house; and if you wish to find a quiet spot to pass the hot season in, I think this will suit you. I may have to be absent for a time, but need not be away long.
>
> My mother and sisters join me in kindest regards to Mrs. Marshall and yourself.[147]

Earlier in June, Mary had sailed to Europe and was out of the country when the clandestine events of the summer and autumn were unfolding. By this time Agnes Lee was starting to show the signs of a serious illness but no one at that time thought it would be fatal. The family was just beginning to recuperating from the death of Rob's young wife, Charlotte Haxall Lee. The "Beautiful Lottie" perished with tuberculosis after only a year of marriage.

The new school year at Washington and Lee was beginning. Mildred was busy arranging the house for the distant cousins who would reside in the household through the academic year. Custis, too, was now entrenched with the details of the new session. Neither of them imagined the tragic events which would encompass the autumn of 1873.

In later years Mildred recalled the circumstances surrounding her sister Agnes' demise.

> She was ill for weeks, but I never realized it—absorbed in housekeeping, company, everything but the comfort of the dear frail form that was so soon to leave us. God knows my remorse now, when I remember my carelessness! About the 1st of Oct I was aroused to a sense of her danger—& moved her from our old room to a brighter sunnier one. She had to lean on me as we crossed the passage, & entered her death chamber, not to leave it until she was carried out in her coffin by her three brothers. Oh, those golden Oct days!
>
> The delicious sunshine thro the open windows, the roses, whose days were also numbered! I used to place them so her tired eyes could drink in their beauty. The sound of the stone-masons, cutting away at the church opposite—went on through those weary days. She said she liked to hear it—"how strong they must be!" Looking down at her own white hands. I forget what day Jinnie Ritchie came—she rode over from the Baths to inquire—and staid until it was over. A ministering angel she was, sitting up *every* night—so strong & cheerful & helpful.
>
> The 12th Oct came—the day my Father died. She was very ill. I road out in the afternoon with poor Mr. Davidson to get some air, she telling me to go, & brought back branches of crimson leaves, with which I decorated his picture on the mantelpiece. She looked, but said nothing. But afterwards (the next day 13th) she spoke of it grate-fully, & said "don't think I am not appreciative of all this

kindness & nursing, because I am silent, but if you knew how much I suffered!"

On the morning of the 14th I was combing her soft brown hair—her eyes had an unearthly brilliancy—& occasionally looking heavenward. The Doctor (Graham) was sent for, & told us she had but a short time to live!

In the afternoon my poor suffering mother was brought up in her chair & sat close to her bedside holding her hand, the tears streaming down her face, but Agnes was hardly conscious—the stupor of death was gathering fast. Later about dusk her mind cleared, & turning to the Doctor said to my surprise, "Doctor must I prepare to live or die?" "To do both Miss Agnes." He went out and we were left alone. She must have seen my tearful eyes, & said, "it is just as well. I never cared to live long. I am weary of life." "How strange I should die between my Father & Annie. He died on the 12th Annie on the 20th!" "You must thank Dr. Graham & Dr. Barton for their kindness—they did what they could." Mildred you must look after my God-children—give my watch to Katherine, & my lace shawl & little work-box to Sally Poor & her little daughter. Little Mildred can have my old clothes—you Mildred must look over my letters & papers. I suppose those that are of no use had better be destroyed. "Perhaps Cousin Markie had better have my *Bible*—you know *Orton* gave it to me!" Then the stupor came in again, & the shadows gathered...Night drew on—We were all collected in that still room, looking wistfully at the slight form on the bed, & listening to her breathing. Dear Jinnie Ritchie was putting hot irons on her feet— Cousin Markie doing all she knew how. I stretched upon the floor, my head splitting with a raging headache. We had induced Mama to go to bed. The Doctor was lying down in Custis' room & Custis was resting in a little back room. I was doing something for Agnes after awhile, when she opened her eyes, & asked in a ringing tone, that will sound forever in my ears—"Am I dying?" I said "Oh

Agnes I am afraid you are—you are not afraid to die?"
"No," & she said something about "My Saviour," &
"going to my Father," (meaning Papa) & "lay me by my
Father." We all stood breathless around her bed. I
managed to repeat the Lords Prayer, & she joined in at "
Forgive us our trespasses," murmuring "ah that's the
part!" Then Jinnie Ritchie said, "Would you like me to
say Rock of Ages?" She assented & listened while those
solemn words were repeated in a firm voice. "Where is
Custis?" I ran for him. He sat on the bed by her side, &
she said in a half caressing way, "you know I have always
loved you—you must not forget me when I am gone." He
stroked her hand, saying "Aggie none of us will do that."
All of us were so choked with sobs we could not speak.
She turned to me. "Mildred take care of the Connors (a
poor family) for my sake." "Mildred, you will forgive my
being exacting at times—you know I was always
contrary!" I forget now what else she said. I remember
saying "you are going to Papa, & Annie & GrandMa," her
again murmuring "by my Father," "Annie"—That was
all—her breathing grew shorter—one gasp-& all was
over for ever!

Day was just about dawning in the East, when her
pure, her heroic spirit took its flight—ah *whither*, who can
tell! I rushed down stairs to tell Mama. Shall I ever forget
that scene—She was standing undressed in the chilly
frosty morning air, my poor suffering, patient Mother, &
when I told her Agnes was dead, cried "my poor child,
that I should have outlived her. Oh that I could have seen
her again!" Mama never rallied from this blow, & died on
the 5th Nov. less than a month after. I laid two roses on
Agnes' dead heart, gathered from the bush Papa planted—
and on the 17th Oct she was laid beside her Father in the
Chapel, where soon after my precious Mother was also
taken—& buried close to the side of her husband.

Agnes was between 32 & 33—just ten years older
than Annie when she died.[148]

Within the period of three weeks, the Lees suffered the loss of both a sister and their mother. All of the remaining Lee children were present except Mary who was still in Europe. On Friday, November 7, 1873, the local newspaper, the *Lexington Gazette and General Advertiser* published the following obituary notice of Mrs. Lee:

> Mrs. Mary Custis Lee died at her home in Lexington on the night of 5th of November, near the hour of twelve.
> The funeral services will be held in the Lee Memorial Chapel today (Friday) at 12 o'clock, and the remains will be deposited in the vault of the Chapel, in accordance with her wish. The places of business will be closed during the services.[149]

The *Southern Collegian* in part, states Mrs. Lee's passing,

> It is enough to say that in intelligence and in refinement of taste, in kindness of heart and attractiveness of manner, in cheerfulness under the heaviest reverses of fortune and her agonies of bodily pain, in sympathy and in benefactions towards the impoverished and suffering people of her country, in her manifold and ceaseless self-denials and labors on behalf of religion and the church of her fathers and of her choice, in all this she was an ornament to her sex, was worthy of her illustrious husband.[150]

After Fitzhugh and Rob returned to their own homes, the routine of daily life was difficult to resume for Mildred and Custis Lee. The eldest Lee child and the youngest Lee child were forced to continue their lives together, but yet separately. Those first few miserable months without her sister and mother were extremely difficult for Mildred. In stillness of the winter, alone with Custis, she wrote in her reverie of an "emptied silent house, where every room echoed with dead voices."[151]

Although Mildred had the opportunity to live with any of her brothers, she chose to aid Custis during commencement in the spring and then remain through the summer. By early autumn she would travel to Rob's home for the colder months.

In the autumn of 1873 a student by the name of Robert F. Campbell began his first year at Washington and Lee University. During his first year at the university he was not impressed by President Lee, but he recalled an event which he said "...has been of considerable value to me as an element in sound philosophy of life."[152] Campbell continued to tell the story which left a lasting impression:

> In my innocence as an undergraduate, I though one of the professors had done me an injustice, and that the right thing to do was to carry it to the president. I did this, and when I laid the case before him, he said, "Mr. Robert, I am sorry for you, and I do not see that I can do anything." He then quoted the following lines, which I have kept in my memory and repeated many times to myself and others:
>
> > 'For every evil under the sun,
> > There is a remedy, or there is none.
> > If there be one, try and find it;
> > If there be none, try not to mind it.'[153]

Campbell said there were rumors among the students that Lee drank, yet he was quick to add, "...but probably none of them ever saw him under the influence of liquor. As you know, in his bearing toward others, he was a perfect gentleman." Campbell concluded his remarks by repeating a story his brother John related from a conversation with Professor Harris.

> Prof. Harris had no bitterness in his make-up, and this gives more point to his remark, which was this, "John, you know, I think that his reticence and aloofness is due to a feeling that he is just a little better that the rest of mankind." [154]

Although Custis gave the appearance of detachment, he was very much to the contrary. He was congenial and eager to help anyone in need. He always placed himself last. There is a story told by a local Lexington gentleman named William Patton who was at one time a clerk in a gentleman's shop named Larrick Gents Clothing Store, Lexington. He remembered General Custis Lee as "courtly in manners to the clerks and everyone with whom he came in contact. Frequently when waiting to be waited on and his time coming, he would stand back and offer his place to some insignificant person, saying that he had plenty of time and they probably were in a hurry, in the most deferential way. "Sir, won't you take my place and be waited on as I have plenty of time." Mr. Patton recalled him wearing black ties, and saying "William, have you English [cravat] seven-eighths?"and when told that he had, he would say, "Please give me six." And he mentioned once someone saying to the General, "I saw you a moment ago on the street pass an old colored man, who took off his hat and you bowed and touched yours," and General Lee replied "Yes, I never allow anyone to exceed me in politeness."

In another incident, a gentleman by the name of Colonel Merriweather Jones reported an anecdote about Custis that he recalled from his cadet days at the Virginia Military Institute. Jones said he saw General Lee hold the limit gate for an old colored man who was driving a horse and a wagon, and touched his hat to the colored man as he went through and gave a pleasant salutation.

Along with his extreme politeness, speculation also surrounded Lee's quiet lifestyle. Frequently, stories surfaced about him having an alcoholic condition. This gossip was utterly erroneous and insulting. During the interview with William Patton, he told the interviewer that he had heard a report "in Lexington that General Lee drank and would get on sprees, but that no one ever saw him as he kept close in the house if such was the case."[155] Nevertheless, a visiting professor of history from the University of Virginia, Richard Heath Dabney informed his friend Mr. Dold, then Mayor of Lexington, that during his brief visit of period of three weeks to deliver his lectures to the students of Washington and Lee he resided at the President's house. "I enjoyed my association with

General Custis. He was a generous host, and we both drank and enjoyed champagne daily. This was rather more than I had been accustomed to, and I found it very grateful. Almost invariably we had the same delightful stimulant at night."[156] It is a common fact that Victorian gentlemen, in an effort to be a good host, would offer their guests, the gentlemen, various aperitifs as well as after dinner liqueurs. Apparently, champagne was the alcoholic beverage of the wealthier social strata. Since there exist nothing of explicit documentation of any alcoholism, the fact remains that such gossip arose from those people such as Prof. Harris, who were perhaps jealous, but most certainly they were ignorant.

Trying to maintain order in his life, he resumed his routine in the President's office. Since Lee was so unassuming, many of his accomplishments went unnoticed, or the credit was given to someone else.

Before Custis Lee replaced his father at Washington and Lee, none of the property east of the campus and facing Jefferson [Bank Street as it was then named] Street was owned by the University with the exception of a small lot of land on which the "Old Hotel" stood. Since the building was used as a student dining room, the structure became know as "Mess Hall."

This strip of land was purchased under Robert E. Lee's administration in the winter of 1867 at a cost of $1750.00. The purpose of this purchase was to afford more living quarters for the massive numbers of students attending the university and to provide relief to the overburden housing situation in the town.

The "Mess Hall" was used for other activities than strictly a domicile for the students. Apparently the students requested permission to use the structure for a hop with the permission of the faculty for the evening of Wednesday, December 2. The request was granted during the executive committee meeting held the previous week. It is presumed that permission was granted at this time to use the facility in order to appease the students who had been denied the year before an extension to their Christmas holiday furlough. Permission of this singular request, opened the door to other student activities being held there, as well as civic organizations utilizing the structure for a meeting place. The use of the structure became habitual until the building was destroyed by fire in 1878.

As some people would suggest, Custis Lee had little or no fore-sight other than what his father had purposed at the end of his tenure at the university. This is far from the truth, as Custis Lee was planning improvement far beyond his father's intentions.

Lee proposed the acquisition of the old Exchange Hotel which was located on the of the Gibbs lot facing the Main Street and directly adjacent to the easterly part of the campus. Originally named the "Mansion House," it was a resting place for weary travelers. Later, it became known as the Exchange Hotel, since it used for mostly commercial traffic.

The structure stood three stories in height with a brick facade. Each floor had a central hall. The ground floor had a large dining room, and the second and third floors had abundant small dormitory-style rooms. The property was an ideal purchase for the university. Jefferson and Henry Streets gave clear access to the rear of the property, where an old stable was erected. Later in Lee's tenure, this stable would be converted into the University gymnasium. After extensive negotiations the property was purchased less than a month after Lee inauguration as President of Washington and Lee University on March 28, 1871, in the amount of $9,000.00.[157]

Nevertheless, it took more than two years before any action could take place in the way of needed repairs to the structure. Yet, the exterior lot in the front of the main building had always been used for student recreation. But the students and faculty had long desired a better place, as well as a gymnasium. Editorials in the *Southern Collegian* supported the need for both of these facilities: "...those who are daily engaged in mental labor, need and must have physical diversion, and until new and better grounds are obtained, the campus will continue to be our field of sports."[158] An immediate result did not occur from this editorial, but in a few months subsequent the students set forth a petition urging the executive committee to take action concerning the use of the old stable on Gibbs' lot for the purpose of a gymnasium.

The use of this structure for indoor sports was deemed practicable and from the September 28, 1874 minutes, the committee decided: "That the stable attached to the hotel property be turned over to the students, now interested in getting up a gymnasium, and that the lumber removed for the building be appropriated towards defraying the expenses of the work."[159]

The following month the *Southern Collegian* reported "The fact that we are going to have a gymnasium is now reduced to almost a "dead certainty" ...We are happy to see all this. We hope that private rooms in college buildings will now cease to resound with the bang of falling Indian clubs and dumb-bells, and a man can possess his soul in peace, with no splinters of shattered furniture to frighten away what few ideas he may have collected. Professors and students subscribed very willingly and freely to the fund."[160] The newly-converted stable served many years as the students' gymnasium.

As was Lee's habit, he quietly went about his work, steadily trying to obtain properties on behalf of the university throughout his tenure as president; of course, in doing so, he was constantly modernizing the university by expanding the physical size of the campus. He relished this part of his duties as president very much since it was somewhat aligned to his beloved engineering.

Within his presidential tenure, Lee managed to acquire additional property "extending from Jefferson street to Main through the University grounds near the lower hotel." Lee continued to include in his request to the Board of Trustees, "it is the opinion of the Committee that this extension would be an improvement to the town as well as to the grounds of the University."[161] The Trustees approved the acquisition of the land as did the town council. The executive committee immediately set out to inquire as to the sale of the portion the lot desired but the actual property known as the Deaver lot was not verifiably acquired until 1880 and other adjacent properties were not obtained until 1889 as well as property willed to the university from the estate of Mrs. Susan A. Roberts located on Jefferson Street. It should be noted that "the policy of General Custis Lee of extending the Campus to the east had been to a considerable extent accomplished, but there still remained the Governor Letcher house and three others on the east corner.[162]

Toward the end of Custis Lee's tenure as president, he was able to acquire the long sought after Letcher property situated on Main Street in the amount of $8,000.00. The motion to purchase the property was made by William Henry Fitzhugh Lee, brother of the president. W. H. F. Lee joined the Board of Trustees in 1888 and served until his death on October 15, 1891. Two years after this proposal, the purchase was completed on May 1, 1891, at the amount $7,000.00, one thousand dollars less than originally demanded.

By procuring this large brick house, the university had another structure it could utilize as a professor's residence; as well as an extension of the northeastern boundary of the campus to Main Street via Baley's Alley. This gave a clear right of way to Main and Jefferson Streets with the exception of two small lots: the Gillock and Wintfield lots located between the Letcher and Gibbs lots. These two small pieces of property were finally obtained by the university in 1913.

As a result, it was abundantly clear that "this extension of the University ground eastward and town-ward seems to have been a plan conceived by Custis Lee, and later years have completely confirmed his wisdom."[163]

Throughout the years of Lee's tenure at the university, his workload of interesting topics were very few and it took years to bring to fruition any major project. Yet, he had another preoccupation which was becoming paramount in his mind—the recovery of Arlington.

Although R. E. Lee tried to recover Arlington, he found the fight futile, but Custis never gave up hope. Less than six months after his mother's death, he set a plan in motion for the extrication of Arlington. Early in April of 1874, during the First Session of the 43rd Congress of the United States, his petition was presented to the Senate that requested a "Memorial of G. W. Custis Lee, of Virginia" "setting forth—His claim to "Arlington," and proposing to convey that estate to the United States upon payment of just compensation, and asking Congress to pass a law to provide for the adjudication of his title, and to ascertain the fair value of the property. The petition was referred to the committee on the Judiciary and ordered to be printed.[164] This legal argument was designed to show the Congress how Custis was wrongfully deprived of his property even though the United States had already paid the property taxes on the estate of $26,800.00 for the eleven-hundred acre estate therefore the Senate considered the property already purchased. To add insult to injury there were men elected to this august body who still wanted retribution for the war and the very name of Lee was repugnant to them. Consequently, the burials continued and the petition became a nonentity.

He spent the summer of 1874 in a similar manner as to other post-war summers. He kept up with his personal correspondence and lacked the enthusiasm for beginning another academic year. He wrote to Captain J. J. White, who was vacationing at White Sulpher Springs:

Yours of the 10th did not reach me until yesterday. Please thank our friends for their kind inquiries. I am very glad that you have found your visit so pleasant and profitable, and hope you will stay long enough to get the full benefits of the company, and the water. I am afraid that Mr. Tucker and Col. J. can not be got away, although I have no doubt that a visit to the "White Sulpher" would be of great service to both of them. I had heard that Miss Belle Harrison had been quite sick. Both Mildred and I are very glad to know that she is better. When you see her, please remember us very kindly. Everything here is about the same as when you left, except the Chapel which was struck by Lighting night before last. The fleur-de-lis (or whatever it is) which surmounts the tower was shivered and some shingles were knocked off the roof of the tower as the current passed to the tin gutters, where it seems to have been conducted away by the metal. There was no other injury, so far as we have been able to ascertain. Prof. Campbell is repairing damages. You have of course heard of the death of Mrs. Kilpatrick. It was a great blow to our whole community, and has fallen heavily upon the poor Dr. & the young ladies of the family.

The remains of Col. Sellers reached town last Tuesday morning by the Packet boat, and were interred near the family residence. Maj. Sellers, also brought on the remains, started this morning on his return to Galveston. As this is the first day for several weeks that I have attempted to write, you must make all due allowances. Your immediate family & friends are well, & would all join us in kindest regards and they know of my wishing.[165]

Since the end of the war many former officers of both armies wrote to Custis requesting mementos from his father and other Confederate heroes. These requests lingered on for many years, as witnessed by the following letter:

> Your two letters, respectively of the 11th & 22d. ult. reached me in due time. The first was not promptly acknowledged, because I then hoped to procure for you in a short time, the desired information in regard to some of the Confederate officers referred to. In this, however I have been disappointed. Since the arrival of the second letter, I have been prevented by illness, and the pressure of business which would not admit of delay, from replying to either of them.
>
> Genl. Wm. R. Terry resides in Liberty, Va. Genl. R. L. Gibson, No.5 Caronlet St., New Orleans, La. may possibly be able to put you in the way of getting the autograph of the late Genl. L. A. Stafford, and of some of the others named by you. I have given your list to Col. Wm. Preston Johnston, of this place, who is now engaged in arranging the papers of his father, the late Genl. A. S. Johnston, and who promises to send you all of the autographs asked for that he may come across. With regards to the maps, I do not recollect to have seen then, but, when Col. Chas. Marshall—Marshall & Fisher, Attorneys-at-Law, Baltimore, Md.—undertook to prepare a biography of my father, some years ago, I sent to him all the maps and papers, bearing on the war, which I could find in our house. If he has the maps you wish for he will no doubt let you have them for a time.[166]

By November, he and Mildred had visited William Henry Fitzhugh Lee. It is presumed that Custis took this opportunity to discuss with his brothers his plan to resign from Washington and Lee with a view of actively working toward regaining possession of Arlington. In a letter to his wife, W. H. F. Lee wrote from Ravensworth, "Custis & Mildred I wrote you left-on Thursday and Bob went Friday."[167]

After he and Mildred returned to Lexington, Custis submitted his resignation, citing a decline in his health, with the remedy suggested by his doctor to live a more active life. The Board of Trustees was very reluctant to accept his resignation. Therefore, Lee suggested a leave of absence for a year without pay. He was granted a year's leave to recuperate and think about his future.

Even though Lee was technically on sabbatical, he remained in Lexington much of the academic year, departing on short trips to Richmond to see his old friend and his physician, Dr. Hunter McGuire and to spend the summer at White Sulpher Springs.

In January, he wrote to Dr. J. Wm. Jones of his intention to meet with him in Richmond in a few days, "The enclosed letter will explain itself. After you have done with it, please send it to Col. Marshall, as it may possibly be of some use to him. I expect to start this evening or tomorrow morning for Richmond, and hope to meet you."[168] His visit to Richmond was brief and by mid March he was once again in Lexington.

He continued his leave from the university in a tranquil but relatively active manner. He became more social by taking walks with a kinswoman who resided at the Lexington Hotel nearly daily. According to a former employee of the university, he and the lady would stroll along Main and Washington Streets through both campuses and then return to the hotel where he would bid her adieu until the next day. Mr. Dold, the mayor of Lexington recalled that General Custis was a striking figure; tall with military bearing and a fine physique. Dold considered him much handsomer than his brother William Henry Fitzhugh Lee while he admitted he never saw Robert E. Lee, Jr..[169]

Within weeks of his return to Lexington, he received notice of a settlement from the estate of the Lee children's great aunt, Mrs. W. H. Fitzhugh. Custis and his brother William Henry Fitzhugh Lee served as executors to Mrs. Fitzhugh's estate. Custis received a monetary payment in securities totaling the sum of $24,000.00. [170] By acknowledging this settlement, he relinquished all other claims to the physical estate, therefore giving clear title of the property known as Ravensworth to his brother and his heirs. Nevertheless, Ravensworth would become his home after he finally retired from Washington and Lee University in 1897.

Quickly, the spring became summer and he would make his annual sojourn to White Sulpher Springs for the season. Custis kept up with his correspondence with his private secretary at Washington and Lee University, Captain J. J. White, in a series of notes and letters throughout the summer at "Old White":

> Your note of the 23rd inst. reached me yesterday (Sunday). As you do not allude to Mrs. White's health, I trust that she continues to improve and hope she will soon be quite well again.
>
> I will write today to Rev. Dr. Barr in behalf of Rush, and give him the best recommendation I can.
>
> I have taken a box at the P. O. here, and hope that my letters will come straight hereafter. Its number is 85.
>
> Please mention to Mr. Dold, if you think of it when you next see him, that I have received his note on Genl Bragg's letter to me.
>
> When I arrived here last Wednesday evening, I was told that it had been raining here constantly for the past 20 days.
>
> It continued to rain until Saturday, when it cleared away—I hope for some time. Yesterday was very pleasant and so is today.
>
> Among your friends and acquaintances here; are Mr. & Mrs. Taggart, Mr. & Mrs. Richard Norris, Dr. Thomas, Maj. Mathews, Genl. & Mrs. Johnston, Genl. & Mrs. Gilmer, Genl. St. John, ect. ect. I understand that Mr. Corcoran is going to the "Old Sweet". When he gets there, I will go over to see him.[171]

A few days later Lee wrote another letter to J. J. White:

Yours of the 29th inst. reached me this morning; and from Mr. Bayly and Fitz Lee, which you forwarded. I am very glad to know from yourself that Mrs. White continues to improves in health, and sincerely hope that it may soon be completely restored. Please remember me very kindly to her.

I will write a few lines to Mrs. Newcomb and am glad to have another opportunity of writing to Mr. Corcoran. I hardly know what to say to Mr. Bayly. Some of the Trustees suggested that in acknowledging the receipt of Mr. Bayly's clerk, which arrived while you were so closely occupied with Mrs. White, I should express the wish to hang the portrait of his brother in our gallery. This I did and you have seen his answer. Probably it will be best to put off definite action in the matter until we all get home again, and until we (of W. & L. U.) can see our way more clearly. I will write to Mr. Bayly somewhat to this effect.

Your friends here inquire very kindly of Mrs. White and yourself. Dr. Henry Alexander has arrived to stay some days.

It continues to rain, and the hope of pleasant weather, which concerned the visitors about a week ago, has left them. Some have already left in search of sunshine, and many others, I think, will follow their example before long, if the rains continue many days more. Mr. & Mrs. Taggart are as jolly as ever. Mrs. Richard Norris has been quite ill, but is now right well again. Our friends, Mr. & Mrs. Baker, son & niece, of Baltimore, with some New York people, started this morning for the Warm Springs, The bell of the place, Mrs. Chas. Huger of Mobile, is to go away this afternoon.

When you next see Mr. Dold, please thank him for the catalogue, and for the copies of the "Alexandria Gazette," which he has been sending me, and which he need not trouble himself to send me any longer, as I get the papers here. I should like, however, to have the "Lexington Gazette" & the "Southern Churchman" sent me. As these are both weeklys, there will be but little trouble in sending them together.[172]

The following month he wrote again to his secretary in order that he may keep up with the events at the university:

Yours of the 25th inst. reached me a day or two ago; for which I am much obliged. I have not written you oftener, to _____adding to your correspondence, and other troubles.

I am truly glad to learn from yourself of Mrs. White's continued improvement in health, and hope that she will soon recover her strength altogether.

Col. Allan, who came directly here from Lexington, gave me full accounts of the recent action of the Board of Trustees, and told me also that he had seen Mrs. White, and that she seemed to be doing very well. I agree with you that the Board acted wisely in not filling the Chair of Modern languages at this time; and I trust that they will be able to make satisfactory arrangements for the Law school at their meeting to-day— if Judge Wilford declines, which I fear from all I can learn will be the case. Mr. Wirt Henry, also is here now, suggests the name of Mr. Wm. A. Maury, of Richmond, son-in-law of Commodore Maury, for the law Professor. It is very doubtful, however, I think, whether he would accept. You may know that he was for a time Prof. of Law in Richmond College. Mr. Henry regards him as not only one of the most promising, but one of the most scholarly lawyers in the State. I mention this only for what it is worth.

Our company here is not now so large as it has been; but is still quite respectable in numbers, and very good in other respects. Mr. C. H. McCormick arrived last night but I have not yet seen him. Genl. Lilly is still here.

I hope you may be able to take a trip somewhere before the opening of the session. I can return any day, if desirable, and will start at once on receipt of a telegram from you. Everyone says that I improve greatly, and I think I am better that when I came here. The wet weather has been somewhat against me; but I trust it is nearly over now. It is raining again to-day; but we have had some pleasant days during the past two weeks.

I want to be in Lexington a week or ten days at least before the opening of the session.

My sister Mary joins me in kindest regards to Mrs. White and yourself— and other friends would do likewise, did they know of my writing—[173]

Custis and Mary Lee arrived back at Lexington several weeks prior the opening of the autumn session at Washington and Lee University. The session began in the same manner as it had for years: welcoming the new and continuing students, directing them to the appropriate professor for scheduling of their courses and locating housing for the students during the academic year.

By late October, Custis had time to respond to personal correspondence from old friends and acquaintances. He had received a letter of application for membership into the Virginia Division of the Army of Northern Virginia from his former colleague Captain George B. Purcell. All these years later Custis was happy to oblige Captain Purcell:

> I return herewith your application for membership in the Virginian Division of the Army of Northern Va. Your statement is correct to the best of my knowledge and belief; and I have therefore signed the certificate, as requested.
>
> I take occasion to add that, during our association in the organization for "Local Defense", and afterwards at the Va. Mil. Institute your conduct both as a gentleman and a soldier was always unexceptionable. With kind regards and good wishes I remain,[174]

In early November an interesting prospect occurred which would benefit the university's science department. President Lee received a letter from Henry Augusta Ward, a professor of Natural Science at the University of Rochester and an accomplished paleontologist. In cooperation with a number of American universities, he established "cabinets," or small natural history museums, in areas which had never had then previously. Ward's communications with Lee concerned the establishment of such a "cabinet" or display at the university, consisting of fossils and taxidermic specimens, as well as bleaching the bones of Traveller to add to this exhibit. Throughout the three years of correspondence with Ward only one letter remains from their communications:

[Copy of the original letter written by a secretary]

Since you left this place I have had some conference with the members of our Board of Trustees with reach, in reference to the subject of your recent communications and find that their views agree substantially with those I prescribed to you.

I think I have mentioned that the Board of Trustees have charge of the financial affairs of our institution, and that their next regular meeting will not be until the latter part of June next. It would be very difficult, if not impossible, to get a quorum for business at this season of the year, should a special meeting be called. While the Trustees with whom I have counseled, can not absolutely promise the appropriation of One Thousand Dollars, as proposed, they have good reason to believe that every effort will be made at the first meeting of the Board to meet "Mr.____'s" [actual benefactor was Lewis Brooks of Rochester, New York, who anonymously contributed money for the museum] generous offer and feel assured that if there be from lack of ability, and not from want of inclination, to do so.

They do promise to fit up the room for the reception of your collection, and to defray the expenses of transportation, putting up, &c. Our institution is much in need of such a series of casts, fossils and minerals, as you have, and its authorities would doubtless have made arrangement before this time to procure it, had their available means been sufficient to justify the necessary outlay. They gratefully appreciate the kind proposal of "Mr._____," [Brooks] and will thankfully accept for the institution whatever he may be pleased to give toward securing your valuable collection.

I have sent you by mail, according to promise, a copy of Dr. Jones' Book, and now enclose as copy of Prof. Henry's letter, as requested and with the hope that this may find you safe at home, I remain [signed G. W. C. Lee, along with his hand written note on this letter: W. & L. University Lexington, Va. 17 Nov., 1875—G. W. C. Lee—Accepts conditionally the offer of Mr._____, made through Prof. Henry A Ward, to present a museum to W. & L. University—Duplicate][175]

Included in his year end report to the Board of Trustees, President Lee provides a lengthy report concerning the proposed museum:

In November last, Prof. Henry A. Ward, of Rochester, N. Y. introduced by Prof. Henry, of the Smithsonian Institution, visited this place, and made a statement to the following effect;

A gentleman, who desired to be known only as a friend of this institution in the State of New York, was willing to aid it in procuring a Mineralogical, Geological, and Zoological Cabinet, provided such a cabinet was needed in the institution. This gentleman, Mr._____,would contribute $1600.00 for the cabinet, if the authorities of W. & L. University would add to that the sum of $1000.00, and bear the expense of the hall, freight, and mounting.

In response to Prof. Ward's proposition after conference with such members of the Board of Trustees as were within such, a correspondence took place of which the following copies and extracts of letters give the more important features.

> Prof. Henry to the Presdt. of W. & L. U.
> Smithsonian Institution,
> Washington, 8 Oct. 1875.

Dear Sir:

I beg leave to introduce to your acquaintance the bearer of this letter, Prof. Henry A Ward, of Rochester, N. Y., who has established a wide reputation and has done good service to the cause of education in this country by reproducing casts of the most celebrated specimens of the organic remains of the old world.

I am much gratified to learn through him that a friend of the cause of science & education in this country has offered to present to Washington & Lee College of Va. a full set of Prof. Ward's casts, & I doubt not you will be glad to receive them not only as a testimony of good feeling of a gentleman from the North towards your college, but also as a valuable accessory in the line of education. The cast are admirable illustrations, derived from authentic sources, of the extinct animals of former geological periods & will be of great importance in illustrating the subject of paleontology. I beg leave to commend Prof. Ward (who visits you in regard to the above mentioned proposition) as a gentleman of scientific reputation and well worthy your confidence and esteem. The above letter came by mail several weeks before Prof. Ward arrived here, when he explained that Prof. Henry had altogether understood Mr.___'s proposition. [Copies of letters written in response from Lee were not kept or included in the annual report.] Nevertheless, Lee continues to include all the letters he received on the subject including November 17, 1875 and the following dated November 28, 1875 from Professor Ward:

I duly received your letter of the 17th with its enclosure

I had already written to Mr_____ giving him an account of my visit to Lexington, And a report in accordance with the facts. In that report I laid considerable stress upon the importance to your cabinet of a series of <u>Minerals</u>, to introduce normally the Geology. I mentioned this as my own idea, which he might chose to accept or decline. A few days since I called upon Mr._____repeated the story of my visit and read him your letter. He was much pleased that the institution is willing, so far as able, to meet him by paying a position towards the cast of the cabinet. It assured him that the collection was wanted, which is a point on which he seems to have wanted assurance. He now says "You may tell Presdt. Lee that if the College will meet the expenses of transporting, & mounting; & fitting a suitable room with suitable cases, I shall not expect them to so any further." That settles the $1000.00 question without any need of further consideration. And I am very happy to be able to announce further that Mr._____ increases that sum of his giving to $6000.00. For this sum I am directed to prepare for you the Rocks, Fossils & casts of Fossils of which we spoke together, and to further add a $1400.00 collection of Minerals, and $2,000.00 of Zoology (stuffed animals, skeletons & invertebrates). The total is not large for the ground which is to be covered, but by a careful housing of the specimens I shall be able to make a very full and effective cabinet; one, I will say, which will be much more symmetrical, and have far more practical scientific value that have the majority of our college cabinets. Mr._____gives this very earnestly,—in fact he seemed to lead me on to suggest more and more things. But, he is I find, very decided and ever sensitive on the point of not having his name appear. When I rather urged the point of [it], he said "Mr Ward I am afraid that you will almost make me sorry that I took up this matter." So I now see his full wishes, and I write to request that from this early date the gift be spoken of as from a friend of the college <u>in</u> <u>New</u> <u>York</u> State. (I do not mention it in our city) I hope to, some time, visit the college with him, and then you will have the pleasure of knowing him by name, and personally.

Yours respectfully
(sgd.) Henry A. Ward

Please ask Prof. McCormick to hurry me along, as freight, the bones of "Traveller". I enclose tags for the box. Thanks for the book which came duly, and will be highly appreciated.

(sgd.) H. A.W.

18 Dec., 1875

In an interview with Mr._____immediately after my return from Lexington, he raised the donation to W. & L. University to $6,000.00, as I wrote you, by making minerals $1,200.00; Rocks $200.00, Fossils $800.00; casts of Fossils $1,600.00; Geological Landscapes $200; Zoology, $2,000.00. These sums grew under our hands rapidly on a short hour's talk. The Zoology had not been anticipated by me, and when it was suggested I fixed $2000 as about a proper quotum of material in this department to balance the others. And I thought this about right until at the commencement of this week I worked carefully through the series, to see what would be required. Choosing my vertebrate material (skeletons & stuffed specimens) by what should be represented in a cabinet of this scope, and the Invertebrates by the same rule, modified a little by my ability to furnish the special forms, I closed by adding up (from my printed M.S.S. catalogues) the total cost. I was annoyed to find to be $2800.00 for this Zoology. I went around to Mr._____and explained to him just how the matter stood. He listened carefully, and told me that if I thought that was what was needed, to "go on and finish it." So, this difficulty was over, and the cabinet now stands at $6,800.00. I send you by to-day's mail four plans of the cabinet hall, intended to assist you in planning the disposition of cases, &c.

The sum will really be small for the material which we now have to put in it, and it is only by aid of gallery on three sides with cases above and below, and by covering all available wall surface that we shall get all in. But I think once in place it will look very nicely—will, in fact, make a graphic & imposing display. There will surely be nothing at all its equal in display or in scientific & educational capacity—south of Washington, although many cabinets (running as they are so apt to do on specialities) may exceed it in number of specimens, or in some individual departments. It would on some accounts be well if you had a second hall somewhere near at hand for the Zoology. It would crowd the other hall less, & would virtually double the apparent scientific wealth of the institution. The cost of cases would be the same, and the cost of gallery would be saved.[176]

From the details of this last letter the proposed museum was nearing fruition and by mid-Spring the whole plan would be completed.

Early in February, 1876, Lee was continuing his communications with J. William Jones pertaining to data that Jones had utilized in his manuscript on General Robert E. Lee. Now, Lee wanted the data sent to another gentleman, " I enclose a copy of a letter, recently received from the Hon. Joseph W. Taylor, which will explain itself. The M.S. [manuscript] requested does not seem to be here, and thinking that it may have come into your possession, when you were preparing the Personal Reminiscences of my father, I venture to ask you- provided, of course, the M.S. is in your possession—to send it, at once to Mr. Taylor, prepaying the express charges, and letting me know the amount, so that our Treasurer may refund it to you."[177] About ten days later Lee once again writes to Jones on the same topic:

I acknowledge with thanks your favor of the 8th inst.

and would have written to you before, but for waiting to hear for Mr. Jones in reference to Mr. Taylor's M.S. I am sorry to say that he thinks it has been destroyed. If so, it will put Mr. Taylor to considerable trouble and labor to reproduce it. I am very glad to learn from yourself that the Society-is getting on so well, and hope that its condition will always be as satisfactory and more so. I am glad to know that you are going to take up the resources of the South, &c. If you would like to leave a copy of this letter, send me a line by Postal Card, and I will send it to you. I wish indeed that Col. Marshall could get through with the material in his possession, and turn it over to you. The first good opportunity, I will say something to him on the subject. I have no doubt that he would be glad to give you access to any reports you might wish to examine. Your many friends here would join me in kind regards and best wishes to you and yours, did they know of my writing—[178]

In addition to his considerable personal correspondence, Lee spent a large part of his professional time continuing his correspondence on expanding the property holdings of the university and completing the final details of the museum which was given to the university in the spring of 1876.

In March, he received a letter from an attorney in New Orleans in reference to real estate that the university was trying to obtain, known as the Bayly property.

Yours of the 9th, reached me yesterday, & as I know that you must feel considerable anxiety about the large interests which you represent in the Bayly matter I hasten to give you such information as I have already collected.

The house of Bayly and Pond has been declining in credit and esteem ever since the destruction of their shore by fire about two years ago, and their failure took no one by surprise. The public is very harsh in its criticism upon them, although I must say that the junior partner seems to get the larger share of censure. The stories which I heard on the streets to the extent of their indebtedness to the estate of R. H. Bayly were of so alarming a character that I felt no hesitation in at once approaching Mr. Bayly in order to get his statement in the matter. I asked in as delicate a manner as possible to avoid giving offense by the idea that I suspected any breach of trust, and first assured myself by a call on one of the committee of creditors engaged in examining the affairs of the firm that the estate of R. H. Bayly appeared as a creditor for $1600 or $1700 on the statement furnished by the firm to the committee. I next saw Mr. Bayly, himself, who gave me the same figures, but added that the debt was merely a nominal one, as the estate was his debtors for about the same amount independently of the legacies to himself, and that he never had & never would entangle the affairs of the estate with those of the firm. He further informed me that no real estate has been parted with except one piece in the city which has been accounted for.

I have withdrawn the record of the succession from court, and shall examine it thoroughly. It is meager and useless factory—no account having been filed since May 1873—but I hope to be able to find out enough to prevent the necessity of any legal steps. If I am not successful in my efforts your only safe course will be to call upon Mr. B. to file an account, but I desire to avoid this, if possible, as it will be looked upon as a hostile measure. It will probably be some time before I can send you a full account of this matter, but I shall do so as soon as possible.

With kind remembrances to all Lexington friends, especially your sisters, I remain[179]

Continuing with university business, Lee received two letter in the spring from Professor Henry A. Ward of Rochester, New York, in reference to the completion of the "museum cabinets" proposed last November:

Enclosed please find Dft. on Bk. of America, N. York, for $1265.00. This is sent to you by Mr. _____as a further gift to W. & L. University, and is intended to cover the entire expenses of the University on the cabinets themselves; viz; $875.00 due to me, as per agreement, for the mounting, and $390.00 as per your estimate, in letter of the 13th for "freight, insurance, & hauling." In this manner Mr._____presents you the cabinets in place in your museum halls, leaving to you the preparing of said halls and the fitting up the cases.

(sgd.)

P.S. I hardly need tell you, sir, how pleased I am to write you the accompanying letter with its remittance. I called on Mr.____three days ago, and after asking as usual after news from you, he said "Mr. Ward I have decided that that cabinet shall be called the "Ward Cabinet." I told him that would not so and explained why. But he with a pleasant kind of sophistry insisted that as he gave me the money for it I was really the donor and he wished it to be so. Finally I said "But Mr._____I can not afford it, They pay me $875.00 to mount the cabinet, &c., &c., If I give them the cabinet I can not charge them for this." "Never mind that," answered he, "I will pay the $875.00 additional." Glad of the chance to get you the further sum, I made no further objection to his insisting that my name should go with the donation. But sober thought at home told me that this was not at all best, even though you should be willing. So, yesterday, I went and told him that I could not take any unearned honors in this way. I further showed him you late letter, with its enclosed estimates. I suggested to him that as he was giving the $875.00, he might add $390.00 more, and make a clean gift of the cabinets all in place in your hall. He laughed, said, "how one thing leads to another in there matters," and drew his check for $1265.00, which I have transferred into a New York Dft. of like amount, and now enclose. This is not as well as I had some hopes of doing for you, but is still all helps along.

* * * *

He has paid me for the cabinets in full $6,800.00 making his entire gift to your university $8,065.00. I wished to see it an even $10,000.00 and possibly I may yet succeed in this. But I have no hint for him that he purposes doing anything more.

Hoping to hear from you by return mail, I remain

(sgn.) Henry A. Ward

I shall read your letter, as before, to Mr_____ [180]

About a month later, Lee received a telegram from Professor Henry A. Ward from Rochester, New York: "I have got what I anticipated in late letters and much more—will visit you middle of next week."[181]

When President Lee submitted his annual report on the university, he informed the Board of Trustees of the negotiations through his personal comments pertaining to the "museum."

About the 20th April last Prof. Ward made a second visit to Lexington bringing with him fifteen ($1,000.00) Bonds, making the entire donation of our unknown benefactor $25,000.00 in sound numbers; who is understood to approve the plan of applying the unexpended balance of this sum in making cabinets as full and complete as our space will admit of.

The part of the buildings corresponding to Prof. McCullock's Lecture room was originally selected and prepared for the Cabinet hall. This was afterwards enlarged by the addition of two adjoining rooms in the middle building, and can be further enlarged—which is very desirable to give room for a botanical cabinet and some additions to the mineralogy—by adding two or more rooms in the ninth building, which will make the cabinet complete.[182]

Shortly after the completion of the business transactions concerning the new museum for the university, Custis received word from his personal attorneys, William J. Robertson and Francis L. Smith that there may be information coming forth about his claim to Arlington. With this glimmer of hope secured in his mind, he traveled to Burke, Virginia to consult and visit with his brother, William Henry Fitzhugh and his family. Although he was pragmatic where Arlington was concerned, he remained silently sanguine. From Ravensworth, he wrote to Captain J. J. White in Lexington:

> I have written to Bishop Pinckney, in acknowledgement of his note of the 25th ult., which you forwarded to me; and to the effect of that we should expect him in Lexington on the 18th of June next. I also told him that you had written to the Rev. Douglass Forrest in regard to the change of day for our Baccalaureate sermon. I infer that Genl. Pryor has agreed to change his day.
>
> I think I shall finish my business here this week, and hope to return to Lexington sometime next week, taking with me Mildred, who is somewhere about Richmond. I saw Mr. Tucker for the second time yesterday. He seems tired of Washington and anxious to get back to Lexington.
>
> I called on Mr. Corcoran yesterday but he was not at home. Will try him again. I also went to see Genl. Gibson's family, but found them out. The General himself I had previously seen at the Capitol, which is not a pleasant place for me to go to. My brother and sister, here join me in kindest remembrances to your household, and with regards to the members of the Faculty generally, I remain[183]

Unfortunately, he concluded his visit to Ravensworth without accomplishing any further resolve concerning Arlington. Nevertheless, he was urged to remain patient but for how long? As he eluded to in his letter to White, due to Congressional slowness in deciding upon a resolution of the situation, he was becoming more and more bitter and was impelled to regard the Capitol with great destain.

Lee returned to Lexington with nothing more resolved than when he left. As a result, it would be nearly another year before his intellect and emotion would reach its apex and he would decide to sue for his birthright. But for the moment, the university business took precedence.

The end of the session activities took place, the exams and graduation and finally, the President's Report to the Board of Trustees: "I have the honor to submit the following report for the session of 1875-6. The whole number of matriculates during the session is One hundred and fifty-nine, several States..." [184] The student came from as far north as New York, as far south as Florida and as far west as Texas. Of the twelve schools of study the most populated was the school of mathematics. This fact must have given President Lee a great source of pride, since his own academic field was the best attended.

As usual, Lee reported on the conduct of the students and their attendance of chapel services, "The conduct and behavior of the students throughout the session have been very good; and their attention to, and progress in study, fully was good as usual, and satisfactory. There have been conducted, as heretofore, by the ministers of the several churches of Lexington in turn; and the attendance of the students on them has been remarkably good, and gratifying."[185] Lee went on to report on the Young Men's Christian Association, as well as the Library & Apparatus and the Grounds and Buildings, then concluding with his commendation of the faculty:

> The membership for this session is somewhat in advance of that for last session.
>
> Its mission work has been carried on with encouraging success its principal school (the one at House Mountain) having increased for 30 to 40 to about 75 regular scholars.
>
> The weekly prayer meeting has been kept up; and though at times, during the first part of the session, rather poorly attended, it has during the last few months been an object of much interest to the students at large- the hall having been crowded Sunday after Sunday.

The Rev. Mr. Boyle, of the Methodist Church in this town, has been very active and earnest in the interest of the association. It was fully represented in the State Convention, held at Staunton, Va. in December last.

Library & Apparatus

The bequest of the late Dr. Mercer, of New Orleans, has been received, I believe, before the last annual report of the President. Since the date of that report, however, the one thousand volumes of the bequest have been put in place, and make a valuable and handsome addition to our library.

With the exception of some valuable additions to the Chemical Laboratory, there is nothing of importance to note in regard to apparatus.

A portrait of Dr. Bradford, of Pa., presented by himself, has been added to the collection of fine paintings in the Chapel; and compares very favorably with its companions.

Grounds & Buildings

The shingle roof covering of the middle building has been replaced by tin in accordance with the authority granted by the Board last summer. A new roof being found necessary for the cabinet hall, this was covered with tin, and Prof. McCullock's Lecture room, for which a new roof covering would have been required in a few years, was also covered with tin, both for safety for fire and to correspond in appearance on the exterior with the cabinet hall.

The tin coverings of the north and south buildings have been carefully repaired and the walls of the later—in which is the library— strengthened with iron tie-rods. The college buildings, excepting the low dormitories, have now good tin coverings and are comparatively safe.

In writing your attention to the extracts for the

proceedings of the Faculty herewith, and the accompanying reports of the several professors, whose faithful and laborious services during the session about to close can not too highly commended.[186]

With the university business closed for another academic year, Custis was in an increased state of melancholy over the dismal prospects pertaining to Arlington. Now he wanted to press vigorously forward by means of legal devices to secure Arlington. Obviously, he would need to be near Washington, D.C., to actively pursue this objective. Consequently, he requested and was granted another year's leave of absence with the precursor that his resignation was always in the hands of the Board of Trustees and that "nothing would afford me more real gratification than the appointment of some one to the office...who would be of greater service to the institution than I am or can ever hope [to] be."[187]

Although he was granted another leave of absence, he stayed on in Lexington. His attorneys informed him that little more could be done in way of securing Arlington until the spring. He employed himself with personal business correspondence related to his late parents, as well as university business which necessitated his attention.

Late in September, he answered one of his many inquirers for souvenirs related to his father which were frequently addressed to his deceased mother. One such note was written to Harry C. Hines of Newark, New Jersey: "Your note of the 19th inst., addressed to Mrs. R. E. Lee, has been delivered to me. My mother has been dead several years. I enclose an autograph of my father, the late Genl. R. E. Lee, which I hope may answer your purpose."[188] Subsequently, in the autumn, he wrote a note to Colonel Marshall McDonald of the Virginia Military Institute pertaining to some letter he received on the "subject of fish." "I enclosed a letter just received on the subject of fish, &c. If you can furnish the information requested, or let the writer know where he would be likely too obtain it, you will greatly oblige me by writing to him on the subject, as I know little or nothing about it."[189]

He continued in his modified position as President of

Washington and Lee University until late April, answering correspondence of insignificance, as well as the endless flood of
inquiries concerning his father:

> I received this morning your letter of the 16th inst., and
> regret to say that I can give you no clue to the missing
> letters; neither can I tell you anything of Capt. McDermott.
>
> My father's letter books, &c. were destroyed during the
> retreat from Richmond, by those having them in charge,
> for fear they would fall into the hands of the enemy.
>
> It is likely that Col. Charles Marshall (Marshall &
> Fisher, Attorneys at Law, Baltimore Maryland) who acted
> as my father's secretary nearly the whole time that he had
> command of the Army of Northern Va., has copies of
> some of his letters to Mr. Davis. I gave him copies of two
> or three written just before and after the evacuation of
> Petersburg, and it is probable that he has others.
>
> I am indeed sorry that the letters referred to have
> disappeared, as they may be the only copies extant of
> some of them; but I hope they may come to light again.
>
> Please remember me kindly to Mr. Davis when you
> next see him...[190]

Finally after years of being dejected, angry and resentful Custis
decided to fight the United States government by taking his claims
to a higher court.

...in April, 1877, he began his suit in the Circuit Court of
Alexandria County, Virginia. He filed suit in ejectment, under
Chapter 131, Code of Virginia naming Frederick Kaufman, Richard
P. Strong, and an array of others, as party defendants. He sought to
evict all persons from his land. Kaufman was a civilian agent of the
War Department, in charge of that portion of the Arlington Estate
that had been set apart as a national military cemetery. Richard P.
Strong was an officer of the United States Army, in charge of the
remaining portions of the property, which was designated "A
Military Reservation pertaining to Fort Whipple." Both held their

joint possession under orders of the Secretary of War. The long list of other defendants was necessary to the technical, legal details of the suit. Most of them were negro refugees set free by the war, and living in the freedman's village down near the river shore, where the master of Arlington, in happier days gone by, was wont to entertain the picnic sojourners from Washington in the groves of trees near this refugee camp during the war, and there they still remained in 1877. Many of them had for years been at work in and about Arlington, doing the manual labor incident to the Government's beautifying of the grounds of the National Cemetery. All had to be encompassed in Mr. Lee's suit to recover his property.[191]

It would take another two months before the United States government would proceed with "a petition for a Writ of Certiorari, on behalf of Kaufman and Strong, and the other defendants likewise filed petitions in the United States Circuit Court for the Eastern District of Virginia, on July 6, 1877. The purpose of the writ was to remove the case from the State court and bring it into the United States Circuit Court for trial. On July 9, 1877, the Writ of Certiorari was ordered to issue, by Mr. Justice Robert W. Hughes, of the United States Circuit Court for the Eastern District of Virginia, and in due time in response to that mandatory writ, the cause was lodged in that court."[192]

The following week Charles Devens, the attorney-general at that time, filed for a motion to dismiss General Lee's suit. Devens argued that "the United States was in reality the party sued, and hence the action should not be maintained."[193] Devens' motion stated in part:

> And now comes the Attorney-General of the United States and suggests to the court and gives it to understand and be informed (appearing only for the purpose of this motion) that the property in controversy in this suit has been for more that ten years and now is held, occupied, and possessed by the United States, through its officers and agents, charged in behalf of the government of the United States with the control of the property, and who

are in actual possession thereof, as public property of the United States, for public uses, in the exercise of their sovereign and constitutional powers, as a military station, and as a national cemetery established for the burial of deceased soldiers and sailors, and for the uses and purposes set forth in the certificate of sale, a copy of which as stated and prepared by the plaintiff, and which is a true copy thereof, is annexed hereto and filed herewith, under claim of title as appears by the said certificate of sale, and which was executed, delivered and recorded as therein appears.

"Wherefore, without submitting the rights of the government of the United States to the jurisdiction of the court, but respectfully insisting that the court has no jurisdiction of the subject in controversy, he moves that the declaration in said suit be set aside, and all the proceeding be stayed and dismissed, and for such other order as may be proper in the premises." [Signed: "Chas. Devens, Atty-Gen'l U. S."] [194]

This was a peculiar position for the Attorney-General to submit. He was asserting that since the government "held, occupied, and possessed" the land in question by virtue of a tax-sale certificate, in their opinion having forfeited the title, the government claimed ownership and therefore the United States Circuit Court had no jurisdiction to filed this claim.

...Although the Attorney-General appeared as the champion of Kaufman and Strong, the principal defendants, he specifically informed the court that the rights of the Government were not submitted to the jurisdiction of the court. Who was responsible for the case being taken away from the Virginia State court and removed to the United States Court? Obviously, the Department of Justice through the Attorney-General. Notwithstanding, he directly challenged the court's power to examine into the tax-title to see if Lee had rightfully or wrongfully been deprived of his grandfather's plantation; the court might not sit in judgment of what the United States

Government had done through its officers and agents, and armed forces, acting under the orders of Lieutenant-General Winfield Scott.

> The issue on the Government's Motion to Dismiss was promptly joined by a Demurrer filed by Lee's attorneys, and thereafter the cause tediously wended its progress toward the argument upon this most important questions of jurisdiction which had first to be determined before the cause could otherwise be tried on its merits.[195]

As a result of this legal wrangling, many questions of particular points of law arose. It was clearly understood by the Attorney-General, the consequences which could materialize from this legal "cat and mouse" game. "...if the United States did not strive mightily to maintain the validity of its tax-sale title to the Arlington Estate, it might be faced with the alternative of disinterring the remains of every soldier and sailor buried in that National Cemetery—and the white headstones were increasing day by day."[196] At any rate, nothing definitive happened until the spring of the following year.

While the legal wrangling continued, Custis' attorneys advised him to return to his duties in Lexington, since it was ridiculous for him to stay in the city and continue his "wait and see" vigil. He lingered on at Ravensworth for a little longer and then finally decided to return to Lexington. By this time, the end of the semester was quickly coming to fruition and he began to resolve many university issues which demanded his attention, although he continued his leave of absence. Between the uncertainty of the outcome of his legal case and the usual situation at the university, these issues tended to compound his chronic physical problems as well as create mental distress.

By early September, he departed for the White Sulpher Springs on his annual visit. From "Old White" he writes to his personal secretary, Captain J. J. White in Lexington:

> I send you a case of Sulpher water which I hope may reach you in good time, without breakage, and prove of

some service to you.

I arrived here about 8 1/2 P.M. last Monday, and found the same unsettled weather I left in Lexington, which still continues, and which, I fear, will last until the Equinox.

There are not now here many of the regular comers. Genl. and Mrs. J. E. Johnston go to Richmond to-night. Gov. Matthews & Col. Duncan go out to-morrow morning. Mrs. James Alfred Jones and daughter, Col. Fitzhugh, Lawyer Green, of Richmond & some others remain a little longer. Your acquaintances all want to know why you did not come up, as this has been the most pleasant season for a long time.

Mr. Corcoran, as you know returned home early, in the month. I will write to him about the Alex[andria] Bonds, and go to see him if desirable. My P. O. Box is No. 18; but as there are only between two and three hundred visitors here now, and there melting away rapidly, it will hardly be necessary to the no. to my address.

Please send me my private letters (after you have opened them to determine whether they are private), remember me to the members of your household, and other friends, and believe me to remain very truly yours...[197]

After leaving "Old White" and returning to Lexington, he continued his conditional leave of absence. During this period he rarely left the house for his campus office and he tended to only the absolutely necessary university business. In October, he received a letter from L. E. Hunt of New York offering to give a portrait of Lewis Brooks the benefactor of the university's museum:

Will you please inform me whether or not a fine oil portrait of Mr. Lewis Brooks would be acceptable to the Trustees of your valuable museum.

I would like to furnish them with a portrait of the highest merit, such as the reputed artists of this city Kurtz

& Sarony would not feel ashamed to claim as their own.
An early reply would favor.[198]

Lee graciously accepted the offer of the portrait on behalf of the Board of Trustees. The remainder of the autumn he spent quietly hoping to hear some further communication about the reacquisition of Arlington. No further relevant news would arrive for months.

The dull winter months provided a renewed correspondence with the former President of the Confederacy, Jefferson Davis. Like many former soldiers and politicians both North and South, Davis was collecting data for a book he wished to write pertaining to the establishment and decline of the Confederate government. Just after the new year, Davis wrote to Custis seeking his advice and suggestions. In the following letter Custis was responding to Davis, who expresses a desire to be informed as to his knowledge concerning the conduct which took place at the Andersonville Prisoner of War facility:

> I received last week your letter of the 4th inst., and showed it to Col. Johnston, who said that he would write to you on the subject of your inquiry without delay.
>
> To the best of my recollection and belief, I never heard—before the receipt of your letter of the 4th inst.—of Mr. Hunter's interview with you, in the interests of peace, referred to in the letter published over his signature in the Dec. No. of the Southern Historical Society papers, which I have just read for the first time; nor do I remember to have ever heard a word from you that could be repeated to subject of the Exchange and Treatment of Prisoners. Although a good deal has been published on this subject, it is desirable, I think, to have all the facts clearly set forth in one paper, or series of papers, for the use and information of those who are willing to see justice done in the matter. I am under the impression that there is in one of the Letter-books, which you have had, a short letter from my father to some one who had written to him about the Andersonville prisoners, to the effect that he had no knowledge of their treatment, but presumed that what they

were said to have suffered was due in the main to the reduced and extremely limited his disparagement.

I do remember, however that you were not in the habit of talking to me about public matters out of the line of my duties, and with which I had no special concern. With many thanks for your kind wishes, and with my sincere prayers for the happiness of yourself and household, I remain faithfully your friend...[199]

Lee continued his correspondence with Davis during the winter of 1878. In late February, he wrote a lengthy notandum to Davis relative to activities during the war:

Your letter in reference to the skirmish at Green's Farm reached me some days since; and finding the incidents of the the several raids on Richmond somewhat confused in my memory, I at once wrote to a friend in Richmond under the impression that he could give me all the information desired.

I have received a letter from him, however, to the effect that he was not with me at the time of the Dahlgren raid, and that, although he had tried to get for me the information requested, he had not succeeded in doing so, at least in a satisfactory manner.

To avoid further delay in acknowledgment that the columns under Genl. Kilpatrick and Col. Dahlgren separated after reaching Beaver Dam, on the Central Railroad; the former passing through the upper part of Hanover County into Louisa County, where it took the mountain road and followed it to the Brook turnpike leading into Richmond; the later proceeding rapidly towards the James River Canal, struck it in Goochland County.

In "The Lost Cause" it is stated that Kilpatrick, moving down on the Brook turnpike, came, early on the 1st March, near the outer line of the Richmond fortifications. In the "Southern History of the War" it is stated that Kilpatrick reached the outer line of the Richmond fortifications on the Brook turnpike, at a little past 10 o'clock on the morning of the 1st March. The two accounts agree in the statement that this column of the Federal cavalry never once got within range of our artillery, though in the latter if is stated that a desultory fire was kept up for some hours. They both end with a sentence to the effect that the enemy, after withdrawing, took up his line of march down the Peninsula.

With regard to the Dahlgren column, Mr. Pollard's account [*Southern History of the War*] is substantially this, so far as our purpose is concerned.

After doing some damage to the canal, &c., unable to find the James River on account of high water, it moved down the river road towards Richmond, and, about dark on the 1st March, encountered on this road—which near the city is called the Westham plank road— a force of local soldiers, composed of artisans from the Richmond Armory, and clerks for the departments of the Government at the first fire (musketry only) of the local troops the cavalry broke and fled, and Dahlgren, now anxious only for his retreat, divided his forces so as to increase the chances of escape, the force under his immediate command moving down the South bank of the Pamunkey. Then follows an account of Col. Dahlgren's death, &c.

Pollard puts the column on the Westham road at seven or eight hundred horseman, and states that eleven of them were killed and some thirty or forty wounded by the fire of the local troops. I remember that several men and horses were killed, and some captured; but do not recollect the exact number.

All I distinctly remember of the raid in question is this—Not long before dark on the evening of the skirmish at Green's farm, while riding towards the fortifications in front of the Fair grounds ("Camp Lee"), and not far beyond the later, I met Genl. & Mrs. Preston driving in their buggy towards Richmond. The General in passing made some remark about my being alone and having so

soon gotten rid of all my staff. Soon after this I heard the
rattle of musketry in the direction of the Westham road,
which ceased before I could get to the Intermediate line
of fortifications on that road (the intermediate is the outer
line, as you may recollect, to the left of the Brook turnpike). When I reached this line of fortifications it was
quite dark, and I was told that the "boy company" (a
company of Richmond boys under eighteen years of age,
belonging to the "Department battalion") had had a
"brush" with some of the Federal cavalry, and had
behaved very well. A short distance beyond the fortifications I met the boy-company and some or all, of the other
companies of the Dept. battalion coming in, and was told
in answer to my inquiries, that the boy company had
arrived first at the Intermediate line of fortifications, and
not finding any troops there, had concluded that there was
an outer line, as on the Brook turnpike and to the right of
it, to which they were to go, and that at Green's farm the
company had met the enemy's cavalry &c., one of the
boys was quite badly, thought not severely wounded; and
I am under the impression that one of the clerks, also, was
hurt to the same extent, and that several others of the
battalion were very slightly injured.

I should have mentioned before that, according to my
recollection some or all of the other companies of the
Dept. battalion got up just in time to relieve the boys, and
that at the appearance on the ground of this support the
enemy drew off. I think, however, that most of the little
fighting that was done at Green's farm, was done by the
boy company. I am under the impression that the battalion on the Westham road, which I think was "Armory
battalion", as stated by Mr. Pollard, did not get to the
Intermediate line of fortifications till after the skirmish
was over, and did not go beyond this line.

I can not recollect being on the Brook turnpike, or to
the right of it, during this raid, and should infer form Genl.
Preston's remark to me—before mentioned—that the

"Local Defense" troops were not called out before the afternoon of the 1st March. It is possible, however, that this being the only occasion, so far as I remember of the fortifications on the Westham road, and near it to the right, being occupied, a greater impression was made on my memory by it. It may be that the troops for Local Defense had been on the morning of the 1st March, guarding some of the approaches to the right of the Brook turnpike, and that in the evening they were transferred to the North west of the city, to meet the reported approach of the enemy in that direction. I am quite positive that they were called to this part of the lines in consequence of the reported approach of the enemy from Charlottesville, along the "Three chop", or "Three notch", road. I think that there were some reports afterwards—later in the day—that the enemy's cavalry were on the river road above Richmond, but as I remember, they were thought to be detached parties from the main body on the "Three Chop" road. I am quite sure, however that the troops under my command were ordered to the Intermediate line of fortifications to the North West of Richmond (the outer line in that direction), and no further, and that the affair at Green's farm was accidental. I remember regretting at the time this misapprehension of the boys, which prevented the Federal cavalry from receiving the fire of two battalions, instead of one company. I remember, too, that is was suggested afterwards that this mistake of the boys may have saved the Westham Furnace because the enemy, finding some of our troops in front or advance of the fortifications, would naturally be afraid to scatter for the purpose of destroying property, &c. I think there was no further demonstration against the city that night, or the following day.

I have seen you so often, at so many different points, on the lines near Richmond (all the lines for its defense, I mean) that I can not recall the special times and occasions, except in a very few instances. I do not recollect any incident, which would enable me to say positively whether or not I was with you any time during the raid under consideration. You were no doubt on the Brook turnpike on the 1st March when the approaches by that road were threatened, and if I was there on the lines to the right of the Brook turnpike, or engaged in getting the "Local Defense" troops in readiness to take their places on the lines , if necessary, my not being with you would be accounted for. Upon any movement against the city, the artillery battalions encamped near the lines, being most available would naturally be concentrated on the parts first threatened, while the troops for "Local Defense", getting out later, would be posted on the approaches to the right and left, or both, of those guarded by the troops first in position. You would naturally be at the points most threatened, and in this way I was some-time not with you on the lines.

I am sorry to trouble you with such a long letter, containing so little information; but, not knowing the whole purpose of your inquiries, I have thought it best to send you all I have on the subject, that you may make use of what you need—if any part of it. I have a small package to send you. Is there an Express agent at Beauvoir? If not, how can I send this package? A line on a Postal card will be sufficient for my purpose.

With best wishes for the health and happiness of you and your—in which wishes my brothers an sisters would be happy to join if they had the opportunity—I remain

P.S. Col. Preston Johnston is not now here, he was in Washington when I last heard from him—several days ago.[200]

Shortly after Lee wrote this letter to Davis, he departed for Richmond where Judge Robert W. Hughes of the United States Circuit Court for the Eastern Districts of Virginia was about to render his lengthy opinion in the Arlington lawsuit. This decision took place on March 15, 1878. In part Judge Hughes stated:

We come, therefore, to the questions of law presented

by the suggestions and demurrer. These are two: 1st Whether the Attorney-General's suggestion is of itself sufficient to defeat the jurisdiction of the court over the cause; and 2nd. Whether, supposing it has not that effect ipso facto, the court may look into the grounds on which that officer intervenes; in pursuance of the observations made by Chief Justice Marshall in the case of United States vs. Peters, 5 Cranch, 115—"It certainly can never be alleged that a mere suggestions of title in a State to property in possession of an individual must arrest the proceedings of the court and prevent their looking into the suggestion and examining the validity of title."

"I should compromise the judicial office if I were to devote any serious argument to the first of these questions. The right to every citizen to a judicial determination of a controversy affecting his liberty or property, in which he may be involved, will not be denied at this day in this country. The courts are open to the humblest citizen, and there is no personage known to out laws, however exalted in station, who by mere suggestion to a court can close its doors against him. I have no thought that the chief law officer of the United States, who in the performance of his duty in this cause has entered the suggestions now under consideration, claims for his action any such prerogative as that in question. But even if it were possible to conceive that such a pretension could be made, let it be answered that it is a cardinal tenet of the Constitution that the judiciary are an independent branch of the government, not to be controlled in its dispensation of justice by interference from other departments, and not only empowered but bound to administer the right without fear, favor or affection. It is useless to dwell upon these topics, but it is appropriate to recall what has been said by luminous jurists of a former era in regard to the decision of questions arising between citizens and their government.[201]

In short, the language used by Judge Hughes dismissed the

suggestion from the Attorney-General Charles Devens that the government had the right to the retention of the Arlington Estate. The order dismissing the motion of the government was signed on April 16, 1878 but this was only the first of many battles to come, as the attorneys for both sides strategically attacked and counter-attacked. It would be nearly another year before the case would be sent back to the Alexandria Court House for a decision by a jury.[202]

Custis Lee returned to Lexington before the end of March. From this location he was informed that Judge Hughes had signed the dismissal order against the Attorney-General's proposal. He was happy this small victory came to pass but he realized it would be a long time before an irrevocable decision would be rendered.

As the lawyers played their legal games, Lee returned to his solitary life of answering letters and conducting minuscule university business. While he was in Richmond, he received another letter from Jefferson Davis which was stamped "Missent." In this letter Lee repeats the same information he gave Davis in his earlier extended letter. Here, Lee claims "My memory is very bad..." Nevertheless, one gets the impression that Lee is trying to distance himself from Davis, at least where any wartime activities are concerned, while giving the pretense of being informative.

...Notwithstanding the trouble you have taken to refresh my memory in regard to the attack on the Brook turnpike by Kilpatrick, I can not recall any of the incidents mentioned with distinctness, though I have a sort of shadowy recollection of them, as if I had heard something of them with regard to some one else. My memory is very bad, however, and I have no doubt that yours is more to be relied on, though it is possible that Johnston, or Wood or some other of your aides, was with you at the time.

The "Department battalion" was composed of the clerks from all the departments of the Govt.—not from the Treasury Dept. alone—and of a company of Richmond boys under 18 yrs. old, and it was this latter company that went by mistake to Green's farm, which was not far beyond the line of fortifications on the Westham plank-road to which the "Department battalion" and another (Armory Battalion?) were ordered; and it was this company of boys which first became engaged with Dahlgren's column, and which had the most to do with checking it and perhaps driving if off; though, as I have said before, the rest of the Dept. battalion—some or all the companies—got up in time to help the company of boys— by their presence on the field, at least, if not taking part in the skirmish of this, I am quite sure, and that the other battalion (armory?) remained at the fortifications as a support. I have no distinct recollection of the Marylanders under Marshall Kane, but take it that they did not go beyond the fortifications.

I have come in possession of an English Dressing-gown, which I have thought would fit you, and which I hope may add to your comfort; if not this Spring, at least during the next cold weather. I send it by express to Mississippi City, and beg that you will use it, if it prove suitable; if not, that you will give it in Your name to any one to whom you may think it would be of use.

Mildred is still absent; but I will send her your kind message as soon as I hear where she is. I know that she will be delighted to hear from yourself that you some-times think kindly of her. Always wishing you and yours every happiness, I remain affectionately yr. friend...

P. S. Col. Johnston is still absent—Mrs. Johnston and the "children" here.[203]

Perhaps feeling a little guilty about not being more informative, Lee turns his attention and concerns to the gift he sent to Davis. Lee wrote a note to Major W. T. Walthall in Mississippi City, Mississippi:

About a week ago, I sent to Mr. Davis, by express, a box containing an English dressing-gown, which I thought might suit him. I have within the last day or two noticed in several newspapers a statement to the effect that Mr. &

Mrs. Davis were in the city-of Mexico, [Mexico City] and therefore beg that you will take care of the dressing gown until their return to this country. If you are not now at Mississippi City, please request some one of your friends there to take charge of the package for Mr. Davis. It would be best perhaps to take the gown out of the box, as I could not manage, with what I had at hand, to pack it very well. I wrote to Mr. Davis at the time the package was forwarded, and directed the letter to Beauvoir, Harrison County, while the box was marked for Missi. City,— with all charges prepaid that could be here determined. If there are any other expenses, please do me the favor to pay them for me and inform me of the amount.[204]

A few weeks later he wrote to Prof. J. J. White who was traveling throughout the South and West on behalf of Washington and Lee University in an effort to recruit students and solicit funds:

When your letter from Augusta arrived here I was sick in bed, or I should certainly have tried to meet you in New Orleans with an acknowledgment of your kind consideration. Your letter of the 11th ult. from New Orleans reached me too late, as I thought to answer it to San Antonio; and I determined, therefore, to write to you at Waco. This would have been done last week, but that the weather, or something else, laid me up again; and now there is hardly time, I fear, for this writing to catch you at Waco. I will send it under cover, however, to Mr. Prather, who will probably know how to forward it, and if it never reaches you, you will not lose much.

I am very glad to learn from yourself that you have everywhere received such a cordial reception, though I did not expect you to receive any other, and am only sorry that you have been so hurried in your travels. This is trying and uncomfortable in many respects; but when it is over, I hope may be able to look back on your visit to the South and West with nothing but pleasure; and I am sure that it will result in good, in many ways, to W. & L. U.

Nothing unusual has happened here, I believe, since you left us. There was some little trouble resulting from the election for Final orator— which election came off not long before your departure—but the members of the "Graham" seem to be now quiet, and if the society can get through with the election to be held next Saturday evening without disturbance, I know of nothing else to take place this session, which is likely to give trouble. The Faculty elected Arch Robinson as Valedictorian, and when he declined on the plea of not being able to do justice to the position, Francis Leaull was appointed, and has accepted. The Lit. Societies have invited a number of gentlemen & among them, Genl. Pryor—to address them at Commencement; but that have all declined except Bishop Pinckney, the last one, also has not yet been heard from. Find out if you can whether Miller will be on hand to deliver the Cincinnati oration, as no one here seems to have any definite information on the subject.

Mr. Nielson has sent on the drawings for the basement of the Chapel extension as last proposed. They seem to be all right, though I have not yet been able to examine them carefully.

Col. Charles A. Davidson sent them up to me but I suppose nothing will be done towards going to work until your return. Mrs. White tells me she keeps you posted as to household matters. She and the other members of the family seemed to be very well when I saw them a few days ago.

The Faculty are much as usual and would join me in kind remembrances did they know of my writing. The country is looking green and beautiful—the Spring being more advanced, I think, than is usual for this date.

Hoping that your journey may continue pleasant, and that you may in good time be with us again...[205]

In the spring session of 1878, President Lee took on teaching duties in the Department of Applied Mathematics. This third year course consisted of instruction in geometry, topographical drawing, shades, shadows, and perspective, as well as elementary architecture, applied mechanics and stone-cutting. The fourth year course consisted of applied mechanics and civil engineering with an advance course in "fortifications and gunnery to students that wished it."[206]

Graduation came off as usual, but due to continued episodes of rheumatoid arthritic flare-ups and constant concern over the legal entanglements pertaining to Arlington, Lee felt an obligation to submit another resignation on June 25, 1878, short of the three month mandatory period of notification. Once again it was refused by the Board of Trustees and the summer was spent in the same traditional manner.

As summer turned into the autumn, he was away from Lexington. From White Sulpher Springs he wrote to Captain J. J. White in Lexington:

> Your letters of the 29th ult., & 1st ult., respectively reached me in due time, and would have been sooner acknowledged for for an attack of rheumatism or something else, in my right wrist, which has prevented me for writing for some days past; and although somewhat better to-day, I use my pen with considerable difficulty, as will probably be apparent to you.
>
> I delivered your message to Miss Belle Harrison, who seemed gratified at the remembrance. She is improving slowly, I think though still very weak. Miss Virginia Ritchie is expected up to-morrow morning, and will no doubt be of some service to the invalid. Miss Haskell had taken her departure before your letter arrived. She started for Columbia, S. C. on the evening of the 29th ult., with Col. and Mrs. Macrady (if that is the right spelling).
>
> I am sorry that we have so few students to begin with, but hope that more will come in later in the season. I am very much obliged to you for the disposition of my mite for the yellow fever suffers so as to avoid publicity. Notwithstanding that Barium divides the human race into

two great classes—and into two only—the "humbuggers" and the "humbugged", I believe I prefer to belong to the latter, though it be the losing side.

Genl. Gibson, who is still here, sends his best regards, and thanks for the information about the schools. He thought Mr. Laird's school,, as described to him, just the thing, and though a Roman Catholic himself, I believe, desired his young friend to be in a "good Presbyterian community."

I have not received much benefit from my visit here this time, though Dr. Lake still encourages me to look for good results; and had thought of visiting my brothers, and some other relatives before returning to Lexington, partly because of my health, and partly because I do not feel able physically, or financially, to go to housekeeping again all by myself. I have wished, too, to see Mr. Corcoran again, as before leaving this place he expressed a desire to see me this Fall. Of course, if I can be of real use to the committee, I shall be glad to return to Lexington at once. Mr. Leyburn can probably get along very well by himself, for the present, with some little advice from and the approbation of, some member of the committee.

Most of our company have gone away, and this week will probably witness the close of the season. I may not leave until next week, but will let you know my address as soon as practicable. Please remember me kindly to the Faculty, Mrs. White and the other members of your family and believe me to remain...[207]

From White Sulpher Springs, he traveled to Richmond on his way to visit with his brothers. He wrote to Miss Tunstall from his brother Rob's home named "Romancoke" in King William County, Virginia:

Your very kind letter of the 27th ult., reached me in Richmond, just before I came down here to see my brother Robert, and would have received as it deserved, and earlier acknowledgement, but for my —what shall I call it—illness, thought I don't think I have been in danger of a "sudden caring off". I was, however, very unwell after leaving the White Sulpher, suffered a great deal, and passed many miserable, lonely days in my bed and room. I saw little of nothing of the Fair, or of the visitors to it, excepting a few relations and friends, who came up to my room to see me. As soon as the Dr. would let me, I came down here, where, under the good affairs of my brother and the quiet of the country, I have improved very much, and, as I believe, am quite well again, except in my wrist, which is still stiff and good for nothing. I expect to remain here until about the middle of next week, then go to Richmond for a day or so to see my Dr., return some calls of ceremony, &c., and afterwards visit my brother Fitzhugh at his place, called Ravensworth, the P. O. of which is Burke's Station, Fairfax Co., Va. After my visit to Ravensworth, which must end by the 1st December, as my brother has to be in Richmond about that time, I must, if possible, pay a long promised visit to some relations near Berryville, Clarke Co., Va., and in Winchester, Va. I have promised also to go an see my relations in King George Co., Va, either before I go to Clarke or afterwards. After all this—if I accomplish it, which is doubtful—I suppose I shall have to go back to Lexington, where I can always find something to do, whether regularly on duty or not. I had thought very seriously of going to Lynchburg before going to Richmond, and probably should have done so, but for my attack. I hope to get there yet before returning to Lexington, though I hardly know whether I ought to do so. I have said much more about myself than I intended, and doubtless much more than you care to read. The P. O. addresses are intended for an answer to a remark of yours, which does me great injustice; and, in response to another, which does me like injustice, I beg to say that I mentioned having burned your letter because I was stupid enough to think that what I did was in accordance with your wishes.

Your second letter to the White Sulpher arrived before

I left, and would have been acknowledge, also, before I left, but for the doubt in which its perusal left me as to whether you wished me to write to you again, and through you hardly intended, I trust, to force me to the position of ignoring your letter, your expressions—or some of them—tended decidedly in that direction.

Miss S—was kind enough to invite me, when I last saw her, to drive down to her place below Richmond whenever I might be in that city; but I have not yet been able to do so, and fear that when I return to Richmond I shall not be able to take advantage of the invitation. I believe the models about which you wrote are to be on exhibition after the 13th, inst., and that the selection is to be made before the end of the month. On some accounts I should like very much to see them; but on the whole it is but perhaps that I should keep clear of the matter altogether. Mr. Corcoran seemed to think, before he left the mountains that I had better see them; but if he does not come to Richmond —and he has not been there this Fall, so far as I know—I don't think I shall go to see the models. I have written you a very stupid note, and you can expect nothing better from a very stupid man; but I can and do wish you every happiness, and beg leave to remain faithfully & truly your friend & svt. [208]

Custis communicated with several women through the years, even though his reputation as a confirmed bachelor was strongly established. Another woman he wrote to was Miss Emily V. Mason of Doughoregan P. O. Howard County, Maryland. His note to Miss Mason is similar to the one written to Miss Tunstall, innocent and sprinkled with common knowledge of mundane events and comments on mutual acquaintances. "...Aunt Nannie has not been very well lately. She has been talking of a visit to Dan and to Mrs. Cooper, but I do not know that she will be able to go so far. She is in her usual good spirits, though feeble and practically blind. The other members of the household are well I believe—I have not seen any of them for several days."[209]

His fondness for women never wavered. Yet his insistence on not marrying remains a mystery to twenty-first century observers; while it is quite clear from a nineteenth century perspective. Being part of the upper class in Virginia, a gentleman of his situation was compelled to have an estate or house of his own, a lucrative financial circumstance and lack other obligations. Custis Lee was deprived of all of these components.

His family obligations were obvious to the casual observer, since he was the patriarch of his immediate family. His financial circumstances vacillated as his environment changed. Henry T. Wickham related a story to James L. Howe about a financial situation which arose during this time, "Bonds received from Arlington were kept by R. H. Maury & Co., Richmond. They were rascals—stole the bonds but continued to pay Custis Lee the interest. They burned their books. Miss Mary Lee blamed Custis for the loss, and (to avoid unpleasantness) he paid her her share; much to his financial detriment."[210] This was only one such event which impacted his finances. Again his series of absences from Washington and Lee University plagued his earned monetary payments as president of the facility.

Aside from these incidents, the situation concerning his Arlington Estate beleaguered him the most. On January 24-30, 1879, a designated jury from a special panel was chosen to resume the trial of the Arlington case initiating in Alexandria. After all of the evidence was presented, the attorneys for both sides presented their closing arguments. Of course, Lee's attorneys argued that the jury should find in favor of him, claiming that the government made an error but the counsel for the government contended on two major points:

No. 1. "If the jury believes from the evidence that Philip R. Fendall, for and on behalf of the owner of the property in controversy, prior to the sale therefore by the tax commissioners, on the 11th day of January, 1864, offered to pay the amount chargeable on said property, under the Act of Congress entitled, "An Act for the Collection of Direct Taxes in Insurrectionary Districts within the United States and for Other Purposes," approved

June 7, 1862, and the acts amendatory thereof; and that said offer was refused by said commissioners because it was not made by the owner in person, then said sale was unauthorized, and conferred on title upon the purchaser."

No. 2. "If the jury believe from the evidence, that the commissioners, prior to January 11, 1864, established, announced, and uniformly followed a general rule, under which they refused to receive, on property which had been advertised for sale, from anyone but the owner or a party in interest, in person, when offered, the amount chargeable upon said property, by reason of said Acts of Congress, then said rule dispensed with the necessity of a tender, and in the absence of proof to the contrary, the law presumed that said amount would have been paid, and the court instructed the jury that, upon such a state of facts, the sale of the property in controversy, made on the 11th day of January, 1864, was unauthorized, and conferred no title upon the purchaser."[211]

At this point Justice Hughes expressed his second written opinion in the case. The first was presented on January 28. He realized that the case would be taken to the Supreme Court for its final verdict and therefore wanted to have on record, "the fullest exposition of the legal reasoning actuating his rulings upon the law involved."[212] Justice Hughes' second opinion presented a deliberate analysis and full consideration of the details:

"If the owner had this right to tender or offer payment of a tax through a friend or agent at any time before a sale, and the right was denied him, then it is difficult to see how a subsequent sale to a particular purchaser could, by ex post facto and penal operation, annul that right. A law which makes such discrimination would seem to be unconstitutional, not only in giving to an act performed by government officials under it an ex post facto and penal effect, but also in depriving a person of his vested right in property by a process other than "due process of law," as that phrase is used by the Constitution. The impolicy of such a provision of law is as obvious to me as its unconstitutionality. Its evil would be liable to fall not only upon disloyal but upon the most loyal citizens. A severe illness lasting only ninety or hundred days, would subject the owner of land to the irreclaimable loss of its possessions and of all but two thirds of its value; for the period of advertisement added to the sixty days allowed by the act for redemption, would require an illness of less than hundred days to divest a citizenof his estate. We can imagine, too, a case of even grosser injustice, which might happen by accident, though my respect for the government forbids me to think it could be morally possible by design. It might happen by accident that government, desiring a piece of land belonging to a loyal citizen engaged in its military service, might in time of war order his command to a distant and protracted service, rendering it impossible for him "to appear in person before the tax commissioners and pay the amount of his tax," and thereby bring on a sale of it for taxes, at which sale it would itself have the power to obtain the land irreclaimably. The familiar expedient employed by King David toward Uriah would here be repeated by accident. I doubt the constitutionality of any provision of a law for raising revenues which would subject to forfeiture lands upon which the taxes, when tendered in behalf of the owner, would by its own terms be prohibited from being received."[213]

The jury handed down its verdict in favor of George Washington Custis Lee, the plaintiff. Nevertheless, this loss by the governmental attorneys only gave them further resolve to appeal the decision to the United States Supreme Court.

On April 3, 1879, at Alexandria, the motion to set the verdict aside and in arrest of judgment, was argued and submitted. Counsel for the Government laid much stress upon the case of Carr vs. the United States, a case decided by the United States Supreme Court on March 3, 1879, after Judge Hughes had rendered his first opinion on the jurisdictional question in January of the same year. But notwithstanding the Carr case, a part of the opinion of which he fearlessly pronounced "dictum," Judge Hughes over-ruled the Government's motion, and judgment on the verdict added a third, memorandum opinion to the record of the Arlington case.

[His final addendum was as follows:]

The case has gone to a verdict. Nothing remains to be done except to enter judgment so that the case may go before the Supreme Court on a writ of error, or for execution to issue on the judgment. I should not be willing to order the execution under any circumstance; but I see nothing in the case of Carr vs. United States to require me to discuss this suit at the present time.[214]

As far as Judge Hughes was concerned, the Arlington case as heard in the United States Circuit Court for the Eastern District of Virginia was accomplished. Judge Hughes had completed his ruling and opinion but what did he mean in the course of his opinion by the statement, "I should not be willing to order the execution under any circumstances"?

Simply, that to have ordered the issuance of the dispossessory writ would indeed have created a curious situation, in that, the federal officer charged with the duty of executing it would have found himself confronted with the task of evicting the military authorities of the United States for the Arlington Estate.

In other words, one branch of the Federal government, in this case the Judiciary, could not force or actuate another branch of the Federal government to comply with its mandate. Nevertheless, the Arlington case was sent to the United States Supreme Court under to write of error: the first was prosecuted by the United States in its own name and the second was presented by the Attorney General on behalf of Frederick Kaufman and Richard P. Strong.[215]

Unfortunately for Custis Lee, it would take another three and one-half years before it would presented before the Supreme Court. This was a dreadful blow to Lee. Whereas, the longer the case was prolonged before a final decision could be rendered, the longer the government would have to continue to inter more and more military bodies on his land. Disheartened, Lee returned to Lexington. His chronic arthritis flared up and it seemed to accentuated his melancholy mood over the delay of permanent adjudication concerning Arlington. Nevertheless, by June the Board of Trustees reaffirmed their complete confidence in him and hoped that he would return to his full duties as President of Washington and Lee University in the fall. With the fate of Arlington remaining questionable, Lee decided that he had no choice but to resume his responsibilities at Washington and Lee and try to make the best of it. He would not submit another resignation until June of 1885.

By the autumn semester, he appeared cheerful and willing to continue his executive duties. He persisted with his correspondence to business associated of the university and to friends. Frequently, he would renew old wartime acquaintances. Many of these men were pursuing new post-war careers which were foreign to their backgrounds and principally in the realm of education.

In November 1879, General Daniel H. Hill, then President of the Industrial University in Arkansas, wrote to Professor J. S. Campbell inquiring about the daily lecture schedule performed by professors at Washington and Lee University. Campbell passed the letter onto Lee for a response. As usual, Lee's response was short and to the point:

> In answer to the question in your letter, of the 21st ult. to Prof. Campbell of this institution, I beg to say—
> That our Faculty regulate the number and length of daily recitations; and that, so far as I know, the Board of Trustees have never undertaken to regulate such details of executive management.

With best wishes for yourself and university, I remain...[216]

At the bottom of Lee's note to Hill, Professor Campbell added, "I concur in the above statement." J. S. Campbell Prof. of Chem. & Geology.[217] This letter was a small sample of the type of correspondence he accomplished daily. Most of these written communications were trite inquiries, requesting advice or favors.

Early in January 1880, Colonel Marshall McDonald, a former Confederate engineer and colleague from the Virginia Military Institute requested Lee to write a letter of reintroduction to General Jeremy F. Gilmer of Savannah, Georgia. Custis Lee complied with the request:

> I beg to commend to you my friend, Col. Marshall McDonald, late Prof. of Mineralogy, Geology &c. at the Va. Mil. Institute, whom you will recollect as one of the C. S. Engineers.
>
> He has been for several years the zealous and efficient Fish Commissioner of this State, and is now engaged with the U. S. Fish Commissioner, Prof. Baird, in whose interest—or rather in that of the U. S. Fish Commission—he is visiting the Southern Coast, and streams. Anything that you may be able to do to further Col. McDonald's business or pleasure, in the way of information, advice &c., will be gratefully appreciated by his many friends, one of whom is your friend and servant...[218]

The same day Custis also wrote a note to Marshall McDonald as well:

> You got off from here a day sooner that I expected; and I therefore missed giving you the promised letter to Genl. Gilmer. I went to your home soon after your left, to get your address in Washington; but Mrs. McDonald was not at home and though Miss Rose McCormick promised to send it to me the next day I did not receive it until

yesterday evening. I enclose a note to Genl. Gilmer, and wishing you health, happiness and success, I remain...[219]

Through the course of Lee's tenure at Washington and Lee University, many friends and family members visited Lexington. Custis and Mildred Lee frequently invited this variety of guests to reside with them during their visit. More than sixty years later, a Washington and Lee graduate John M. Glenn, recalled a visit he made to the President's House:

...I had the good fortune to spend several days in the President's House as the guest of General and Miss Mildred Lee. At the same time General Custis' brother, General Fitzhugh (Runy [Rooney]) Lee and his wife and two sons, Robert and Bolling, were staying in the house. It was one of the most delightful experiences I have ever enjoyed. These members of the Lee family were all very fond of each other. The elders were full of fun and vivacity. The two generals were thoroughly congenial and stimulating to each other and showed plainly their delight in being together. Under this genial influence General Custis threw off his sense of responsibility which usually weighted heavily on him, and showed what a charming personality he had.

I always admired General Custis immensely. He was unquestionably a man of good judgment and real executive ability. And he was eminently fair, just and anxious to help others. Miss Mildred was one of the brightest, most stimulating and wittiest women I have ever met. She fascinated me.[220]

The academic year at Washington and Lee University was relatively uneventful. Lee kept up with his personal and business correspondence. As the year progressed Lee became more social. Often he and his sister, Mildred would invite visitors to the town to dining at the President's House. One such invitation was extended to Major Daniel Holt in the Spring of 1881:

Judges Sheffery & Turner, and Col. Pendleton have

promised to dine with Mr. Tucker at my house to-day; and I hope that you may be able to be with us also.

The hour is seven (7) o'clock, to suit the court; but there will be no formality.

I called to see you last evening; but was so unfortunate as to miss you.[221]

With such minor social occasions during the academic year, President Lee's life was tranquil and ordinary. As usual, the graduation events came and went with regularity but the summer provided an unwanted respite of illness from his presidential schedule. Nevertheless, by early August, Lee resumed his letter writing pertaining to university business. In the following letter to Prof. William Taylor Thom, he informs Thom of much university business:

Your kind letter of the 27th June did not reach me until after the last meeting of our Faculty for the session of 1880-81, and until after several of its members had gotten away. It will, however, be brought to the attention of the Faculty at the very next meeting. I owe you an apology for not having sooner made some acknowledgement of you generous in regard to the endowment of a Chair of Literature, and I beg to make it now. I have been so unwell all the summer—part if the time in bed—that I have not been able to give due attention to my correspondence, and other duties; and on this account, my correspondence particularly got into considerable confusion.

I am now trying to straighten it out-though far from being well- and hope to keep it straight hereafter.

I agree with you in all you say in reference to the desirability of a Chair of Literature, and should like very much to see it established, and yourself as its occupant; we have "great expectations", too, in regard to an adequate endowment of this institution, in time; but, of course, there expectations may not come to anything with a reasonably short period. The Alumni will doubtless be so much occupied during the next year in preparing for the Centennial that they may not be able to take anything else in hand until after that's over; but we will see what can be done towards carrying out your views, and the subject can be considered at the alumni meeting next June, if not before.

We are hard at work now putting up a Library building, which we hope to have under roof before frost, and completed altogether before next Commencement. It will not be the handsomest structure of the kind in the country; but will be, I think, as convenient, and well adapted it its uses as any. It is on the site of the South Dormitories, which have been taken down. The stone base of the Library will be about finished this week, and next week, we hope to begin the brick masonry. The building has a capacity for 70,000 vols., as at present arranged; and this capacity can be increased, with but little trouble, or expense, to 140,000 volumes. The building contains six small rooms for offices, a large Reading-room, a good sized Picture Gallery (over the Reading-room), and the Book-room.

We hope in time to get a building to balance the Library, on the site of the North Dormitories this latter to be for Halls for the Literary Societies, or for a Museum. &c.

With best wishes for your health and happiness, I remain...[222]

As fate would have it, the Centennial celebration of the Washington and Lee University was postponed through a "Special Notice" issued by the University on April 17, 1882:

The Faculty of Washington and Lee University take this method of informing the Alumni and other friends of the institution that, a recent order of the Board of Trustees, the Centennial Celebration proposed to be held in June of this year has been deferred to a later day. This action of the Board, adopted with the full concurrence of the Faculty in its propriety, was prompted by the unexpected occurrence of obstacles which seem to be insuperable to such an observance of the occasion as its importance and the expectations of our friends demand.

First, it is now ascertained that the Mausoleum, for the completion of which its was supposed adequate arrangements had been made, cannot, by the time mentioned, be put in readiness to receive the Statue of Gen. Robert E. Lee. Without an opportunity to exhibit the Statue to the visitors at the Celebration, a prime purpose of the occasion would be defeated, and great disappointment among our friends the result.

Secondly, unavoidable delay has occurred in the collection of funds which were relied on to defray the expenses of preparations deemed essential in order to render the Celebration creditable to the institution and satisfactory to our friends.

Thirdly, in consequence of the extraordinary character of last winter and the early spring, the work on the Valley Railroad has been so retarded, we cannot longer hope that his important facility for reaching Lexington will be available until after the time appointed for the Centennial.

With respect to these reasons for delay, we would simply add that when the appointment was made for June of this year, they were not foreseen, nor could have been, by either the Board of Trustees or the Faculty. Our friends will please notice that the purpose to commemorate our Centenary is not abandoned, but only postponed. The Board of Trustees, at the annual meeting in next June, will appoint the particular time for the ceremonies, of which due announcement will be made to our friends and the public generally.

Notwithstanding, the new library structure was named Newcomb Hall and Lee would later take one of the rooms on the southern end of the second floor for his presidential office. Like Lee himself, his office reflected his personality: clean, austere and elegant. The new presidential office was truly reflective of a mathematical mind, along with the accentuated sharp lines of an engineer. At the end of the academic year 1881-1882, Lee provided the Board of Trustees with a lengthy report on the construction and utilization of this new structure.

> The Library and Apparatus of the institution are in about the same condition as at the date of the my last report. A list of the books presented to the Library during the session is given in the catalogue for 1881-1882.
>
> The new Library Building is essentially finished, and ready for the books. Work on it begun soon after the last annual meeting of The Board, and the sum ($20,000.00) mentioned in my last report as promised for its erection had been received by the Treasurer of the institution, and expended in great part in the work of construction. The giver, whose name was not mentioned in my last report, is Mrs. Josephine Louise Newcomb, and the building is intended as a memorial to her husband, the late Warren Newcomb, who himself gave the sum of $10,000.00 to the institution before my official connection with it. In addition to the granite block over the front door bearing the name, "Warren Newcomb," there is to be a tablet over the front entrance door to the Reading-Room with the following inscription, selected by Mrs. Newcomb—

> "This Hall was erected in 1882 by Josephine Louise Newcomb as a tribute of affection and Honor to the Memory of her husband, Warren Newcomb of New York."

> The architect of the building undertook, several months ago, to have this tablet prepared in Baltimore; but it has not yet been received by the contractor.
>
> The following correspondence between the architect and W. F. Poole, of the Public Library, Chicago, who seems to be considered [a] good authority, may be of some interest.
>
> By way of introduction to this correspondence, it is

perhaps proper for me to say that I called Mr. Neilson's attention to Mr. Poole's pamphlet on the construction of Libraries some time last autumn when the masonry of our building was well advanced.

Extract from Mr. Neilson's letter of Nov. 1881.

"My Dear Genl. Lee

After reading again the paper furnished by Mr. Poole, the Chicago Librarian, I concluded to adopt your suggestion of writing to him for a copy; and that idea, by the time I got ready for the letter, developed itself into a notice of our own little affair. I sent him a sketch copied from the photographers plans, and a letter which not only described our building but mentioned some other matters and made also a short defense of our profession. The enclosed letter came back as reply. I think it will gratify you as much as it did me; and for future reference it might, considering the source, be worth copying into some record connected with he Library. * * * * I answered him promptly, saying amongst other things that the second story of cases was a sort of concession to the prevalent idea of piling up, to economize now, that the upper cases would not go in now, and we would trust to the future." (The rest of the letter refers to the dimensions of the shelving, &c.)

Yrs. very truly,
(sgnd.) J. C. Nielson

Copy of Mr. Poole's letter of the 27 Oct.,
1881 to J. C. Nielson

"Dear Sir:

Your letter enclosing a plan of the Library Building of the Washington & Lee University is received, and I have read the one and examined the other with much pleasure.

The ground plan is very excellent and suitable one; and so long as you keep the room in that form I have nothing to criticize, and much to commend; but when you come to put up what you call "over cases" and I call "galleries," I have the same strong objections to urge which I made in my Washington Paper. Calling this arrangement "over cases" does not help the matter. You have space on the floor of the two rooms for shelving 54,550 volumes. By the W. P. Reports of Public Libraries, 1876, the university than had 11,000 volumes. It is fortunate then that the "over cases" are not to spoil this beautiful plan for some time to come. Perforated iron floors, and hammered glass floors, so far as letting light through, or serving any purpose that is useful, are a snare and a delusion. (Here follows a discussion of the dimensions of shelving, &c.)

I mail with this letter a copy of my Washington Paper, as you desired, and also my paper on the "organization & management of Public Libraries," which appeared in the Govt. Report, 1876. On p. 11 you will find some rough sketches of my shelving and dimensions.

I am very much pleased with your plan because it is practical and sensible, and hence I have frankly given my views as to its details. You do not say whether you expect me to return the sketch. I should like to keep it, or if you wish it returned, to retain a copy of it.

We should not agree on the explanation of the enigma. Why the conventional style of constructing libraries has been kept up so long you think the architects have not been remitted to build any original design. I think that as a rule they have not made an original design which is worth building. All the architects have known have followed in the old classic ruts. Librarians and Trustees, on the other hand, have had no ideas of their own, and have turned the matter over to the architect who would make the prettiest design. The Librarian ought to know what he needs, and employ an architect to express it. The combination of the two kinds of knowledge and skill will produce a good

structure. Neither can do it alone. I have written more than
I intended because I have been interested in your ideas and
plans.

Yrs. very truly,
(sgd.) W. F. Poole

~~~~~~~~~~~

<div align="center">

Recommendations

</div>

The Recommendations of the Faculty are respectfully
submitted for your consideration; and with them several
papers strongly recommending
Rev. Henry E. Dwight of the Honorary Degree of
Doctor of Divinity.

~~~~~~~~~~~

I have the honor to be
Very Respectfully,
Your Friend & Svt.
G. W. C. Lee [223]

In the autumn of 1881, one hundred and nine young men
commenced their academic studies, hailing from thirteen states
other than Virginia and the District of Columbia. By the close of the
scholastic year, ninety-eight students remained.

During this instructional year, thirteen departments of study
were offered at Washington and Lee University. The mathematics
department was the best attended, with the department of modern
languages trailing behind with nine fewer students. The enrollment
in the Department of Applied Mathematics was especially gratifying to President Lee, as it gave him an opportunity to return to
classroom. It is obvious that he took great pride in this course from
the statement he included in the Annual Report of 1881-1882 to the
Board of Trustees:

The instruction in this Dept. has been divided, during
the session, between Prof. Moreland and myself.

He had the Junior class in Engineering during the 1st term, and the class in Astronomy during the 2nd term.

I had the Senior class in Engineering during the whole session; the class in Surveying during the 1st term, and the Junior class in Engineering during the 2nd term.

The surveying class numbered 15, one withdrew before the Intermediate Examination, and another did not stand his examination on account of sickness. 13 stood the examination and passed satisfactorily. The Junior class in Engineering numbered 4, one of whom withdrew before the final examination, and another failed, 2 passed satisfactorily. The two (2) members of the Senior class in Engineering pass both examinations satisfactorily, and are recommended for the Degree of Civil Engineer.

Many years later, W. J. Humphreys, a former student of Washington and Lee University, recounted his association with President Lee during his senior year engineering class:

...I frequently saw General Custis Lee and came to know him much better than did the average student. My lasting impression of him is that he was a calm, dignified and scholarly gentleman. He inspired by unremitting, perfect example and never by parade and oratory, even before his own faculty and students. I never saw him give way to hilarity of any kind, nor, on the other hand, appear glum and morose. My most frequently and closest association with General Lee was as a student in a class of two in Civil Engineering—the last class he ever taught. The subjects he covered were essentially portions of applied mathematics in relation to bridges and other structures. The theory and practice of surveying were given by one of the faculty.

Of course for so small a class formal lectures were not necessary, nor given. However, we met with all the regularity and punctuality of an accurately regulated clock, not, as stated, for the purpose of a formal discourse, but for an informal discussion of the subjects covered in the assignment for that day's consideration. Obscurities were cleared up and real difficulties fully removed. In short, as a patient and efficient guide through the maze of whatever topic was under consideration he was perfect—no trace of misunderstanding was left behind.

In the course of my many, but always brief, conversations with General Lee only once did he refer to any important event in his own life. He was speaking of the folly of overconfidence, and illustrated it by his personal experience as a cadet at West Point. He worked hard, he said, during all the first year, and led his class. From this success, he added, came an unwarranted assumption that he could lead his class again the next year, and without working so hard. He tried it, but the results were disappointing. He had been overconfident. Again he got down to real work and eventually graduated at the head of his class.[224]

Late in December 1881, a "Circular" was distributed through the student body from the faculty concerning daily religious services at the Lee Chapel:

> "The Faculty of Washington and Lee University desire to call the attention of the parents and guardians of its students to the fact that although daily religious services are held in the Chapel the attendance in them is left optional. This course has been adopted not through any doubt as to the property and value of such services, nor through any indifference on the part of the Faculty as to whether the students shall avail themselves, or not, of the privileges offered them, but because it is believed that the interest taken in the services and benefit derived from them will be much greater when the attendance is voluntary that if it were enforced by authority and penalties:
>
> "The Faculty, however, regret to say that the results of their efforts to induce a general attendance on the exercises in the Chapel have not been satisfactory. Some of

the students are regular in their attendance; others are seldom or never present. In this state of things, the Faculty deem it proper to ask the co-operation of parents and others having influence with the students, in an effort to remedy the evil. A few word of advice and persuasion coming from home, will often accomplish what no official remonstrance can secure."[225]

After this notice was sent to the families of the students, President Lee reported at the end of the school year that of "Young Men's Christian Association, there is little or no change to report in the membership and work of this useful association. The interest in it has not diminished, although it may not have increased to any great extent."[226]

As always, President Lee was concerned about the deportment of the students. He reported in June, 1882,

The general conduct of the students had been good, and their attendance at morning prayers better than for several years past. All the members of the Faculty, with one or two exceptions, have attended there exercises regularly. The exercises have been conducted, as heretofore, by the Pastors of the churches of the town, and by Dr. Kilpatrick.

In this connection your attention is invited to a copy of a circular issued towards the close of last year, and addressed to the parents or guardians, of all the students then on the rolls of the university.[227]

Finally, Lee commented on the performance of the faculty:

The duties of the Professors have been performed with customary zeal and fidelity, and their labors have been rewarded by respectable progress on the part of the students. For the details of the Professor's work during the session, you are respectfully referred to their reports submitted herewith.

A copy of the Minute[s] adopted by the Faculty on the

occasion of the death of Dr. Thompson is here presented for the information of The Board. The members of the Faculty appointed for the purpose, attended the funeral in a body.

At the end of the spring session, it was common for President Lee to open his house to the students for an informal reception. W. J. Humphreys remembered one such occasion, "...there was little formality but a superabundance of the finest ice cream. I wonder how many of us ever partook too freely at one of those feasts? I did once, the first time I ever saw raspberry ice cream, and missed a "calico" [an informal social event where respectable young ladies and young gentlemen were present] engagement." [228]

Prior to the students leaving on their summer vacation, Lee received a circular and letter from Arthur Gilman, Secretary of the Longfellow Memorial Association of Cambridge, Massachusetts. In the course of the letter from Mr. Gilman, he requested that the faculty and students be informed of the association. In his usual polite and concise manner, Custis Lee acknowledged the notification received from Gilman, "Your circular of the 15th, ult. reached me some days ago, and was brought to the attention of our Faculty at their first meeting after its receipt. It will also be brought to the attention of our students, and without unnecessary delay."[229]

With the student activities for the year completed, Lee met with the Board of Trustees to resolve the issue of the Lee statue installation and the centennial celebration which had been postponed in mid-April. The trustees decided to schedule the installation and centennial celebration for the spring 1883.

Now that the university business was accomplished for another academic year, Custis took his usual sojourn to White Sulpher Springs for a rest from university schedule. In his customary manner, he returned to Lexington a few weeks prior to the opening of the new academic year. Shortly after his return, he received a letter from his attorneys informing him that the Supreme Court had scheduled to hear the Arlington case in October. After a lapse of more than three and one-half years since Judge Robert W. Hughes of the Richmond Court had rendered his decision in favor of

George Washington Custis Lee, an appeal was brought forth on behalf of two writs of error: one prosecuted by the United States in its own name, and the other by the Attorney-General in the names of Frederick Kaufman and Richard P. Strong was finally being heard in the Supreme Court on October 18, 1882.

The Solicitor-General Phillips and Westell Willoughby represented the United States, Kaufman and Strong in the case while General George Washington Custis Lee was represented by William D. Shipman, A. Ferguson Beach and Francis L. Smith of Alexandria, William J. Robertson of Charlottesville, and Leigh R. Page of Richmond. The highest court in the land heard arguments from both sides on October 18 and 19, after which time they retired to their chambers to deliberate on the outcome. Custis lingered at Ravensworth a few days before returned to Lexington to await the verdict and continue his duties at Washington and Lee.

General Lee had arrived back in Lexington just in time for Halloween. As was the custom in many towns, the high school and college-age students play pranks on the unsuspecting public. Washington and Lee was not immune to such revelry and mischief. A former resident of Lexington, John R. Senseney, related the following story in the *Rockbridge County News*, October 26, 1937:

> The students were in the habit of celebrating Hallowe'en night, like students in all other university towns, by taking down signs, carrying away gates, and in some cases damaging property. After one of these escapades, Mayor Dold sent out his officer with instructions to make a list of all damages down, and to make an itemized statement in dollars and cents, also the names of the owners of the property so damaged. When the mayor received the report, he made out an itemized statement and sent it with a very courteous note to General Custis Lee, as president of the University, leaving the justice of his demand entirely to the good judgment of the general. General Lee at once called a meeting of the student body. He told the students that he would demand them to raise the amount, among those guilty of the depredations. He

further stated that he did not want anyone to confess, but would leave this matter up to the conscience of the guilty ones to subscribe the amount necessary to liquidate this indebtedness to the people whom they had damaged by their boyish pranks. He said that hereafter he would expect and demand of each student that he act in a manner becoming a gentleman; and in the future he would send home any who did not hold up the reputation of the University as a class of gentlemen, even if it embraced the whole student body, and in that event he would lock the doors of the University, and await the time until he could fill their places with gentlemen. This had the desired effect of breaking up destructive Hallowe'en parties among the students. But, I have an idea that a great many depredations were committed by town boys and blamed on the students, while the students furnished a "smoke screen" to hide the town boys.

After many weeks, Custis was recalled to Washington, D. C. to hear the opinion of the Supreme Court which was rendered on December 4, 1882 by Justice Miller. The opinion consisted of twenty-eight printed pages from the 106th United States Supreme Court Reports. The case was in part compounded due to the language utilized within the opinion from the justice:

> If this sale was valid and the certificate conveyed a valid title, then the title of the plaintiff was thereby divested, and he could not recover. If the proceedings evidenced by the tax sale did not transfer the title, then it remained in him, and so far as the question of title was concerned, his recovery was rightful.
>
> We have then two questions presented to the court and jury below, and the same questions arise in this court on the record:—
>
> 1. Could any action be maintained against the defendants for the possession of the land in controversy

under the circumstances of the relation of that possession to the United States, however clear the legal right to that possession might be in the plaintiff?

2. If such an action could be maintained, was the prima facie title of the plaintiff divested by the tax sale and the certificate given by the commissioners?

It is believed that no division of opinion exists among the members of this court on the proposition that the rulings of law under which the latter question was submitted by the court to the jury was sound, and that the jury was authorized to find, as they evidently did find, that the tax certificate and the sale which it recited did not divest the plaintiff of his title to the property. For this reason we will consider first the assignment of errors on that subject.

No substantial objection is seen on the face of the certificate to its validity, and none has been seriously urged. It was admitted in evidence by the court, and, unless impeached by extrinsic evidence offered by the plaintiff, it defeated his title...

It is in reference to the clause which permits the certification to be impeached by showing that the taxes had been paid previous to sale that the plaintiff in the present case introduced evidence.

This court has in a series of cases established the proposition that where the commissioners refused to receive such taxes, their action in thus preventing payment was the equivalent of payment in its effect upon the certificate of sale.[230]

Next, the court addressed the questions of the alleged error committed by Judge Hughes of the lower court in the matter of giving and refusing instructions to the jury. Justice Miller concluded, "It is a general rule that when the tender of performance of an act is necessary to the establishment of any right against another party, this tender or offer to perform is waived or becomes unnecessary when it is reasonably certain that the offer will be refused."[231]

> The other point raised was the right to pay the taxes between the advertisement and day of sale in any other mode than by personal appearance of the owner before the commissioners, did not exist in cases where the United States became the purchaser. As it could never be known until the day of the sale whether the United States would become the purchaser or not, it would seem that the duty of the commissioners to receive the taxes was to be exercised without reference to the possibility of the land being struck off to the United States...
>
> It is proper to observe that there was evidence, uncontradicted, to show the Fendall appeared before the commissioners in due time, and on the part of Mrs. Lee, in whom the title then was, offered to pay the taxes, interest, and costs, and was told that the commissioners could receive the money from no one but the owner of the land in person. In all this matter we do not see any error in the ruling of the court, nor any reason to doubt that the jury were justified in finding that the United States acquired no title under the tax-sale proceedings.[232]

Justice Miller further concluded that it had "been ascertained by the verdict of the jury, in which no error is found, that the plaintiff has the title to the land in controversy and what is set up in behalf of the United States is no title at all, the court can render no judgment in favor of the plaintiff against the defendants in the action, because the latter hold the property as officers and agents of the United States, and it is appropriated to lawful public uses."[233]

> The Court then proceeded to discuss at considerable length on what principle the exemption of the United States from a suit by one of its citizens is founded, and what limitations surround this exemption...[234]

After the Justice sited many precedents from English and American law, he finally stated:

The case before us is a suit against Strong and Kaufman as individuals to recover possession of property. The suggestion was made that it was the property of the United States, and that the court, without inquiring into the truth of the suggestion, should proceed no further; and in this case, as in that, after a judicial inquiry had made it clear that the property belonged to plaintiff and not to the United States we are still asked to forbid the court below to proceed further, and to reverse and set aside what it has done, and this refuse to perform the duty of deciding suits properly brought before us by citizens of the United States. It may be said—in fact it is said— that this present case differs, [from a the United States verses Peters, as previously sited] because the officers who are sued assert no personal possession, but are holding as the mere agents of the United States...[235]

Although the judgment of the Circuit Court was in favor of the plaintiff and its result was to turn the soldiers and officers out of possession and deliver it to plaintiff, Mr. Chief Justice Marshall concludes his opinion in this emphatic language: "This court is unanimously and clearly of the opinion that the Circuit Court committed no error in instructing the jury that the Indian title was extinguished to the land in controversy and that the plaintiff below might sustain his action." [Worcester vs. Georgia]

We are unable to discover any difference whatever in regard to the objection we are now considering between this case and the one before us.

After analyzing and comparing a number of other decisions of the Supreme Court, involving the same general principles, Mr. Justice Miller came to the consideration of the case of Carr vs. the United States. It will be recalled that this case had been decided by the Court on March 3, 1879, after Judge Hughes had rendered his first opinion on the jurisdictional question in January (1879), just two months before, although the Carr case had been argued at the October Term, 1878. It was because of this fact that counsel for the Government had counted heavily upon the Carr case at Alexandria in April, 1879, when the motion to set aside the verdict of he jury had been argued. In passing the Carr case, General Lee's long fight for restoration of the Arlington Estate had to cross the most dangerous shoal encountered in its turbulent progress throughout the years since 1878. The learned justice below had analyzed the Carr case at the time he delivered his addendum opinion in April, 1879, and pronounced the very parts of the opinion relied upon by the Government to defeat Mr. Lee's recovery, as "dictum." In the Supreme Court a majority of the learned justices did not falter when the time came either to repudiate the obiter dictum of Mr. Justice Bradley or subscribe to it and deprive Mr. Lee of the right to have his ancestral estate of Arlington...[236]

What is that right as established by the verdict of the jury in this case? It is the right to the possession of the homestead of the plaintiff. A right to recover that which has been taken from him by force and violence, and detained by the strong hand.

This right being clearly established, we are told that the court can proceed no further, because it appears that certain military officers, acting under the orders of the President, have seized this estate, and converted one part if it into a military fort and another into a cemetery. It is not pretended as the case now stands that the President had any lawful authority to do this, or that the legislative boy could give him any such authority except upon payment of just compensation. The defense stands here solely upon the absolute immunity form judicial inquiry of every one who asserts authority for the executive branch of the Government, however clear it may be made that the executive possessed no such power. Not only no such power is given, but it is absolutely prohibited, both to the executive and the legislative, to deprive any one of life, liberty or property without due process of law, or to take private property without just compensation... Courts of justice are established, not only to decide upon the controverted rights of the citizens as against each other, but also upon rights in controversy between them and the government; and the docket of this court is crowded with controversies of the latter class...[237]

It can not be, then, that when, in a suit between two citizens for the ownership of real estate, one of them has established his right title possession of the property according to all the forms of judicial procedure, and by the verdict of a jury and the judgment of the court, the wrongful possessor can say successfully to the court, "Stop here, I hold by order of the President, and the progress of justice must be stayed." That, though the nature of the controversy is one peculiarly appropriate to the judicial function, though the United States is no party to the suit, though one of the three great branches of the government to which by the Constitution this duty has been declared its judgment after a fair trial, the unsuccessful party can interpose as absolute veto upon that judgment by the production of an order of the Secretary of War, which that officer had no more authority to make than the humblest private citizen.

While by the Constitution the judicial department is recognized as one of the three great branches among which all the powers and functions of the government are distributed, it is inherently the weakest of them all. Dependent as its courts are for the enforcement of their judgments upon officers appointed by the executive and removable at his pleasure, with no patronage and no control of the purse or the sword, their powers and influence rest solely upon the public sense of the necessity for the existence of a tribunal to which all may appeal for the assertion and protection of rights guaranteed by the Constitution and by the laws of the land, and on confidence reposed in the soundness of their decisions and purity of their motives. From such a tribunal no well-founded fear can be entertained of injustice to the government or of a purpose to obstruct or diminish its just authority.

The Circuit Court was competent to decide the issues in this case between the parties that were before it; in the principles on which these issues were decided no error has been found, and its judgment is Affirmed.[238]

Those justices who concurred with Justice Miller were Justices Blatchford, Field, Harlan and Matthews. The dissenting votes came from Chief Justice Waite, Justices Bradley, Gray and Woods. Justice Gray delivered the lengthy dissenting opinion which in essence stated that they were "of the opinion that the Court had no authority to proceed to trial and judgment; because the suit, which had been commenced against he individual defendants was thenceforth prosecuted against the United States."[233] Nevertheless, the Arlington case was over and the ultimate verdict was presented, and no further appeal could be requested.

The Government found itself adjudged a trespasser upon the Arlington Estate property by the highest judicial tribunal in the country; holding it by force under rules and regulations of the War Department, against the rightful and legal owner, George Washington Custis Lee. A situation indeed! What was to be done about it? If, by any chance, General Lee had changed his mind about conveying his title to the United States for adequate compensation, as he had theretofore offered to do, there were seemingly only two remaining alternatives: First: that the Government would have to disinter the remains of every soldier and sailor buried in their Arlington graves, as well as remove the military post occupying other portions of the estate, on Second: it could ignore the decision of the Supreme Court and continue a trespasser as theretofore. Fortunately, Lee was magnanimous in victory.[240]

In the true image of his father, Custis Lee generously agreed to sell all of the land occupied by the government as a military post and cemetery to the United States at the purchase price of one hundred and fifty thousands dollars, a fair market value at the time. It would be three months before the closing formalities of the case would be finalized. Once, again Lee returned to Lexington during this interim period.

Toward the end of December, President Lee issued a letter to the students on behalf of the faculty and himself pertaining to the reading room located in the new Newcomb Hall:

> The Faculty congratulates the students on the increased facilities afford them for literary culture and enjoyment by the opening of the Reading Room in Newcomb Hall. It is the earnest wish of the Faculty that the advantages thus offered my be realized, in the highest degree possible, by all connected with the University; and in order to this end, they have published some Regulations for the government of the room, to which they desire, through this paper, to call the attention of the students. The rules which have been adopted are deemed essential to the orderly conduct and success of the Reading Room, being, in substance, such as are prescribed for rooms of a similar character in other places. The propriety of those that are designed to secure full order and quiet is so obvious that nothing need be said to enforce them.
>
> The last two Regulations have reference to the protection and becoming appearance of the room itself and its contents; and respecting each of these a single remark will suffice:
>
> FIRST, it is due to the generous friend whose noble benefaction enabled the University to erect the Hall, that the building in all its parts and appointments should be carefully preserved from wanton or needless injury and defacement.
>
> SECOND, from its character and its position in the Hall it is safe to assume that the Reading Room will

attract the particular notice of all visitors of the University grounds. It must be the wish of the students, no less that of the Faculty, that this room and all belonging to it should be found, at all hours, in a condition to be inspected without discredit to those who use it or those who have it in charge.

The Faculty feel assured of the co-operation of the students in the endeavor to render the Reading Room, as it ought to be, an ornament as well as a valuable auxiliary to the University.[241]

Apparently, Dr. George W. Bagby, the state librarian, was present for the opening of the new library. Bagby and Lee were acquainted during the war when both were stationed in Richmond. During these years, Bagby, a trained medical doctor, started to develop a literary avocation. Bagby rapidly gained a reputation for his writing skill and became something of a syndicated columnist throughout the South. After the war he went to New York to pursue a career in journalism but soon returned to Virginia where he became the editor of the *Southern Literary Messenger*. After his departure from Lexington, he wrote to President Lee from his home in Richmond. Lee was exceedingly grateful for Bagby's contributions of time and knowledge; therefore, he wasted no time in responding to Bagby's letter:

Yours of the 20th duly received. As you would go, I am glad you had a safe journey home—and I trust it was not uncomfortable. If I had known that you wished my photography I should have had great pleasure in giving it to you. I shall not forget you when we come to catalogue our books; and hope that we may some day make it worth your while to become our Librarian.

I can't now say when I may be in Richmond again; but shall certainly try to find you the first time I am in your city, and pay my respects to Mrs. Bagby and the little ones.

All your many friends here would be glad to join me in kind remembrances, if they knew of my writing.

Hoping to see you here again soon, and with best wishes for your health and happiness I remain...[242]

At long last, Lee received notice from his attorneys that Congress had reconvened. In the course of their various discussions, the Arlington case was presented and the following resolution was approved:

On the third day of March, 1883, the 47th Congress of the United States appropriated one hundred and fifty thousand dollars with which to purchase the Arlington Estates property, and on March 31st. General George Washington Custis Lee signed a deed conveying the land to the United States, which he acknowledged before a notary public on April 24, 1883.

This deed was submitted to Attorney-General Benjamin H. Brewster, who on May 8th informed Secretary of War Robert Todd Lincoln, by a "manuscript opinion," that it would pass a good title to the Government. Consequently, the United States legally obtained the Arlington estate. The deed was registered in the Alexandria Court House on May 14, 1883, just ten days short of the twenty-second year anniversary of the occupation of the estate on May 24, 1861 by Federal troops.[243]

This was a bittersweet triumph for Lee. He obtained financial compensation for the Arlington Estate, as well as closure to this chapter of his life, but he had lost his home irrevocably and the foes of his father retained their hateful position on his most beloved property.

During the early years of the 1880's, Leslie Lyle Campbell was a student at Washington and Lee University. In an interview dated January 17, 1939, Campbell remembered well his former teacher G. W. C. Lee, President of Washington and Lee University:

It was the privilege of the writer [Campbell] to be a student at Washington and Lee in the 80's, when General

Custis Lee was the President of the University. Today we again see him walk with steady, firm military step from his home on the Campus to his office on the second floor of the southern end of the Main College building, now next to Newcomb Hall.

The daily passage of the erect, dignified figure across the Campus reminded many of the majestic form of his heroic father. His walk was a continual reminder of the dignity of the man. His regular attendance at morning Chapel services, in the basement of the Lee Chapel, brought a holy hush and a quiet benediction as he entered the door. In those days, in front of the Lee Memorial Church, there was a narrow two parallel-plank walk. When General Custis Lee, in good or in muddy weather, met a student or a citizen on this walk, he stepped off the planks to let the other pass.

Before Newcomb Hall was built, when there was no place for the students to read or study in the college buildings, the writer sat one cold wintry day on the stone steps that led to the door through which General Lee came down from his office, and saw the student studying in the winter chill he invited him to go up and study in his office. His gentle, generous offer, though declined, will not be forgotten. The writer treasures one of General Custis Lee's visiting cards, written in his own strong hand. The general was not above doing things spurned by lesser men. His private secretary in the 80's W. C. Ludwig, a classmate of the writer, told that after he had written General Lee's letters in long hand, General Lee read and sealed the letters and put on the stamps himself, and carefully pressed down each marginal preformation of the stamp until it clung smoothly to the envelop. In the 80's the College gymnasium was in an old stable, down on the Campus, near the College gate on Jefferson Street. The old stable contained one trapeze, two hand rings, a cross-bar, and a pair of parallel bars. The floor was covered with a tan bark from the Chalkley tannery on

Henry and Randolph Streets. The Professors' cows slept on the floor each night. General Lee's readiness to co-operate with the students was shown when a committee of Will Hamilton and the writer approached him with the daring request that a new gymnasium by set up in the large room on the second floor of Newcomb Hall, in the room intended to be used as an art gallery, where price-less portraits were to be hung. General Lee cooperated wholeheartedly with the committee, overcame whatever Faculty opposition there was, and soon the new gymnasium equipment was installed in the sacred precincts in Newcomb Hall.

There were few serious infractions by the students during the writer's days at College. When the College walks were painted with red hatchets in honor of "Old Hatchet," General Lee quietly let it be known that he was much pained by the incident, and the students in the future sought to do nothing that would wound General Lee.

One clear afternoon, when House Mountain seemed but a stone's throw away, four rampant students, W. C. Ludwig, J. W. W. Bias, Paul M. Penick, and the writer, struck out to see the sunset and the sunrise from the top of the mountain. As the students walk on, the mountain receded, and only allowed weary feet to reach the top about midnight. After a sleepless night, by a fire that reddened their eyes with smoke, the sadder, if not wiser students made their weary way, breakfastless, direct, back to College, which they reached several hours after their first classes. Bedraggled and faint, they made their way in trepidation to General Lee's office. As was his custom, General Lee arose, and stood quietly, while the students endeavored to explain, that they had expected to reach home in time for breakfast and for College. All the General said to the luckless students was: "Young Gentlemen, the next time you leave town to spend the night, it would be well to get permission before you leave."

The writer was taught Applied Mathematics by General Custis Lee in the 80's. The class was held on the third floor of the southern end of the Main College building, immediately above the Law Lecture Room of that day. In the Applied Mathematics room was a collection of fairy-like figures, of single and double warped surfaces, made of threads extending between mathematical curves. Along these ladders ascended and descended mathematical fairies. It would be a joy to enter this fairy land again, in the presence of the presiding genius.

It was General Lee's custom to send the students in Applied Mathematics to the black-board, where they drew intricate diagrams and wrote out the proofs of the propositions. If during a student's explanation of the drawing and the proof, there occurred some hitch, General Lee quietly came up to the students at the board, and in gentle humility indicated where the trouble lay. No tone of voice, no expression of face did ought to "call the student down," or make him feel badly; he was sent glad, on his way along the correct mathematical path. General Lee, as a teacher, he never stooped to the level of the professor who vents himself in sardonic wit or flabby pedantry. He was always the gentle, the strong, and courteous gentleman. He had graduated first in his class at West Point. Like the truly great, he was the helper to all. Professor Charles A Graves, who was in charge of the University Law School while General Custis Lee was President, once wrote of him: "He had the reputation among the students of being the most courteous of gentlemen, and the most brilliant of Mathematicians."[244]

Throughout the winter and spring of 1883, Lee maintained a correspondence with G. W. Bagby. By mid-June, he wrote once again to Bagby:

I am sorry to learn from your letter of the 10th inst— received last evening that you are still and invalid; but sincerely hope that you may soon begin to mend and in good time be well again.

I will send you the photograph, with pleasure, as soon as I can get it from Mr. Miley; and if my hand continues in as good condition as it now is, I shall be able to put my name on it, too.

Mr. McBryde has been quite unwell since he returned from the Council; but seems to be recovering his health steadily, through slowly. I have not been able to see much of himself and wife since they went to housekeeping, as I have been away, Mr. McBryde has been sick, &c. &c. I am happy to be able to say that they have both made a most favorable impression here.

Your many friends in our little town, would, I am sure, be glad to join me in kind regards and remembrances if they knew of my writing. Dr. Kilpatrick is not at all well, through he is attending to his college duties. Genl. Smith & others are about as usual. With best wishes for the health and happiness of you and yours, I remain...[245]

Shortly after Lee wrote this letter to Bagby, the gentleman died. Despite this tragic event, Lee continued to correspond with his widow periodically.

Near the end of June as the academic year was ending, President Lee submitted his Annual Report to the Board of Trustees. In part he was most concerned about the classes he taught, the buildings and grounds, as well as the recommendations of the faculty:

Department of Applied Mathematics
Acting Professor G. W. C. Lee
Report for the session of 1882-3

The introduction in this Dept. has been continued by Prof. Moreland and act. Prof. Lee—the former having charge of the classes in Surveying and Astronomy, and the latter those in Descriptive Geometry, Shades and Shadows and Perspective, and in Civil Engineering proper. For surveying and astronomy, see Prof. Moreland's report.

~~~~
Civil Engineering

Senior Class—There was but one student in this class: he continued in it the whole session, but did not get through his examinations satisfactorily.

Intermediate Class—No students

Junior Class—Seven students started in this class at the beginning of the session; but at the beginning of the second term it only had three members. Two of them three passed the Intermediate Examination with distinction; and all three passed the Final Examination with distinction. As to conduct and deportment, I have never had anything to complain of in my classes.

Respectfully submitted,
G. W. C. Lee, Actg. Professor [246]

Buildings and Grounds

I venture to make some suggestions under this head, and in the order of their importance according to my judgment, that the Board may consider then at the proper time.

1—Take down and rebuild the S. W. wall of the building in which is the chemical Lecture-room, old book-room. Engineering-room, &c. It is proposed to make a Law Lecture room of the old book-room, and a law-library of the present office of the President. The estimated cost of this work is from four to five hundred dollars.

2—Grade the grounds about the Chapel and Newcomb Hall, using the earth to fill the lots next to Jefferson Street. Before doing this, it is very desirable to get possession of the lot just below the chapel belonging to Lewis Hughes, and to remove the house, &c. now occupied by him. Mr. Walker—who was so successful in removing Mrs. Wallace, and who has been in negotiations with Lewis for more than a year— Tells me that Lewis' lot and improvements are worth about fifteen hundred dollars, and that the has always asked three thousand dollars for his lot, house, &c. Lewis is now wiling to exchange his property for the "Palmer Property" on Main Street, which can be bought, according to Mr. Walker for two thousand dollars.

Mr Walker seems to be decidedly of the opinion that it would be best to make the exchange with Lewis without unnecessary delay, as he may change his mind.

3—Finish the Nat. Philosophy room. To do so according to the original design will cost about two hundred dollars.

4—Convert the building known as "Paradise" (the building containing the Law Lecture-room) into a "Museum" or an extension of the present "Museum" which s now much too small. It is desirable among other things, I think, to get rid of the students' rooms in this building. The estimated coat of his work is from one to two thousand dollars, according to the way in which it may be done.

5—Complete the spire of the Chapel and put a clock in the tower. The cost of the clock would be about Five hundred dollars. To finish the spire would cost somewhat more.

6—Build a Professor's residence on the lot next to Prof. Nelson's, a suitable house could probably be built now for Five thousand dollars.

7—Replace the north Dormitories by a building to balance (correspond with) Newcomb Hall. Such a building could contain Society Halls, &c. or could be appropriated to other useful purposes.

8—A Building near the front gate with its S. E. face on Jefferson Street, and its N. E. face on the road leading into the University grounds, would be very convenient. The lower story, or basement, would make a good

Gymnasium, which is greatly needed; and the main story would be available as a convenient and comfortable Public Hall, which would be very useful to the University, and to the town generally. The chapel would then be reserved exclusively for religious exercises.

~~~~~~

I have not mentioned the four Professor's houses in the above list, although they ought to have, as soon as practicable, a thorough overhauling. In addition to general repairs, each house should be furnished with a good cistern, as all the University buildings are frequently cut off from the water supply of the town. Three of the Professor's houses have one small cistern each; but these cisterns— which have been several times repaired— are of little of no use. Without having made an estimate in detail, I should say that one thousand dollars would not be too much to appropriate to the Professor's houses.

~~~~~~

Extract from a letter from Col. E. P. C. Lewis to the President

Hobokan, N. J. March 26, 1883

* *

I send by freight today, addressed to you, a Marble Medallion (life size) of your illustrious Father. It was a present to me from America's distinguished sculptor, the late W. H. Rinehart—It was taken for a photograph and was closely criticized by my mother in Rinehart's Studio in Roure, at his request; and he altered it at her suggestions— This makes it doubly valuable to me.

I desire to present it through you, to Washington and Lee University— If agreeable to you I should like it to be unveiled at the same time as the Monument next summer.

****

Rinehart was a great admirer of Genl. Lee and put his whole soul in this work; but he never had the pleasure of seeing him.

Sincerely yours,
(Sgd) E. P. C. Lewis

The medallion above referred to, is for the present with the oil painting in the chapel.

Recommendations

The appended and other recommendations of the Faculty are respectfully submitted for your consideration and action; and with there letters from Dr. Vincent S. Bradford, and Mr. H. O. Claughton recommending the Rev. Charles R. van Rourondt of New Jersey for the Honorary Degree of Doctor of Letters (D. S.) The naming of Wm. T. McAuslane, Glasgow, Scotland and McBryde, Presdt. University of South Carolina, were presented to the Faculty for their consideration.

The former is mentions in connection with the Honorary Degree of D. S. and the latter in connection with that of S. S. D.

~~~~~~~

I have the honor to be,
Very Respectfully,
G. W. C. Lee

With the formalities of the academic year over, the little town of Lexington swelled with many visitors, as the time drew near for the dedication of Valentine's recumbent sculpture of General Robert E. Lee and the proposed "Centennial Commencement." The author Ollinger Crenshaw states in his book, *General Lee's College,* about the event, "The statue was indeed placed in the mausoleum; but that event so fully overshadowed everything else that little was heard of a centennial observance."[247] A local "tongue-in-cheek" columnist, "G. Whillikens" writing for the Lexington Gazette commented, "...Our Centennial was a big thing. There was a very few under Brigadier there. We are mightily please about it. We are so tickled we think of having another when the Valley Road is completed."[248] Not far from the truth, the University's Centennial Committee ultimately decided to rescheduled their celebration for June of 1885.

By August, Custis was able to steal away to White Sulpher Springs for his annual vacation. But all too soon he had to return to Lexington to begin making plans and arrangement for the academic year of 1883-1884.

The new academic year started off as usual with little or no deviation from a regular autumn session. The faculty was assembled. The incoming freshmen were nervous and the new senior class was confident about their last year at Washington and Lee University. President Lee welcomed the students and directed them to the appropriate professors to help them establish their autumn schedule.

General Lee continued to teach applied mathematics. He immensely enjoyed teaching; the students had great respected for his knowledge and teaching skill. Lee was a serious educator but the lessons the students experienced with him would last their lifetime. The autumn session seemed to fly by, soon it was Christmas, then New Year's Day and then the beginning of the spring session, 1884.

Nevertheless, Lee was able to travel to Richmond and Petersburg to spend the Holidays with his siblings. While he was in Richmond visiting several other friends and acquaintances, he had a visit at his hotel from Major Isaac H. Carrington, the former Confederate provost marshall of Richmond during the war and whom Custis communicated with regularly at that time. Through the years they had maintained a causal correspondence and Carrngton would sometime act as liason for the University but now Carrington sought more than Lee's friendship; he needed Custis' advice. Although the problem is not specifically mentioned, it apparently was a legal matter where Carrington needed character references and legal support. Of course, General Lee wanted to help him, if possible. Before mid-February, Lee had seen Carrington in Richmond and received two letters from him after he arrived back in Lexington. By February 12, Lee wrote a letter of reassurance to Carrington:

> I received you letter of the 5th, inst., some days ago; and should have written to you at once, but for the uncertainty of our mails on account of the heavy rains, floods, &c. From what you said to me that Monday morning, I did not much expect you at the hotel in the evening, although I was there packing up, &c. I trust you are safely over the troubles in your family.
>
> Your letter of the 10th, inst. has just reached me. I will show it to Judge McLaughlin to-day, and not mention it or its contents, to any one else. Judge McLaughlin has been quite sick; but I am in hopes that he will be well enough to travel the later part of this week or the first of next. I am in hopes, also, that, if the Judge can go to Richmond, it will not be necessary for me to be there, too. Of course, I will go if you consider it necessary, though my classes lose a good deal whenever I leave here during the session. Genl. Wickham and Mr. Pollard are "all right", I think, and you can manage the rest (that need any management) better than any one else. If Judge McLaughlin has any suggestions to make, I will write to you again—or he will write himself. In the meantime, I remain...[249]

Custis did what he promised for Carrington by giving his letter to Judge McLaughlin but there lacks documentation of the letter's contents or that Lee himself left Lexington for Richmond on Carrington's behalf.

In early May of 1884, Custis wrote another note to Carrington apparently loaning him money. The sum was five hundred dollars, a very substantial amount in 1884. Again, the reason is not mentioned for the loan. "I think I have a bond of $500.00, executed by Lancaster & Co., in my Bank box in Richmond. Maury & Co. have the key of the box, and I will request then by this mail to attend to the matter for me."[250]

During this period of communication with Carrington, Lee remained at his post in Lexington. It is assumed that Lee attended all of the meetings associated with the functions of the university. As usual, Custis presided over the faculty meetings. Among the concerns of the faculty were scholarships [February, 25, 1884]; a scheduling change for the university to close its second session in June to the third Thursday of the month instead of the fourth Wednesday on the month, [May 12, 1884]; and the format of a certificate for awarding honorary degrees, [June 9, 1884].[251] Aside from the university business, he had time to write to his one of his Maryland cousins, Miss Emily V. Mason of Westwood, Maryland:

> I have just received your note of the 10th inst.; and forwarded by today's mail one of our catalogues to Gov. Carroll, and a pamphlet copy of Maj. Daniels' address— delivered her last June—to you. After several months absence, Mildred returned here last Monday. Mary was in Washington City...Next week, and the week after (Commencement Week), would not be pleasant for you, but after the 28th inst., we could, I trust, take good care of you. After your kind and friendly efforts in my behalf, you may judge how hopeless are my matrimonial prospects.[252]

Within two days of writing to "Miss Emily" once again he was conducting the end of the academic year business. At the meeting of the Board of Trustees on June 16, they agreed to confer the degree of Doctor of Philosophy to J. T. Akins and the renewal of a scholarship in chemistry be reinstated due to the recently defunct Wilson Scholarship.

Meeting again on the 23rd, the Board of Trustees recommended to award fourteen Bachelor of Law degrees, one Bachelor of Arts degree, as well as the previously mentioned the doctoral degree to J. T. Akins. They gave two honorary degrees: a Doctor of Divinity to Professor James F. Latiner and a Doctor of Laws degree to Bishop A. M. Randolph.

The next day the faculty held their last meeting of the academic year 1883- 1884. Among the topics discussed and recommended to the Board of Trustees was the payment to W. St. Saunders for the instruction of elocution and oratory classes in the sum of $225.00 from the University account and thereafter request the students to pay a sufficient sum directly for this additional course of study. In addition to this recommendation, the faculty resolved to have this course under the control and supervision of the President and faculty. The faculty thought it prudent to furnish the requisite assistance in mathematics and modern languages. They suggested that the following sums be allocated for this purpose:

> For instruction in Elocution & Oratory $225.00
> Assistant Instruction in Mathematics $150.00
> "   "   in Modern Languages $175.00

In addition to this compensation it will be necessary for the students receiving instruction in Elocution and Oratory to pay a suitable fee... If the Board cannot see its way to a satisfactory provision for instruction in Modern History for the ensuing session, the Professor of Modern Languages, English & Modern History would be willing to mark out a course of reading for students in that subject, such as would be equivalent to the present course; such course of reading to be accompanied by an Intermediate and Final Examination, and to be considered, if successfully passed, sufficient for students who are candidates for degrees.

The following resolution was adopted—

Resolved-That the Board of Trustees be requested to make the following changes in the requirements of the A. B. degree.

1. Scheme A. (catalogue p. 30). Change so as to read:- The entire course of Latin, Greek, Rhetoric, Moral Philosophy, and Modern History or English Literature; the Intermediate course of English; the

entire course of German and the Junior course of French <u>or</u> the entire course of French and the Junior course of German, Chemistry, Mineralogy, and Geology <u>or</u> the Junior course of Natural Philosophy, Surveying and Astronomy.

2. Scheme B. Strike out the words "<u>the course of Chemistry; the Junior Course of Natural Philosophy, an elementary course of Surveying and Astronomy</u>," and insert the course of chemistry, mineralogy, and Geology or the Junior course of Natural Philosophy, Surveying and Astronomy.

3. Scheme C. Strike out "the Intermediate course of English" and in the last line for the words "the entire course of" substitute <u>the Intermediate course of</u>.

This proposal was signed by John L. Campbell, Clerk of the Faculty.

On the same day, President Lee wrote his Annual Report to the Board of Trustees. The sections of this report, which contains the most interest, are the buildings and grounds report as well as the Lee's closing recommendations. The report of the buildings and grounds were stated as follows:

The S. W. wall of the building containing the Chemical Lecture-room was taken down and rebuilt last summer, as authorized by The Board. The old Book-room has been in use during the whole session as the Law Lecture-room, and the President's Office adjoining as the Law-library. Owing to objections raised by some of the citizens of the town, and the unfavorable weather, last autumn, for out-door work, Lewis Hughes (our Head-servant) could not be moved until this spring. The grading of the grounds about the Chapel and Newcomb Hall was consequently deferred until towards the 1st of May. It has been very well done under the immediate superintendence of Mr. Wm. G. McDowell, C. E. an alumnus of the University, and a citizen of the town, After the grass has grown on the "cuts and fills", the improvement to the grounds will, I think, be quite apparent.

While on this subject it is proper for me to say that the widow of the late Gov. Letcher is willing to sell her home and grounds (at the Eastern corner of the University grounds) to the University. The terms are — $1000.00 cash in October next (when the next payment on the Peabody claim is expected), $1000.00 cash within 12 months after the first cash payment; and the balance of $6000.00 within five to ten years at 6 per cent interest, the interest to begin upon the delivering of the property to the university. Mrs. Letcher has had some applications for her garden, to be used as small building lots, but prefers to sell the whole property together, and to the university. She states that the property, with improvements, cost more than $8000.00, and that she must sell as soon as practicable. Several members of the board are so much better judges of the value of this property that I am, that it is needless for me to go further into the subject of price. I have thought, however, that it would be well for us to get control of this property, and eventually of that between it and the "Blue Hotel." The "Letcher House" might be rented as a boarding house, or used as a residence for one of the Professors, until such time as the University could afford to remove it; and the other houses referred to—of comparatively little intrinsic value—could be rented for the same time. This is probably not the best investment for immediate returns that could be made, but it would not, I believe be a bad investment in the end.

The old stable of the "Blue Hotel", which has been used as a Gymnasium for a good many years, was sold and taken down this spring. It was in a very dilapidated condition, considered not altogether safe, and in the way of the grading of the grounds. It will be necessary, I presume, to give the students another Gymnasium of some kind, where they can amuse themselves and take exercise during the months and days unfavorable to out-door exercise. A building larger and better than the old one could be erected, I suppose, for $500.00 more or less. I am expecting every day a design and estimate for such a structure from Mr. Neilson, archt. His sickness, and some misunderstanding as to the time this design would be needed, have delayed the preparation of it as soon as it comes it will be submitted to you, with another design and estimate furnished at my request by Mr. Wm. G. McDowell.

In my last report I recommended the turning of the Building called "Paradise" into an addition to the Museum accommodations. I shall not now trouble you further, on this subject, than to submit the "plan and specifications" just received from the architect. The Gymnasium recommended should, I think, have precedence of the Museum addition, unless they can both be begun about the same time, although the later is very desirable. The Professor's houses, too, still appeal for some attention and consideration as between the Museum and the Professor's houses I hardly know which ought to be taken in hand first. I am in no doubt as the Gymnasium as I think one of some kind ought to be ready for the boys before the cold weather.

Recommendations.

The appended recommendations of the Faculty are respectfully submitted for your consideration and action. Some matters brought before the Faculty, yesterday, for the first time, could not be gotten into proper form in time for presentation to you with this report. They will be submitted as soon as possible, and with the hope that you will not be inconvenienced by the delay. Several of the gentlemen recommended, during the session, for Honorary Degrees, have recently received them from other institutions of learning; and their names are not, therefore, now presented by the Faculty of W. & L. University.[253]

Finally, all of the end of the academic year activities were concluded and Custis was free to be more social while directing his correspondence to other topics unrelated to the university. Once again he wrote to Miss Emily V. Mason of Westwood, Maryland:

> I have received your of the 26th ult., and will request the Supt. of the Va. Mil. Institute to send two of his "Registers" to the addresses you give. I will give your message to my sisters, who would have some for you, I am sure, did they know of my writing to you. I am sorry we can not have the pleasure of expecting you here shortly; but hope we may have the pleasure of meeting you somewhere before very long.
>
> I remain, with best wishes for your happiness.[254]

On the same day as he wrote to "Miss Emily," he wrote to Colonel Mc Donald of the United States Fish Commission:

> The "Commencements" here are just over; and I take the first opportunity of acknowledging the receipt of your letter of the 24th ult., and of the plans and specifications of the Fish ways for the Great Falls of the Potomac; for which I am very much obliged to you. I will examine the Plans, &c. with much interest, I am sure, as soon as I can find a little spare time. I should like to see your boat way model at work, and hope you may make a great success of it, both for your sake and for that of the world in general.
>
> I was in Washington for a little while this last Spring, and about the same length of time the Spring before, but did not have time either trip to do more than attend to the business that took me there. I did not know whether you were in town or where you stayed when in Washington, and was not able to get as far as the Smithsonian Institute for the purpose of making inquires.

My acquaintance in England and Scotland is very slight, but I will try with the aid of my sisters to get up some letters for you and send them to Washington in time for you.

With kind remembrances to Mrs. McDonald and the children and with best wishes for a pleasant journey for you and safe return, I remain...[255]

A few days later he responded to a letter from Mrs. Parke C. Bagby of Richmond:

I have received your letter of the 2nd inst., and have consulted Dr. Kilpatrick with reference to the subject of it. We think that it may be well for your canvasser to visit this town, especially as she will be so near to it. Many persons, who receive printed circulars, put them aside with the expectation of attending to the at some more convenient season, which never comes.

You had better keep, I think, for the present at least, the bundle marked "Lexington Material."

Although your husband greatly over valued what he was pleased to term my kindness to him, I am none the less grateful to him for his kind remembrance of me.

It will give me great pleasure to call upon you the first time I go to your city and if I can ever be if use to you I hope you will not fail to let me know how.[256]

In September, Lee communicated with Mrs. Bagby again. This time he was responding to a postal card she sent along with a packet of information her late husband, George W. Bagby, wished Lee to receive. In this return acknowledgement, Lee encloses a money order for the shipping fee: "I have just received your Postal Card of the 9th inst., and enclose Money Order for $4.00, payable to you at Richmond, Va."[257]

Prior to the beginning of the autumn session, Dr. and Mrs. James A. Quarles and family moved to Lexington, as Dr. Quarles had accepted a position with the Washington and Lee faculty. As it was General Custis' habit to welcome any new neighbor to town, he promptly called on the family. Miss Mary Quarles, later Mrs. Reese Turpin of Kansas City, Missouri recalled his welcoming visit:

...I remember the morning he called to welcome us to our new home in Lexington, Virginia and to Washington and Lee. He wore no beard then, but a mustache and with his iron gray hair, erect carriage and courtly manner I felt I had never seen a more handsome man. The General was the kindest of neighbors and many a time there was served at our table some delicacy he had sent Mother. I recall on one occasion Patterson, his butler, appeared bearing the largest tray I had ever seen. It held some very fine Lynnhaven oysters on the half-shell. I have never forgotten that appetizing lay-out.[258]

On a less personal note, Mrs. Turpin revived other anecdotes pertaining to activities at the university.

Have you heard of the occasion when the students hung in effigy either a Professor of one of the town's officials by way of expressing their displeasure over some act, or ruling of this individual? The hanging took place right at the corner of our yard, the body swinging from a large limb that protruded, over the walk as you go towards Newcomb Hall. In the midst of the ceremonies Gen. Lee appeared on the scene, and if the earth had opened and swallowed the participants in this orgy they could not have more instantaneously and quietly disappeared. Another incident I recall was when the General sent for a student who was not at all measuring up to the requirements of W. & L. to come to his office. The General broke the news so gently and pleasantly to the student that his name would be erased from the register at the student body, that on meeting some of his fellow students after the interview he remarked to them, "Gen. Lee is the finest man I know and he is so kind, he told me that I couldn't be feeling well and would better return home." With one accord his listeners shouted "Why boy, don't you know you've been fired?"

Not so much to the credit of my dear brother, Gus, although he did not realize the full extent of his wrong doing, being but a young boy, not yet in College, he was so interested in some rowing machine, as I recall, that had been installed in the little Gymnasium under the hill, he thought he would like to try his skill in its manipulation. Finding the door locked, he sought entrance through as open transom. The General heard of this misdemeanor and made an opportunity for a conversation with Gus. During the interview, the General reminded the young boy what the Bible has to say of one who enters not through the door but climbs up some other way.[259]

Now, with the academic and social correspondence subsiding, President Lee departed Lexington for his annual visit to the "Old White." He needed to rest and socialize with old friends who would frequent the resort each summer also.

Quickly, the summer weeks became the autumn once more and Lee returned to Lexington to start the new autumn session. As the fresh young faces started to arrive, Custis Lee, now fifty-two years old and a veteran of fourteen years as President of the university, settled into another year at W. & L. but now he was seriously hoping it would be his last year at the school.

The academic year began as usual and nothing eventful occurred in Custis' quiet life until late February, 1885 when he received a letter from General Henry Heth requesting a letter of recommendation for the position of Commissioner of Indian Affairs within the Department of the Interior. Custis obliged his old friend with a letter to L. Q. C. Lamar, Secretary of the Interior:

Genl. H. Heth informs me that he is—or will be— an applicant for the office of Commissioner of Indian Affairs, and seems to think that a letter from me may be of use to him.

While I know but little of the duties of the office in

question, I do know that Genl. Heth was a faithful and gallant soldier in both the U.S. and C.S. armies, and that he had, prior to the late war between the States, long service among the Indians. I believe him to be a gentleman of the highest character and standing, and am sure that his appointment to any office foe which he is qualified would be conducive to its best interests, and very gratifying to his army comrades, and friends generally.[260]

Heth successfully obtained the position of agent from the Office of Indian Affairs but his tenure was short lived.

Apparently the wear and tear of the previous year took its toll on President Lee's health. The constant physical discomfort sparked an extended period of depression and a sullen mood of inferiority which lingered on through the entire winter and into the spring. The old self-doubts and the irrevocable loss of Arlington still haunted him. Despite this, he carried out his presidential responsibilities by sending graduation invitations to many people including General F. H. Smith of the Virginia Military Institute, "I enclose some programmes of our approaching Commencement exercises, and extend a cordial invitation to the officers and cadets of the Va. Mil. Institute to all or any of them that is may be convenient and agreeable to them to attend." [261] His mind was once again set on retiring from the post held for fifteen years.

On June 16, 1885, G. W. C. Lee submitted his third resignation to the Board of Trustees of Washington and Lee University:

Owing to the state of my health, and other causes with a statement of which it is not necessary to trouble you, I am unable to serve you longer as President of W. & L. University; and, therefore, hereby tender my resignation of the office with which I have been for so long honored, with the request that it may be accepted, to take effect at any time within the three months required by law that may be most convenient. If you have any difficulty— on such short notice, of providing for the instruction in the Department of Applied Mathematics, I will gladly take charge of that Dept. until you can secure the services of a suitable instructor, or until I am forced to leave this climate or account of the condition of my health.

Sincerely thanking you for the courtesy, kindness, and consideration that I have received at your hands, I have the honor to be, with my best wishes for the success of your efforts for the prosperity of the venerable institution committed to your care, and for your individual happiness.[262]

Once again the board was able to induce him to withdraw his resignation by pointing to his exceptional service at the facility and by offering several incentives in order that he would continue as their President:

Genl. Lee having withdrawn his resignation of the Presidency, this Board tenders him its warm thanks for this expression of his willingness to continue in the high office, the duties of which he has heretofore so ably and satisfactorily discharged. The Board also expresses the hope that a visit to a warmer climate during the coming winter will result in permanent benefit to Genl. Lee's health and to this end the Board requests that he will accept a leave of absence from Nov. 15th to May 15th next or for such period during the coming session as may be agreeable to him or advised by his physician.

The Board also authorizes the Executive Committee to make such appropriation as may be necessary to employ a private Secretary for Genl. Lee, he to select such secretary.

The Board also authorizes the Executive Committee to make the necessary arrangements for the instruction of the classes taught by Genl. Lee and for the discharge of the duties of President during his absence.[263]

President Lee declined the offer of the leave of absence, as well as the employment of a private secretary. He did, however, choose to instruct his classes in the Department of Applied Mathematics during the fall session.

Nevertheless, the closing events of the academic year were still at hand and the Centennial celebration was yet to be held. The long awaited Centennial Commencement ceremony was conducted smoothly and reverently with many notable personages present. The keynote speaker was the Reverend Dr. Moses Drury Hoge of Richmond, while Colonel J. T. L. Preston, husband of Lexington's most celebrated literary figure, Margaret Junkin Preston, read her commemorative poem, Centennial Ode. Unfortunately, there was a discord placed upon the Centennial events with the death of Dr. John L. Kirkpatrick, Chairman of the Department of Mental and Moral Philosophy at the university. Dr. Kirkpatrick was appointed during the administration of Robert E. Lee. At that time there was a slight controversy over his appointment to the position, as he was a Presbyterian clergyman in realm of a Episcopalian facility, yet he was elected to the position. He was a good man who would be sorely missed.

On Thursday, June 25, Custis Lee wrote a brief note to General Francis H. Smith in reference to the funeral arrangements for Dr. Kirkpatrick:

> The officers and cadets of the Va. Mil. Institute are respectfully invited to Dr. Kirkpatrick's funeral, which is to take place from the Presbyterian church to-morrow morning at ten (10) o'clock. You and Col. Lyell are invited by the family to be pall-bearers; but if either or both of you should be prevented from accepting, any other two members of your Faculty would, I presume, be acceptable. The pallbearers are requested to meet at the President's office, Newcomb Hall, at nine (9) o'clock to-morrow morning.[264]

By Monday June 29th, Custis Lee was rapidly on his way out of town. Too busy with last minute details for his departure, he requested a student secretary, J. M. Allen, to respond in his stead to General Francis H. Smith in reference to the invitation to attend the

Virginia Military Institute's graduation ceremony:

> Genl. Lee, who is unable to write this morning and who expects to leave town this evening, requests me to express his regrets that he will not be able to accept your kind invitation to attend the Va. Military Institute Commencement. Some of our Faculty, however, will be present. Genl. Lee desires through you to make his apologies to the Board of Visitors for not having been able to pay his respects to them. With Genl. Lee's kind regards and best wishes, I have the honor to be...[265]

Seemingly, Custis could not leave the area fast enough to take refuge at White Sulpher Springs. He truly needed a long rest and rehabilitation for his arthritic joints and disheartened mind. The old friends and frequent periods of self-imposed solitude at the resort was a respite for this weary man. His spirit, as well as his body, needed to be rejuvenated before he could resume his commitment to Washington and Lee University. After what must have seemed like a very short summer, Custis returned to Lexington and began again.

The new academic year began very much like the other years. He continued to function as president of the university as he had agreed to do. The only joy he possessed was the instruction of his beloved mathematics classes. The autumn session came and went, while Custis remained in Lexington through the winter and spring, not heeding the advice of the Board of Trustees to take a leave of absence for the winter.

Aside from his presidential duties, he continued with his personal correspondence. The following is a series of letters to Major Isaac H. Carrington pertaining to acquiring funds for the support of the university:

> I received yesterday your letter of the 22nd inst., and have shown it to Judge Edmondson, and Capt. Wm. A. Anderson, members of the Ex. Committee of our Board of Trustees. We are expecting Judge McLaughlin tomorrow, and have thought it best to wait for him. Capt.

Anderson said he would write to you this evening. As far as I am concerned, I would leave the matter for you to manage as you may think best.[266]

The next letter was written on February 15:

Your letter of the 13th, inst. was received yesterday, and handed to Capt. W. A. Anderson, who goes to Staunton this morning, and expects to be in your city next Wednesday night. I am very glad that Mr. Pollard [Edward A.] has introduced the amount desired by us, and hope that the Legislature may give it to us now, and be done with the matter.[267]

The final letter in this series is dated March 4. This note implies that Carrington was able to provide Lee and the university officials with good news about the requested funds.

Your letter of the 2d. inst., was delivered to me last evening; and that of the 3rd this morning. I have shown them both to Judge McLaughlin, and we are very much obliged to you for the cheering information furnished so promptly.

It was Prof. John L. Campbell, who died recently, and not his son, John L. Campbell, Jr. who is still our Treasurer. I presume the later will drop the "Jr." from his signature, and simply sign his name as John L. Campbell, Sr.

Please excuse the efforts of a rheumatic hand, and believe me to remain...[268]

There was no further communication between Lee and Carrington after this point. Carrington would succumb to illness in 1887. It is unknown if any letters of communication between Lee and Carrington's family occurred.

Through the remainder of the spring, Lee continued the best he could yet he constantly gave in to the physical ailments and nothing seemed to bolster his spirits. Not even letters from his brothers, friends or associates would boast his morale.

General Francis H. Smith sent him a packet of letters which seemed to elevate his spirit, as he responded to Smith in his usual courtly manner: "I return the letters you were kind enough to give me the privilege and pleasure of reading, and thank you very sincerely therefor."[269] A few days later he wrote to Smith again, this time in reference to a memorial tablet: "Immediately upon the receipt of your letter this morning, I wrote to Mr. Nelson, sending him the inscription for the Memorial Tablet to the Rev. Wm. Bryant, and am in hopes that he may be able to have it ready for the consecration of the church. If he is at home, I shall probably hear from him in the course of a few days, and will promptly let you know the result."[270]

Lee continued to conduct business from his house, as he was frequently unable to leave the premises for the short walk to his office. He was so ill, in fact, that he did not attend the commencement ceremonies. Due to this single act, he urgently reminded the Board of Trustees that he was ready to leave the office at any time they thought it prudent to do so.

As many of the graduates were leaving Lexington for their homes throughout the country, President Lee was able to rally himself to bid them a fond farewell. John V. McCall remembered the event, "That afternoon (after graduation, June 1886) General Custis came down to the train to bid students goodbye and putting his hand on my shoulder he kindly said, "Mr. McCall, go back to Texas & send us a few good boys." I replied "Why few, General? Why not many?" The General responded "Mr. McCall, Washington & Lee would like in the future as in the past, to lay the stress on the kind of men she sends forth, rather then the number."[271]

After the university business had concluded for another year, Lee slipped away to his usual vacation spot. He left "Old White" earlier than usual so he had time to visit Richmond and his brothers at their respective homes named "Ravensworth" and "Romancoke" before the next academic session. All too soon he again returned to Lexington, now with a new resolve to try to work even harder and to overcome the old doubts and disappointments.

Once the students and faculty had settled into the new academic year, Lee summoned various students to his office to discuss their different issues and problems. W. J. Humphreys, a returning student, was requested an interview in President Lee's office. Mr. Humphreys remembered the event vividly:

> General Lee's private office was visited only, of course, on his special "invitation." My one such invitation came in the late fall of 1886 when I was just beginning to recover from an attack of typhoid fever. I was anxious to get back to my classes, but actually was in no condition to do so. He talked to me in an exceedingly kind manner and while commending my desire to go on with my studies told me that my physician with whom he had consulted strongly urged against my trying to so any more work this session. He then added, softening the information with a friendly smile, that if I insisted on attending classes he would just have to dismiss me from the University. He advised me to go home for a long recuperative rest, and then return to the University the next fall to complete the course I had begun. This I did. I saw in General Lee a dignified scholarly gentleman. I found him a patient and thorough instructor. I knew him as a kindly and wise friend.[272]

The remainder of the university sessions were relatively uneventful and mundane, but General Custis did his duty in all things and as he had advised a student long ago, "For every evil under the sun, There is a remedy, or there is none. If there be one, try to find it; If there be none, try not to mind it." Although he suffered great physical hardship, he tried "not to mind it."

Late in April 1887, he received a letter from Colonel Marshall McDonald, who had attempted in vain to obtain the personal possession of Lee family from Arlington House. Custis' response to McDonald reveals an insight into the man, as well as his most personal resolve:

> Your kind letter of the 28th, ult. was duly received, but I have not been able to acknowledge it with my own hand

before to-day.

When President Johnson ordered that the "Arlington relics" should be returned to my mother, to whom they belonged, Congress passed a violent joint resolution that they should not be so disposed. For this reason, I have always thought that an act of Congress would be necessary for their restoration to the family. I am now the less obliged to you, however, and to Prof. Baird for your good offices in the matter, and only ask that you will not give yourselves too much trouble in my behalf. I have never made application for the removal of my political disabilities and never expect to do so; nor do I care to petition Congress for the return of the relics; nor do I wish trouble my friends—who doubtless have troubles enough of their own—to trouble themselves on my behalf.

I should like very much to get away from my present duties, and have several times made an earnest effort to do so, but without success. It seems to be intended that I should end my days here, and possibly it is just as well even from my stand point, as I am too good for nothing, now, I take it, to undertake anything else.

Trusting that you and yours are well and happy, I remain, as always, very sincerely, your friend...[273]

As June approached, the graduation and other end-of-the-year activities commenced.

This was a particularly rewarding time for General Lee, as he was the first recipient to be presented an honorary Doctor of Laws degree from Tulane University in New Orleans, Louisiana. It was an equally proud moment for the past professor of Washington and Lee University and his old friend, President William Preston Johnston to confer this honor. Although Lee was unable to attend the ceremony, his old friend expressed the view of many past associates and students who knew George Washington Custis Lee by stating: "He has borne the weigh of a great name so well, that no one can think him an unworthy successor, in his last great work, to Robert E. Lee. He is as good a man, and of as royal a nature, as is alive on earth."

Even as these words were being spoken at the Tulane University commencement ceremony, General Lee was busy in his office writing letters. One letter of immediate importance was to General Francis H. Smith of the Virginia Military Institute in reference to a visit by Virginia's Governor Fitzhugh Lee:

> Some days ago, I received a letter from the Gov. to the effect that he was coming here today, would bring his wife with him, and that they would stay at my house if convenient. I have just received another letter from him (dated yesterday), in which he says that he finds it impossible to come, and requests me to express his regrets to you that he can not attend the Commencement exercises to-morrow.[274]

Even though Governor Fitzhugh Lee did not attend the graduation ceremony for the Virginia Military Institute, Class of 1887, General Custis Lee did attend the commencement. With all of the customary celebrations over, Lee slipped away for his annual summer retreat.

Returning in the fall to start the new academic year, he was more resolute to his situation. He did not offer another formal resignation until June, 1893. In the fall of 1887 a new student named Wade H. Ellis arrived at Washington and Lee. He later recalled a few brief anecdotes about General Lee:

> I have the most vivid and imperishable memories of Gen. Custis Lee who was President of the University when I was a student there in 1887, it was a fact which I think was known by others which was the courtly and gracious habit of General Lee whenever he met one of the students on the campus, or elsewhere, of taking off his hat in acknowledgment of a similar salute for the student. I have seen him so this many times. I also recall a rather amusing incident that occurred just in front of Gen. Lee's house one fine spring day when two ladies who had stopped to see him, were leaving his home. One of them said, as they started off; "We are going for a walk down

the campus." Gen. Lee bowed politely and said with an intriguing smile: " I hope you will enjoy it, but don't hurry back, for I'm busy." They all laughed at the joke, and I never forgot it.[275]

The mutual respect and cooperation between Washington and Lee University and the Virginia Military Institute regularly brought forth school-wide invitations for special programs and lecturers. That same spring the eminent lecturer Professor Richard Heath Dabney of New York City came to Washington and Lee to deliver a series of seven addresses on historical subject matter. President Lee took this opportunity to invite the Virginia Military Institute's population to attend the lectures:

These lectures will be delivered in the Chapel or in the Y.M.C.A. room. Unless some notice be given to the contrary the first lecture will be given tomorrow afternoon at 6 o'clock punctually.

> The officers and cadets of the Va. Mil. Institute are cordially invited to attend these exercises; and I take this occasion to say, what I trust is already well known, that the officers and cadets of the V. M. I. are always expected at and invited to, all of the exercises at W. & L. U. of which the Faculty have any control. I was sorry to hear yesterday that you were suffering from a bad cold. I trust you are better to-day.[276]

This was only one of such lectures and other intellectual ventures offered at the University. The lyceum supported various organizations, among which was a debate society. Wade H. Ellis, a student at Washington and Lee from 1887-1889, recalled an anecdote:

> In 1888 or 9 I engaged in a contest for the debater's medal. There were two students on each side and the subject for debate was "Which has done more for America, the Puritan or the Cavalier?" The medal however, was won without regard to the subject but just

for the best address, and I am still the proud possessor of that token. My recollection is that this was one of the few occasions where Gen. Custis Lee sat as one of the judges, and I think John Randolph Tucker was the other.[277]

By early June, President Lee was expressing his gratitude for the information sent to him from General Smith, as well as extending another invitation to General Francis H. Smith and all of V. M. I. family to join them in the Washington and Lee "exercises."

Many thanks for the programmes and Registers. I send herewith some of our programmes and catalogues, and a copy of our last Alumni catalogue. We shall have some bound numbers of the letter before long, and one of them will be sent to the Va. Mil. Institute Library of course. You and all connected with the V. M. I., have a cordial invitation to the exercises at W. & L. U. You will find the seats on the platform—or those in rear of it— more comfortable than the benches of the auditorium. The back stair-way is always open to the officers of the V. M. I., and their friends.[278]

Closing out the academic year with his Annual Report to the Board of Trustees, President Lee included an interesting report on the topic of "Building and Grounds":

The new Professor's house was finished and occupied, about the 1st of last September, and is a very comfortable residence. It appears somewhat high in comparison with the other residences near it; but a less conspicuous shade of color on the roof, and the growth of trees in front of the house, would hide this fault almost, if not quite, altogether.

There has been but little damage to property during the session; and, with the exception of the blowing down (with gunpowder) of one of the old Locust trees in front of Newcomb Hall, there has probably been no premeditated damage.[279]

White Sulpher Springs, West Virginia, 1868
G. W. C. Lee seated on right with friends;
Jeremy F. Gilmer left & Joseph E. Johnston
right standing center
The Greenbrier Archives, West Virginia

White Sulpher Springs
Lee Family Cottage
Photograph by Author

White Sulpher Springs, West Virginia, 1868
G. W. C. Lee third from the left standing.
Mary Custis Lee, third from the right
seated with striped dress
The Greenbrier Archives, West Virginia

White Sulpher Springs,
West Virginia, 1888
G. W. C. Lee, standing center with friends
Special Collections, Leyburn Library,
Washington and Lee University

Shortly after the commencement exercises and other events had concluded, General Custis departed for White Sulpher Springs to spend the summer with his friends, General and Mrs. Simon B. Buckner, their son Simon B. Buckner, Jr. and Mr. and Mrs. George A. Robinson and their daughter, Rosa, as well as Colonel and Mrs. William Preston Johnston and Miss Mattie Harris. Refreshed from a summer of relaxation and little commitment, Lee returned to Lexington determined to do his best in spite of his physical difficulties.

The autumn and winter quickly became the spring again. Lee spent several weeks through the late spring communicating with distant cousins and other family member:

I am very much obliged to you for the invitation contained in your last kind letter, and for your account of Rooney's condition. As soon as I heard of his illness, I wrote to know if I could be of use, whether I should go to Washington, &c. and was promised that I should be informed as soon as my services were required. I hear on all sides that Rooney is convalescing satisfactorily; but not knowing how ill he has been, I can not form a very good idea of his present condition. Last week I had a letter from my brother, Rob, who had just heard of Rooney's illness. He did not say whether he expected to go to Washington but, as the journey is a short one for him to make, and as he is master of his own time and movements, I think it likely that he has been or will go, to see his brother. I wish Rooney could get away from Washington, as the life there does not seem to suit him. I suppose he will go south as soon as he is well enough to travel; at last accounts, he was to go to Thomasville, Ga., which I believe is a comfortable place with a good climate for weak lungs. The little son of our neighbor, Dr. (Prof.) Quarles, has had quite a severe attack of pneumonia, but is not convalescing rapidly. Mrs. Lizzie Letcher Harrison's baby has had an attack of the croup; but is well over it, I believe. I trust Presdt. Harrison will let Col.

McDonald and Capt. Yeatman alone. I saw a notice in the Alexa. Gazette some time ago to the effect that the court of claims would reconsider the Ravensworth case. Hoping that cousin Edmund and may continue to be free from pain; a with love to him, Miss Minnie, Capt. Yeatman & yourself, I remain—Affectionately yours...[280]

Lastly, he wrote a series of notes to General Smith, a packet of data on the state's debt: "At the request of Prof. Richard M. Smith of Randolph Macon College, I send you by bearer a package of pamphlets on the subject of the State debt, which he wishes distributed among the officers and cadets of the Va. Mil. Institute."[281]

Then, there was a series of acknowledgement notes for the Fiftieth Anniversary; the first written on Lee's behalf by W. H. Winfree and the others written by Lee, himself. "Genl. G. W. C. Lee, who is not well enough to write desires me to acknowledge, with thanks, the receipt of an invitation to be present at the Semi-Centennial Celebration, July 3rd and 4th, 1889, of The Virginia Military Institute; and to express the earnest hope of being able to take part in the Exercises of her Fiftieth Anniversary."[282] The next two communication are written by Lee to Smith in reference to the golden anniversary of the Institute, the first date June 17, "I have received your note of the 15th inst. with the accompanying invitations, and will try to distribute the latter to the best advantage." Then, on June 22, he wrote the following to Smith: "It is made my pleasant duty to transmit the accompanying Extract from the Minutes of the Board of Trustees, which will explain itself. If you will let me know on what days, and at what hours, you will use the Chapel, it will be ready for you."

The Fiftieth Anniversary of the Virginia Military Institute was celebrated on June 25, 1889. This event added to both commencements at V. M. I. and Washington and Lee University. It provided a happy closure to the end-of-the-year activities of the two facilities. Later in the year a published document entitled the Semi-Centennial Report of the Superintendent of the Virginia Military Institute, June 25, 1889 was distributed. General Lee was grateful to receive a copy late in November of that year.

With the retirement of General Francis H. Smith in December 1889 and his untimely death in March of 1890, General Scott Shipp became Superintendent of the Virginia Military Institute.

Custis Lee and Shipp were old friends who taught together at the Institute in 1865. They continued a warm and professional relationship through the years. Once again both men were on the same professional plane at their respective schools. Shipp continued in the position of Superintendent at the Institute well after Lee retired, but even then their relationship continued until Lee's death. As with Shipp, Lee's communications were generally of the professional realm and of mutual concern to both schools: "I received your letter of the 4th inst., and beg that you will extend to the Committee of the Virginia Legislature, on Schools and Colleges, the cordial invitation of our Faculty to visit this institution at such time as may suit their convenience. If you can let me know that proper time, a delegation of this Faculty will call upon the Committee."[283] The following week he sent another communication to Shipp in reference to the arrangements for receiving the Committee of the Legislature:

I received your note of the 13th inst. last evening, and will be on the lookout for the Committee of the Legislature. It was stated in one of the newspapers, a day or two since, that the Committee would visit the State Institutions in Staunton today. If so, they will probably come here tonight, and visit the V. M. I. to-morrow morning. If you can manage to let me know in time, a committee of our Faculty will meet them at the V. M. I. or anywhere else that may be most convenient to the visiting Committee. As the greater number of our Faculty go to dinner about 2 P. M. it would be more convenient to us to meet the Committee of the Legislature before 2 or after 3 P.M.; but his matter of dinner is of no particular consequence.[284]

The Committee of the Legislature met with President Lee and the faculty members. Although the enrollment was lower than in years, the committee from the state recognized the high educational standards set forth by its educators as the foundation of the university. The Committee of the Legislature realized that the economic status of the state paralleled itself to the school's situation. All in all, the committee was pleased with Washington and Lee University. Yet, the university was not without its troubles.

Early in March, a student had succumbed to illness on March 6 at the boarding house where he lived with other university students. On the morning of March 7 Lee responded to Shipp's letter of condolence:

> Many thanks for your kind letter. The remains of the late Claude Sublett are to be taken to Richmond, to-night, on the 8:30 train. There will be no funeral services here, but the students will probably accompany the body from Mrs. C. U. Figgat's residence to the train, leaving the house about 8 P.M. I suppose.[285]

Later that same day Lee was compelled to write again to Shipp:

> Since writing to you this morning, our students have had a meeting, and appointed a Committee to draft Resolutions; and will meet in the room under the chapel, at half past seven (71/2) this evening, to adopt the Resolutions, and go thence in a body to Mrs. Figgat's house, so as to accompany the corpse to the train. This is all the students propose to do, so far as I am informed.[286]

As soon as this unfortunate event was over, the students quickly returned to their university classes and the faculty got their lives back to the normal daily routine.

In late April, Custis received a small package with an enclosed note for his Maryland cousin, Miss Emily V. Mason. She had sent him a book written by a Confederate officer. He was grateful to receive it and in turn he invited her to visit Lexington.

> I have just received your note of the 30th, ult., with the accompanying book—Letters of a Confederate Officers,

&c.—that you have been kind enough to send me; for both, please accept my best thanks. Mildred is still in Washington City, and will go from there, I presume, to our brother Robert's place, below Richmond, where she will probably remain until towards the last of May. I do not expect her here until early in June. I have my two nephews with me, and shall be glad to take care of you and Miss Carroll whenever you may be able to get here, but hope you will be able to stay more that one day. The train on the valley branch of the Balt. & Ohio Ry is due here at 8-15 P. M. You can come here, also by Charlottesville & Lynchburg, and get here by 6 P.M., if you make connection with the Richmond & Allegheny Ry. at Lynchburg; but this connection is somewhat uncertain as the margin is small. Both routes will take you through Washington City, from which to Lynchburg, you take the Va. Midland Ry. There is no change of cars between Baltimore and this place by the Balt. & Ohio Ry. By the other route you change at Washington and Lynchburg. Let me know on what day, and by what route, to expect you, and I will meet you at our station (Lexington). With best wishes for your happiness, I remain Faithfully yours...[287]

It is not documented whether Miss Mason and her party ever arrived for a visit, but it is certain they would have been welcomed guests at the President's house.

As mentioned in Lee's letter to Miss Mason, his "two nephews" were with him at Washington and Lee University. In February, 1939, Dr. George Bolling Lee, son of William Henry Fitzhugh Lee recalled, "My brother and I boarded with him during our time in Lexington and naturally knew him very intimately, having lived four years in his house on the campus."[288]

President Lee struggled through the physical act of the graduation ceremony at Washington and Lee out of personal duty, but he was not so inclined toward the obligation to attend the Virginia Military Institute commencement. On June 26, 1890, he sent a message to General Scott Shipp: "I have been wishing particularly to attend your

Graduating Exercises to-day; and also, your Reception; but am really not well enough to go out."[289] Several weeks passed before Lee was able to travel to White Sulpher Springs for his annual vacation.

After many weeks of rest, Lee's chronic rheumatoid arthritis subsided well enough for him to continue once again at his post in Lexington. The disease from which Lee suffered was inherited from the maternal side of his family. His condition would vacillate from a state of near complete debilitation to a height of prolonged remission. Nevertheless, Lee was always in some particular stage of discomfort during the period of the mid-1880's. Stress tended to escalate the arthritic spasms which occurred without warning, yet he felt it was his responsibility to continue the best he could.

Lee had a multifaceted position as president of the university. Frequently, potential students would inquire about the university and sometimes about V. M. I., also. Lee would answer the inquiries with at letter and catalogue to the prospective student along with a note to General Shipp: "The accompanying letter seems to be intended rather for the V. M. I. that for W. & L. U. I have sent the writer one of our catalogues, and a note to the effect than his letter would be handed to you."[290] Another aspect to his position was that of disciplinarian and overseer of all student activities. A former student from Harrisonburg, Virginia recalled an annual autumn ritual of building a bonfire: "On one occasion the students had a bonfire on the campus. When it was at its height General Custis came down from his house, with his lighted lantern, walked several times around the fire, and then returned to his house, without saying a word to anyone."[291]

Around Halloween or late in the fall, the students from Washington and Lee would raid the grounds of the Virginia Military Institute and abscond with one of their cannons as a prank. Tired of this annual escapade, General Shipp wrote a note to General Lee with hopes that he could locate the guilty boys. General Lee responded, "I have just received your letter of the 21st inst., and am very sorry that some of our students have been again misbehaving themselves at the Va. Mil. Institute. I will do my best to put a stop to such misconduct; the only trouble is to find out who are the guilty ones. I will try to see you shortly;"[292]

During the last years of his tenure in the 1890's, Lee declined many of the daily university activities he faithfully participated in the past. He was more and more absent from the daily chapel services and typically he would arrive well after classes started each morning at his office, if at all. Harry B. Lewis of Ohio, a former student in those years, remembered:

> When I went to Washington and Lee he [Custis Lee] was little known to the students and seldom, if ever, seen by them. I never saw him on the campus or in the chapel. I never would have seen him but for the following incident:
>
> Some of us had the feeling that the university ought to have a Glee Club, and one was organized with George E. Lenert as director. Then Banjo and Mandolin Clubs were organized. Some calls began coming for our services, and later plans were made for a tour of some of the southern cities. I was appointed to confer with President Lee to lay the matter before him, and, if possible, secure his permission. I called at his home, but got nowhere. He positively refused to grant our request. Again and again I called, but he was adamant. "We were there to study, and not to go gallivanting around the country, —a lot of irresponsible boys," he said, "and that he would not risk the reputation of the institution." At last, in desperation, I told him that Mr. Lenert,—who was older than most of the boys,—and I would assume responsibility for the conduct of the boys while on tour. I also suggested that it seemed to me that the free advertising it would give the university was worth considering. At last he yielded. "But mind you, he said, "I shall hold you and Lenert responsible, and no member of the clubs will be excused from any class work, and all back work will have to be made up."
>
> And so the tour was made, and proved to be a great success. Much favorable publicity was given to our performances, and we were most cordially treated and enthusiastically welcomed in every place. So greatly

pleased was President Lee that I learned, after leaving Washington and Lee, —that he had set aside, a room for the use of the clubs, and had a grand piano installed for their use. The years, with their joys and sorrows, their victories and defeats, have come and gone, leaving marks upon us all. But as I walk in my beautiful garden of memory toward the sunset, I shall never cease to be grateful to God for giving me those happy days at Washington and Lee, for my association with the man I met there, and for the fellowship of the princely men of the faculty, than whom there were never finer.[293]

Through the early 1890's, Lee periodically wrote to General Shipp in his own hand or by proxy. Most of the letters to Shipp are related to corresponding academic business. As in April 1891, Lee asked his private secretary, W. E. Darnell, to send a thank you note on his behalf to Shipp: "Genl. Lee, who is not well enough to write, desires me to thank you for your note of the 27th inst. and the accompanying package from Dr. Perry. Genl. Lee hopes to be able to write to you or see you in the course of a few days." [294] Apparently, Lee recovered well enough to communicate to Shipp in his own hand by early June about the University's pending graduation: "I enclosed some programmes of our coming Commencement Exercises, which all the officers and cadets of the V. M. I. are cordially invited to attend, at their convenience and pleasure. We have been disappointed in Senators Colquitte & Gray's not coming; but they were obliged to decline (after accepting) at too late a day for us to supply their places."[295]

Lee's recent recovery sustained him through the regular and executive meetings of the Jackson Memorial Association, as well as through commencement of Washington and Lee University.

In July, the Jackson Memorial Association was to dedicate the monument to General Thomas J. Jackson at which Colonel F. W. M. Holliday, then Governor of Virginia, was to deliver the oration.[296] The secretary of the Jackson Memorial Association, J. K. Edmondson, wrote the Governor:

The Jackson Memorial Association of Lexington,

have with unanimity selected you to deliver the oration or address on the occasion of the unveiling of the Heroic Bronze Statue on the 21st of July proximo. Your selection has been greeted by great delight & enthusiasm by the Old Veterans & the people generally. The occasion is going to be one of great `eclat—an immense concourse of the Old Veterans & other, will be present, judging from present indications. Capt. Thomas D. Ranson, a member of our Association & of our Executive Committee has been appointed to present in person your appointment & urge your acceptance & I write with him in urging your favorable decision...[297]

The Governor responded that he was not able to accept the invitation to speak at the unveiling of Jackson's statue. Nevertheless, the dedication was conducted on the July 21, 1891, with an estimated crowd of 30,000 people in observance, as General Jubal A. Early delivered the keynote address.[298] After this celebration concluded, Lee went on his usual retreat for the remainder of the summer.

After his return to Lexington for the new academic year, Lee's health wavered the entire year. The autumn was not a happy time for the Lee family, as Custis received word that his brother William Henry Fitzhugh known as "Rooney", and who had a history of lung and heart trouble, died suddenly at Ravensworth in Burke, Virginia on October 15th. Rooney Lee was in his second term as Congressman from Fairfax County in the House of Representatives when he expired. Quickly, Custis pulled himself together and managed to make the necessary arrangement for his brother's internment into the Lee Chapel mausoleum adjacent their parents and sister. The loss of Rooney was a severe blow to Custis. Custis and Rooney were very close as boys and men. This was a difficult time in which to start the new academic year, but he persevered.

He managed to continue his communications with Shipp and to comply with the year-end duties for the concluding academic year, 1891-1892.

In the winter, 1892, Lee wrote via John L. Campbell, the Clerk

of the Faculty, to General Scott Shipp on the subject of a joint resolution to have "the Faculty of the Virginia Military Institute be
invited to unit with the Faculty of this institution in the delivery of
the proposed course of lectures and that the officers and cadets be
invited to attend these lectures." [299] He wrote other communiques to
Shipp also pertaining to "your last Register which you were good
enough to send me, and for which I am very much obliged to
you,"[300] "...the use of the Chapel to the Va. Mil. Institute for the
Readings by Dr. Page, next Friday (I Believe), for the Jackson
Memorial,"[301] and once again information concerning the
Washington and Lee commencement as well as "The Faculty are,
beside, specially invited to the Alumni dinner at 2 P.M. on the 15th
inst.; and it is hoped that some members of the Faculty will respond
to the toast that will be offered to the V. M. I."[302] Lee was in fairly
good health at this period toward the end of the 1892 spring session.
He was able attend the faculty meetings and write in his own hand
the recommendations for the Honorary Degrees.

> The accompanying recommendations for Honorary
> Degrees came too late to be considered by the Faculty;
> but are submitted to you, at their request,that you may
> have before you the whole list to select from.
> For L. L. D.
> Judge Wm. J. Robertson recommended by the Hon. J.
> R. Tucker; Harris Taylor, Mobil, Ala. recommended by
> the Hon. J. R. Tucker and Prof. Graves.
> For D. D.
> Rev. J. Henry Hundley, recommended by a number of
persons.[303]

Although he personally wrote the recommendations for the
honorary degrees, he did not personally write the entire Annual
President's Report to the Board of Trustees. But he did sign it as
accurate at the conclusion of the Buildings and Grounds and
Necrology Report:
> The interior of the main (middle) building, including
> the Lecture Rooms, is in a very shabby condition; and the

other old buildings, that have not been prepared recur for special purposes, are much in the same condition, there has been no general renovation of the buildings since the time of the gift for the Museum by the late Mr. Lewis Brooks, who after the Museum was set up, gave some money for there renovation of the buildings. The usual appropriations for Grounds and Buildings are barely sufficient for current needs, and a special appropriation of from one to two thousand dollars will be required to put the buildings in good condition.

The Faculty has asked that the room in the third story of the Main Building, which has been used as a lecture room, be put in good order this summer. I think it very desirable that this should be done. The room will probably need a new floor and ceiling, blackboards, benches and probably another window. Prof. Humphreys has been requested by the Faculty to have an estimate of cost made. I am in hopes of having a steam heating apparatus in Newcomb Hall by next autumn. The best reliable bid I could get last summer amounted to something less than $4000.00 The boiler is to be put in the boiler room of the new Engineering Building, and the same boiler can be used for heating the Chemical Laboratory above.

Necrology

David Sirrus Read of Roanoke, Va. in his second session here, went home after the December Examinations to spent the Christmas Holidays. He had an attack of "La Grippe," [influenza] and died from the effects of it in a short time. Several of his particular friends among the students represented the University at his funeral.[304]

After the activities surrounding the annual commencement, Lee made is journey to White Sulpher Springs. The "Old White" was still the same but now many old friends were not returning due to loss of personal fortune or death.

It was becoming more and more difficult for Lee to return to Lexington and to motivate himself to continue as president of the university. There existed a combination of circumstances which nagged at him: the grief over the loss of his brother, the dismal financial situation, decline in the student population at the university, and the worry over his own health. All of these conditions only served to increase his distress and exacerbate his physical condition. He worked diligently through the autumn, trying to overcome his anguish by attending to university business and punctually presiding over the faculty meetings and becoming more removed from the Lexington social circle.

By early winter 1893, he resumed writing more socially again, reaching out and acknowledging others. At first, he wrote a simple informational reply to Mrs. Parke C. Bagby, Corresponding Secretary of the A.P.V.A. in Richmond, with his brother, Rob's address, "Your Postal Card to Capt. R. E. Lee has just been received and forwarded to him, 1320 F. Street, N. W. Washington, D. C."[305]

Toward the middle of February, Rob Lee and his family visited Custis in Lexington before returning to Washington, D. C. Upon his return, Rob Lee learned of the death of their cousin Margaret Hunter. This event brought about condolence letters from both Custis and Rob to "Cousin Margaret's" immediate family:

> I arrived here last night from Lexington, and heard of your great loss for the first time-and this morning received your letter-my heartfelt sympathies are with you all-But with you more than anyone-I have known her, admired her and loved her all my life.
>
> Custis and I were talking of her the other day in Lexington. We had no idea that she was even sick. He said he thought she was the finest woman he had ever known.
>
> We were talking of her the very day she died—There is nothing that I can say or do that will help you any— But my thoughts and sympathies haven been with you all the time since I heard this sad news. My love to your children.[306]

Custis' own note of condolence is equally touching:

> Your note of the 18th unst. reached me last Saturday
> evening and was naturally the cause of surprise and grief
> to me as I had not heard of Cousin Margaret's illness. In
> fact my brother, Robert, who was here for a day or two
> last week, mentioned that he had seen our cousin not long
> before, and that he had never seen her looking better. You
> and yours have my tenderest sympathy; and I should have
> written at once, but that this is no train from here on the
> valley branch of the Baltimore and Ohio Ry. on Sunday.
> Not knowing where to address you, just now, I will send
> this to my brother in Washington with the request that he
> will forward it to you.
>
> With sincere good wishes for yourself and the chil-
> dren, and all the other members of the family, I remain,
> very truly yrs.[307]

Two weeks later he was back to his normal routine of communication with General Scott Shipp, thanking Shipp for material of
mutual interest, such as *The Fifty-third Annual Report of the
Virginia Military Institute*, and discussing disciplinary actions
towards students of Washington and Lee who violated the campus
of V. M. I.: "If the boys concerned have any sensibility, they can not
but be grateful for your magnanimity; and your action must have
the best effect whatever our Faculty may do in the matter."[308]

In early May, Professor James J. White of the university
passed away. Immediately, General Shipp sent his condolences on
behalf of the officers and cadets of V. M. I. in the form of Minutes
from the Academic Board. Lee acknowledged this gesture in the
following letter:

> I duly received the copy of the Minuets of the
> Academic Board transmitted by Capt. Mallory under date
> of the 6th May 1893; and read it to our Faculty, last
> Monday afternoon, at the weekly meeting. By the
> Resolution of our Faculty, was requested to acknowledge

the receipt of the Minutes, and to express to your Faculty our grateful appreciation of the kind and valued sentiments that you have been good enough to express in regard to our late friend and colleague, J. J. White. Even at this time General Lee's health had started to deteriorate even further. He was so ill by June that he did not have the strength to write another resignation to the board of trustees. Lee requested a visit from John L. Campbell the treasurer of the University for the purpose of expressing his wishes again to the trustees of Lee's desire to resign. Lee's condition did not improve and Campbell needed to make two attempts before he could finally visit Lee with the reply from the trustees. Once again the trustees refused his resignation in a manner regarded as "affectionate sentiments." But from a political point of view of the university, one of the trustees William McLaughlin confided in Campbell that he thought Lee's resignation at this time would be disastrous. [309]

Consequently, Custis Lee was once again forced to stay in Lexington. This single act prolonged Lee's recovery for many months and for the first time in many years he was confined to his house during the summer.

Although Custis Lee was nearly 61 years old, he was not permitted the retirement he so disperately desired and needed. Instead, as always, he placed himself last and continued at the university for more than three years until he was finally released from the commitment. During the summer of 1893, his friends and neighbors were generous loaning him books, bringing flowers, vegetables and fruit in the hope it would give him some comfort.

By late summer he was able to write his own thank you notes again, "I return with many thanks the books you were kind enough to lend me, some time ago; should have returned them before, but did not know until last evening that you were at home again."[310] However, only a few days later, Lee was compelled to ask Thomas E. Marshall, Jr., a private secretary, to write to his old friend, Edmund R. Cocke of Oakland Plantation: "General Custis Lee, who is still confined to his house by illness, desired me to acknowledge, with thanks, the receipt of the documents that you have been good enough to send him; and to tender you his best wishes for the happiness of yourself and household."[311]

Through October his health improved enough for him to return to his presidential duties, but as before he would either arrive late at the office or conduct the university business from the house. Students saw very little of him except for formal occasions. As part of his presidential duties, he had a brisk communication with General Scott Shipp, yet always amiable:

> At the request of our Faculty, Mr. J. R. Tucker will deliver an address on the Life and Character of the late Prof. James J. White, in the Chapel at 11 A.M., next Saturday, 11 November, 1893. The officers and cadets of the Va. Mil. Institute are cordially invited to be present on the occasion and the officers are especially invited to seats on the platform, where places are always reserved for them.[312]

Then, later in the day, President Lee learned that Mr. Tucker was not available on the designated date and time and quickly informs Shipp of the change in arrangements:

> I have learned since writing to you, this morning, that Dr. Graham has forbidden Mr. Tucker from speaking next Saturday, owing to the condition of the latter's throat. I will give you due notice when the address will be delivered—I mean the day of its delivery.[313]

A few days later Lee had the grim job of informing Shipp of the death of one of the Washington and Lee students from typhoid fever. Although Lee invited Shipp and the V. M. I. family to attend the young man's funeral, he suggested that if anyone at V. M. I. was apprehensive about attending the funeral not to do so, yet on the other hand he correctly advised that the disease was spread via food or drink:

One of our students, George Andrew Warwick of the Law School, died last evening of typhoid fever. His funeral will take place, this afternoon, from the Chapel, at 4 o'clock; and the officers and cadets of the Va. Military Institute are respectfully invited to attend. If the cadets attend in an organized body, their place will be in the lead of the procession; if they attend as individuals, they had better go with the students. If any of the officers of the V. M.I. attend, they had better go with our Faculty. While I believe that it is the opinion of physicians generally that typhoid bacteria can only be taken into the system in food or drink, and not from the air that is breathed, I would not wish the officers and cadets to attend the funeral if there be any apprehension of danger, or danger, in so doing, or if for any other reason they do not care to attend.[314]

Toward the end of October, Lee received a letter from his old friend, General Thomas T. Mumford but as Lee explains in the letter, he does not answer it until early December, 1893:

I am very sorry to have been so long in answering your letter of the 30 Oct. last; but, for the past year, I have hardly been able to do more than to attend to current business, after a fashion, with the aid of a stenographer; and since my illness, last June. I have been confined to the house pretty much all the time.

I read with much interest your paper, and did not notice any errors excepting a few slips of the pen, &c. some of which I corrected in pencil as I read along. I do not think that you have given too much prominence to your own services; but I think that, when you are preparing your paper for publication, it may be well not to call attention too conspicuously to Genl. Lee's part in Genl. Jackson's movements, but to let the facts speak for themselves, and to say no more than is absolutely necessary about Genl. Lee in your preface or conclusion, or both. Of course every one, who knows anything about military matters, knows that no part of an army can be independent of the other parts; and although it has been the habit of writers, North and South to speak of Genl. Jackson as a "free lance"-even after he became the commander of the 2nd Corps in the Army of Northern Virginia acting altogether on his own responsibility, such a notion has no foundation in fact or common sense, and there would be no one more prompt to repudiate such nonsense than Genl. Jackson if he had the opportunity to do so. Still, as many people choose to believe otherwise, it is hardly worth while to set them right even if were possible to do so. If I have not returned your paper on the battle of Five-Forks, please let me know, and I will try to find it. I was obliged to change my stenographer, last August, and have not had the opportunity of showing the new one where to look for papers, &c. with every good wish for you & yrs, I remain...[315]

Lee continued to work out of the President's House through the winter and spring session. After commencement, he was able to take his vacation at "Old White." Upon his return to Lexington, he was fully recovered from his illness which incapacitated him for the past year. Now, he wished to become more visible on campus. One former student, who was an incoming freshman in September of 1894, recalled a slight encounter with President Lee:

My experience had extended little beyond a town of 2000 inhabitants and the surrounding farming district. I was never of a very aggressive disposition, especially at that stage of my life, so you can readily imagine the unimpressive bearing I must have presented. In those days members of the Faculty sat at tables in the reading room in Newcomb Hall and helped the Freshmen with their entrance problems, even advising them about such matters as boarding houses, etc. I had completed these matters and was standing by myself watching the proceedings while waiting for a friend. Out of the corner of my eye I saw General G. W. C. Lee, who was President of the University at that time, standing about ten feet away—also alone. He was looking in my direction and as I am too diffident to face him squarely, my desire to see more of so distinguished a man caused me to continue to watch him in this manner. Apparently he was considering whether he should speak to me and after at least a minute, which seemed to me much longer, he advanced slowly and in almost a diffident manner asked if he could help me in any way. When I replied in the negative he moved away without saying more and continued to stand alone watching the boys coming and going.

You can well imagine how strong and lasting an impression his courtesy, as well as his apparent diffidence, made on my Freshman mind.

When I came to General Lee's office to matriculate, he looked at me quite a while, as if hesitant to speak, and then approached me and spoke to me in a very pleasant and encouraging way, wishing me a pleasant and successful course.

The young student, A. Fred White who recorded the above account had only one other encounter with General Lee, in his entire tenure at Washington and Lee University, "...on one occasion when for some reason I called to see his Private Secretary, who lived in his home. The General answered the door bell himself and, with a few words of direction, handed me a lighted candle to help me find my way to the second floor."[316]

The new academic year was successfully started and Lee's health was good. He work diligently, as was witnessed in a note he wrote to General Scott Shipp, "If you have a copy of the late Genl. G. W. Cullum's Register of the Graduates of the U. S. Mil. Acady— I am not sure that this is the correct title of the book— please let me have, at your convenience, the address of the publishers, as I have so many calls upon me for information of all kinds that I must get the last edition of the Register if possible."[317]

By mid-winter of 1895, Lee once again had the unpleasant duty to inform Shipp of the death of yet another student, Joseph Price Mitchell:

It is with sincere sadness that the undersigned announces the death of Joseph Price Mitchell, who died this morning about five o'clock. The funeral will take place from the Grace Memorial Church at 11 A.M. on the 11th instant.

The faculty and students are requested to attend the funeral in a body, and their place in the procession will be immediately after the family of the deceased.

There will be Suspension [of classes] on next Monday.[318]

Through the winter and spring, Lee's health vacillated, but he managed to finish the spring session with his usual care for details, as seen in these two notes to General Scott Shipp in reference to a firing range on the Virginia Military Institute property which was adjacent to the Washington and Lee campus:

I do not think that there can be any objection to your using the range as heretofore. It may be that the matter will have to be decided by the Ex. Committee of the Board of Trustees, whose day for meeing is the last of each month. I will enquire into the matter, however, and let you know the result as soon as possible. Am always glad to see you, but did not expect an acknowledgment of the letter, I sent it to you because I thought that you might have seen some of the newspaper accounts of Mr. S. D. McCormick's address.[319]

Two days later Lee wrote to Shipp again:

Mr. Jno. Campbell, who is acting Proctor of the College, visisted your range yesterday with Col. Rockenback; and does not see any reason why you should not use the range as heretofore, and does not think that it will be necessary to bring the matter to the Ex. Committee of the Board of Trustees. Mr. Campbell says that Col. Rockenback will keep a lookout for the students going to their boat-house, etc. You had best therefore make use of the range as you have been doing in the past.[320]

The familiar end-of-the-year events proceeded as usual without any problems, and Lee made his plans to travel to White Sulpher Springs in Greenbrier County, West Virginia, for the summer. During his vacation at White Sulpher Springs, all of his personal mail was forwarded from Lexington. From this forwarded mail, he received a letter from a woman who was one of his father's favorite Virginia belles, "Miss Norvell."

Norvell Caskie was the only child of Mr. and Mrs. James K. Caskie of Richmond. Mrs. James K. Caskie, mother of "Miss Norvell" was related to Mrs. Robert E. Lee through her Aunt Nellie Custis Lewis. In 1868, "Miss Novell" became engaged to A. Seddon Jones of Orange County, Virginia. A short time later her father died and it was discovered that the Caskie family fortune was dissolved, leaving her invalid mother and she in desperate straights. She married Jones and spent many years living on a farm near Rapidan Station, Virginia. Ultimately, she and her husband returned to Richmond where she lived out her final days.

In the summer of 1895, "Miss Norvell" wrote to General Custis inquiring about the university as a possible facility of higher education for her son. He was happy to hear from her, and he took the opportunity to reply while at "Old White."

> I have improved so much in health since I came here, that I shall probaly be able to go through the next session at W. & L. University. If you would like to send your boy to our college, I shall be glad to have him live with me. If you conclude to send him to Lexington, send a postal card to the Clerk of the Faculty, W. & L. University, Lexington, Va. for a catalogue, and let me know, here, as soon as convenient, that I may have his room got ready

for him. My chambermaid, who is a man, is to be married on the 5th Sept., and has asked for a leave of absence, and I should like him to get the room ready before he goes away. The college fees are $80.00 for the session of nine months, $5.00 of which goes to the Gymnaisium; your son will have no other expenses except his clothing, laundry ($1.50 a month) and books; the latter are not expensive in the lower classes. Please remember me kindly to Mr. Jones, and believe me to remain, very sincerely yrs.[321]

Apparently, "Miss Norvell's" son did attend Washington and Lee University in the fall of 1895.

Lee returned to Lexington from White Sulpher Springs renewed and ready for work. He was anxious to continue and relished the university duties and even found time in the beginning of the new academic year to respond promptly to a letter he recieved on September 17th from General Bradley F. Johnson in reference to the Lee family's collection of Washington letters:

I have received your letter of the 17th inst., and send you by express the box of papers referred to by Prof. Nelson. According to my recollection there are other papers in the box than Genl. Washington's, but you need not open them unless you care to do so. I think that the bundles are labelled in my mother's handwriting, and I think also that she published some of the letters in a book, edited by herself, entitled Recollections, &c., of Washington by G. W. P. Custis. When you have done with the letters, &c., please return them to me in the box—C. O. D. I duly received the copy of your work on Washington, that you were kind enougth to send me; read it with great interest; wrote to you at 18 North Avenue, Baltimore, Md., thanking you for the book and telling you how much I liked it. I have some other letters here of Genl. Washington's, somewhere, but the ink is so faded that the letters generally cannot be made out; I may be able, however, to have the faded ink brought out. The paper is nearly gone, too.[322]

The autumn proved to be a particularly good period in Lee's life with little physical distress and the little problems with the students, but the university expenses were extreme and the enrollment was in decline. With this economic plague continuing into the spring session, Lee felt he was induced to write to the Board of Trustees in early May, 1896:

> In view of the probable increase in the expenses of the University, and the probable decrease in the number of students owing to the abolishment of Preparatory classes, I respectfully request that my annual salary be reduced to $2,400.00. Allowing $400.00 per annum for expenses of Type-writer, type-writing and copying machines, &c., there will remain a net salary of $2,000.00, which is about the amount recieved by each of the Professors excepting those in the School of Law. I further ask that this reduction be made to take effect at the beginning of the next quarter, 1 July, 1896.
>
> Hoping that you may grant this request, which has been duly considered, I remain, very sincerely...[323]

Lee's request was taken seriously by the Board of Trustees. Moreover, the board thought his proposal was not necessary, but they acquiesced to Lee's wishes.

He spent most of the summer in Lexington anwsering correspondence and extending polite thank you notes, yet with a touch of humor in notes to General Shipp, "I have received a copy of the Annual Report of the Va. Mil. Institute for the session fo 1895-1896, for which I presume I am indebted to your kindness. I am very glad to have the Report, and to note your remarks on various topics. Thanking you very much, as our English friends say..."[324]

Lee managed to escape Lexington to Greenbrier County, West Virginia, for a few weeks. But all too soon it was time to resume another acedemic year. One former student recalled an incident that occurred the autumn of 1896 which reveals how Lee was beginning to decline in the use of his faculties:

John Campbell's office used to be (as it was later) a general loafing place for the Faculty. On one occasion when I was there on some errand, "Old Nick" and "Old Alec" were sitting there, the former tipped back with his chair on two legs and the latter as always erect in his chair, and General Custis came in, removed his hat (as always) and transacted his business with "Mr. John," remaining standing all the time. After going out he almost immediately returned hunting his hat. I noticed that he was unconsciously holding it in his hand, but would of course not venture to tell him so. Presently Mr. Campbell said: "Why, General, I think you have it in your hand." "Why, so I have," said the General with some embrassassment, and immediately went out. At that time he was beginning to show some signs of absentmindedness.[325]

Shortly after this incident, Lee lasped into another bout of his physically limiting rheumatoid illness. Once again, he was impelled to place before the Board of Trustee another resignation dated December 29th and written in his own hand:

Gentlemen:—I regret to have to trouble you with my personal affairs; but is is perhaps better to do so now than at some future time, when you may be more pressed with business.

I am utterly useless here, with but little probablity of ever being more useful to the university, and therefore desire to be relieved from duty as its President.

I should like my resignation—which is hereby tendered—to take effect on the 1st July next, or at any prior date that may be deemed best by The Board.

I have no faults to find nor complaints to make, and only wish to vacate the office, to which I was appointed by your Honorable Body nearly twenty five years ago, because I am unable to perform its duties.[326]

George Washington Custis Lee was the seventh President of the University. He maintained the longest tenure of any of the preceding presidents, including his father, Robert E. Lee. He was sixty-four years old, and it was time for Lee to retire. The Board of Trustees of Washington and Lee University finally had the courage to release this man from their manacle and accept his resignation.

Endnotes

[1] Robert E. Lee, Jr. *Recollections and Letters of General Robert E. Lee.* 173.

[2] Joseph H. Crute, Jr. *Derwent: Robert E. Lee's Sanctuary.* 41-42.

[3] Ibid., 42-43.

[4] Letter from Robert E. Lee to Robert E. Lee, Jr., dated July 10, 1865, Virginia Historical Society.

[5] Letter from George Washington Custis Lee to Francis H. Smith, dated July 17, 1865, Virginia Military Institute Archives.

[6] Letter from Robert E. Lee to Robert E. Lee, Jr., dated July 22, 1865, Virginia Historical Society.

[7] J. William Jones. *Life & Letters of Gen. Robert Edward Lee.* 385-386.

[8] Lee, Jr. 175.

[9] Ford, Gerald R. *Remarks upon signing a bill restoring rights of citizenship to General Robert E. Lee,* dated August 5, 1975.

[10] Letter from George Washington Custis Lee to Francis H. Smith, dated August 18, 1865, Virginia Military Institute Archives.

[11] R. E. Lee, Jr. 176.

[12] Joseph H. Crute, Jr. *The Derwent Letters.* 28.

[13] Ibid. 30.

[14] Crute. *The Derwent Letters.* 28.

[15] Letter from George Washington Custis Lee to Alfred Landon Rives, dated October 19, 1865, Leyburn Library, Special Collections, Washington and Lee University.

[16] Letter from Francis H. Smith to Scott Ship, dated September 1, 1865 Virginia Military Institute Archives.

[17] Couper, William. *One Hundred Years at V.M.I.* 119-120.

[18] Letter from Robert E. Lee to Fitz Lee, dated September 1, 1865, Virginia Historical Society.

[19] Crute. *The Derwent Letters.* 125.

[20] Letter from George Washington Custis Lee to Francis H. Smith, dated October 2, 1865, Virginia Military Institute Archives.

[21] Letter from Robert E. Lee to MaryAnna Randolph Custis Lee dated October 3, 1865, Virginia Historical Society.

[22] Letter from Robert E. Lee to MaryAnna Randolph Custis Lee dated October 15, 1865, Virginia Historical Society.

[23] Annual Report of the Superintendent, dated June, 1866, Virginia Military Institute Archives.

[24] Letter from George Washington Custis Lee to Alfred Landon Rives, dated October 19, 1865, Leyburn Library, Special Collections, Washington and Lee University.

[25] Letter from Robert E. Lee to MaryAnna Randolph Custis Lee dated October 27, 1865, Virginia Historical Society.

[26] Letter from Robert E. Lee to Mildred Childe Lee, dated October 29, 1865, Virginia Historical Society.

[27] Letter from Robert E. Lee to MaryAnna Randolph Custis Lee dated November 5, 1865, Virginia Historical Society.

[28] Lee, Jr. 195.

[29] Ibid.

[30] Letter from George Washington Custis Lee to William Washington, dated November 30, 1865 Special Collections Department William R. Perkins Library, Duke University.

[31] Letter from Robert E. Lee to Eleanor Agnes Lee, dated December 5, 1865, Virginia Historical Society.

[32] Lee, Jr. 209.

[33] Letter from George Washington Custis Lee to Alfred Landon Rives, dated January 25, 1866 Special Collections Department William R. Perkins Library, Duke University.

[34] Letter from Robert E. Lee to William Parker Snow, dated February 13, 1866, Leyburn Library, Special Collections, Washington and Lee University.

[35] Letter from Robert E. Lee to Annette Carter, dated May 19, 1866, Leyburn Library, Special Collections, Washington and Lee University.

[36] Letter from Robert E. Lee to Robert E. Lee, Jr. dated June 13, 1866, Virginia Historical Society.

[37] Letter from George Washington Custis Lee to Alfred Landon Rives, dated June 2, 1866 Special Collections Department William R. Perkins Library, Duke University.

[38] Lee, Jr. 239.

[39] Ibid., 241-242.

[40] Letter from Robert E. Lee to MaryAnna Randolph Custis Lee, dated August 2, 1866, Virginia Historical Society.

[41] Letter from George Washington Custis Lee to Adam Badeau, dated

August 18, 1866, Special Collections Department William R. Perkins Library, Duke University.

[42] Letter from Robert E. Lee to Annette Carter, dated August 30, 1866, Leyburn Library, Special Collections, Washington and Lee University.

[43] Letter from William Henry Fitzhugh Lee to Eleanor Agnes Lee, dated September 26, 1866, Virginia Historical Society.

[44] Lee, Jr. 245-246.

[45] Letter from James T. Earle to Francis H. Smith, dated December 15, 1866, Virginia Military Institute Archives.

[46] University of Maryland Time line web site: www.inform.umd.edu.

[47] Letter from Francis H. Smith to James T. Earle, dated December 21, 1866 Virginia Military Institute Archives.

[48] Letter from Robert E. Lee to Mildred Childe Lee, dated December 21, 1866, Virginia Historical Society.

[49] Letter from George Washington Custis Lee to James T. Earle, dated January 14, 1867, Virginia Military Institute Archives.

[50] Letter from George Washington Custis Lee to Francis H. Smith, dated January 14, 1867, Virginia Military Institute Archives.

[51] University of Maryland Time line web site: www.inform.umd.edu.

[52] Letter from George Washington Custis Lee to Alfred Landon Rives, dated February 19, 1867, Special Collections Department William R. Perkins Library, Duke University.

[53] Lee, Jr. 259.

[54] Annual Report of the Superintendent, dated July, 1867, Virginia Military Institute Archives.

[55] Conte, Robert S. *The History of the Greenbrier America's Resort*. 66.

[56] Freeman, R.E. Lee Vol. IV 325.

[57] Letter from MaryAnna Randolph Custis Lee to Robert E. Lee Jr. dated August 6, 1867, Virginia Historical Society.

[58] Bond, Christiana. *Memories of General Robert E. Lee*. 30.

[59] Ibid., 36-38.

[60] Ibid., 49-51.

[61] Letter from Robert E. Lee to Robert E. Lee, Jr. dated October 26, 1867, Virginia Historical Society.

[62] Letter from Robert E. Lee to Annette Carter, dated November 1, 1867, Leyburn Library, Special Collections, Washington and Lee University.

[63] Lee, Jr. 286.

64 Ibid., 287.

65 Ibid.

66 Lee, Jr. 288.

67 Letter from Robert E. Lee to Annette Carter, dated March 28, 1868, Leyburn Library, Special Collections, Washington and Lee University.

68 Ibid., n.d.

69 Lee, Jr. 313.

70 Ibid., 319-20.

71 Lee, Jr. 322.

72 Ibid., 324.

73 Letter from Robert E. Lee to William Henry Fitzhugh Lee, dated October 19, 1868, Virginia Historical Society.

74 Lee, Jr. 333.

75 Lyle and Simpson. *The Architecture of Historic Lexington.* 164.

76 Lee, Jr. 334.

77 Letter from Robert E. Lee to William N. Burwell, dated February 15, 1969, Virginia Historical Society.

78 Letter from Robert E. Lee to Robert E. Lee, Jr. dated February 27, 1869, Virginia Historical Society.

79 Freeman. R. E. Lee. Vol. IV 381.

80 Lee, Jr. 343.

81 Letter from Robert E. Lee to Robert E. Lee Jr., dated April 17, 1869, Virginia Historical Society.

82 Virginia Military Institute Archive, File Z.

83 Annual Report of the Superintendent, dated June, 1869, Virginia Military Institute Archives.

84 Lee, Jr. 358.

85 Letter from Robert E. Lee to Charlotte Taylor Haxall Lee, dated July 9, 1869, Virginia Historical Society.

86 Ibid., 363.

87 Lee, Jr. 370.

88 Letter from Robert E. Lee to William Henry Fitzhugh Lee, dated December 9, 1869, Virginia Historical Society.

89 Lee, Jr. 381.

90 Ibid., 384.

91 Lee, Jr. 385.

92 Freeman. R.E. Lee Vol. IV 442.

[93] Lee, Jr. 389.

[94] Ibid.

[95] Lee, Jr. 389.

[96] Lee, Jr., 390-391.

[97] Ibid., 394.

[98] Letter from Robert E. Lee to MaryAnna Randolph Custis Lee, dated April 11, 1869, Virginia Historical Society.

[99] Lee, Jr. 398.

[100] Ibid., 405.

[101] Ibid., 411.

[102] Letter from Robert E. Lee to Annette Carter, dated May 20, 1870, Leyburn Library, Special Collections, Washington and Lee University.

[103] Letter from Robert E. Lee to Margaret Hunter, dated June 8, 1870, Leyburn Library, Special Collections, Washington and Lee University.

[104] Annual Report of the Superintendent, dated June, 1870, Virginia Military Institute Archives.

[105] Lee, Jr. 414.

[106] Ibid., 419.

[107] Lee, Jr. 427.

[108] Ibid., 430.

[109] Letter from Robert E. Lee to Fitzhugh Lee dated September 19, 1870, Leyburn Library, Special Collections, Washington and Lee University.

[110] J. William Jones. *Personal Reminiscences of General Robert E. Lee.* 447-450.

[111] Lee, Jr. 440.

[112] Freeman. R.E. Lee Vol. IV, 490.

[113] J. William Jones. 455.

[114] Ollinger, Crenshaw. *General Lee's College.* 176-177.

[115] Ibid. 177.

[116] Letter from George Washington Custis Lee to Charles Marshall, dated December 5, 1870, Leyburn Library, Special Collections, Washington and Lee University.

[117] Letter from George Washington Custis Lee to Walter H. Taylor, dated December 6, 1870, Stratford Hall Library and Archives.

[118] Virginia Military Institute, File H.

[119] Virginia Military Institute, File Z.

[120] Virginia Military Institute, File H.

[121] Ibid. File I.

[122] Virginia Military Institute, File J.

[123] *The Southern Collegian*, dated February 11, 1871, Leyburn Library, Special Collections, Washington and Lee University.

[124] Ibid.

[125] *The Southern Collegian*, dated February 11, 1871, Leyburn Library, Special Collections, Washington and Lee University.

[126] Virginia Military Institute, File G.

[127] Letter from George Washington Custis Lee to Charles Marshall, dated March 1, 1871, Leyburn Library, Special Collections, Washington and Lee University.

[128] Letter from George Washington Custis Lee to Thomas F. Balfe, dated May 10, 1871, Leyburn Library, Special Collections, Washington and Lee University.

[129] Letter from William Preston Johnston to George Washington Custis Lee, datedJune 17, 1871, Leyburn Library, Special Collections, Washington and Lee University.

[130] Letter from W. Allen to George Washington Custis Lee, dated June 19, 1871, Leyburn Library, Special Collections, Washington and Lee University.

[131] Annual Religious Statistics of W and L University, dated June 12, 1871, Leyburn Library, Special Collections, Washington and Lee University.

[132] Annual Report on Washington and Lee University from George Washington Custis Lee to the Board of Trustees, dated June 19, 1871, Leyburn Library, Special Collections, Washington and Lee University.

[133] Annual Report of the Superintendent, dated July, 1871, Virginia Military Institute Archives.

[134] Lee Jacobs, *Cry Heart*. 169-170.

[135] Letter from MaryAnna Randolph Custis Lee to Mildred Childe Lee, dated March 1, 1872, Virginia Historical Society.

[136] Letter from George Washington Custis Lee to Charles C. Jones, dated May 6, 1872 Special Collections Department William R. Perkins Library, Duke University.

[137] Letter from George Washington Custis Lee to Charles C. Jones, dated May 17, 1872 Special Collections Department William R. Perkins Library, Duke University.

[138] Letter from George Washington Custis Lee to J. William Jones, dated

July 19, 1872, Private Collection.

[139] Letter from George Washington Custis Lee to S. W. Somerville, dated December 9, 1872, Leyburn Library, Special Collections, Washington and Lee University.

[140] Letter from George Washington Custis Lee to M. R. Patrick, dated March 31, 1873, Leyburn Library, Special Collections, Washington and Lee University.

[141] Crenshaw, 197.

[142] Ibid., 197-203.

[143] Howe, James Lewis. Historical Research & Misc. Notes on G.W.C. Lee, File #186 dated June 22, 1940, Leyburn Library, Special Collections, Washington and Lee University.

[144] Ibid.

[145] Howe, James Lewis. Historical Research & Misc. Notes on G.W.C. Lee, File #186 dated June 22, 1940, Leyburn Library, Special Collections, Washington and Lee University.

[146] Ibid.

[147] Letter from George Washington Custis Lee to Charles Marshall, dated August 4, 1873, Leyburn Library, Special Collections, Washington and Lee University.

[148] Lee. *Growing up in the 1850's The Journal of Agnes Lee*. [Recollections of Mildred Lee] 112-116.

[149] MacDonald, 299.

[150] Ibid.

[151] Coulling, *The Lee Girls*. 180.

[152] Reminiscences of Robert F. Campbell, dated July 7, 1939 File R-8a, Leyburn Library, Special Collections, Washington and Lee University.

[153] Ibid.

[154] #142 G.W.C.Lee Papers, F.5, dated April 10, 1940, Leyburn Library, Special Collections, Washington and Lee University.

[155] Letter from W.E. Dold to James Louis Howe, dated July 24, 1941, Leyburn Library, Special Collections, Washington and Lee University.

[156] Ibid. 8.

[157] Building and Grounds -1-2, Leyburn Library, Special Collections, Washington and Lee University.

[158] Ibid., 3.

[159] Building and Grounds -4, Leyburn Library, Special Collections,

Washington and Lee University.

[160] Ibid., 5.

[161] Building and Grounds -7, Leyburn Library, Special Collections, Washington and Lee University.

[162] Building and Grounds -9, Leyburn Library, Special Collections, Washington and Lee University.

[163] Ibid.

[164] Larner, ed. Columbia Historical Society, Vol. 31-32, 182.

[165] Letter from George Washington Custis Lee to J. J. White, dated August 14, 1874, Leyburn Library, Special Collections, Washington and Lee University.

[166] Letter from George Washington Custis Lee to Charles C. Jones, dated October 31, 1874, Special Collections Department, William R. Perkins Library, Duke University.

[167] Letter from William Henry Fitzhugh Lee to Mary Tabb Bolling Lee, dated November 17, 1874, Virginia Historical Society.

[168] Letter from George Washington Custis Lee to J. William Jones, dated January 27, 1875, Museum of the Confederacy.

[169] Letter from W.E. Dold to James Louis Howe, dated July 24, 1941, W. & L.

[170] Notice of executor settlement on the estate of Mrs. W. H. Fitzhugh, dated March 20, 1875, Leyburn Library, Special Collections, Washington and Lee University.

[171] Letter from George Washington Custis Lee to J. J. White, dated July 26, 1875, Leyburn Library, Special Collections, Washington and Lee University.

[172] Ibid. dated July 31, 1875.

[173] Letter from George Washington Custis Lee to J. J. White, dated August 28, 1875, Leyburn Library, Special Collections, Washington and Lee University.

[174] Letter from George Washington Custis Lee to George B. Purcell, dated October 25, 1875, Leyburn Library, Special Collections, Washington and Lee University.

[175] Letter from George Washington Custis Lee to Henry A. Ward, dated November 17, 1875, Leyburn Library, Special Collections, Washington and Lee University.

[176] Letters from Henry A. Ward to George Washington Custis Lee, dated October 8, 1875, November 28, 1875, and December 18, 1875, Leyburn

Library, Special Collections, Washington and Lee University.

177 Letter from George Washington Custis Lee to J. William Jones, dated February 7, 1876, Museum of the Confederacy.

178 Letter from George Washington Custis Lee to J. William Jones, dated February 17, 1876, Museum of the Confederacy.

179 Letter from E.B. Kruttschnitt to George Washington Custis Lee, date March 16, 1876, Leyburn Library, Special Collections, Washington and Lee University.

180 Letters from Henry A. Ward to George Washington Custis Lee, dated March 17, 1876, Leyburn Library, Special Collections, Washington and Lee University.

181 Telegram from Henry A. Ward to George Washington Custis Lee, dated April 14, 1876, Leyburn Library, Special Collections, Washington and Lee University.

182 Washington and Lee University Annual President's Report for the Session of 1875-1876, submitted by George Washington Custis Lee, dated June 19, 1876, Leyburn Library, Special Collections, Washington and Lee University.

183 Letter from George Washington Custis Lee to J. J. White, dated May 4, 1876, Leyburn Library, Special Collections, Washington and Lee University.

184 Washington and Lee University Annual President's Report for the Session of 1875-1876, submitted by George Washington Custis Lee, dated June 19, 1876, Leyburn Library, Special Collections, Washington and Lee University.

185 Ibid.

186 Washington and Lee University Annual President's Report for the Session of 1875-1876, submitted by George Washington Custis Lee, dated June 19, 1876, Leyburn Library, Special Collections, Washington and Lee University.

187 Crenshaw. 179.

188 Letter from George Washington Custis Lee to Harry C. Hines, dated September 30, 1876, Leyburn Library, Special Collections, Washington and Lee University.

189 Letter from George Washington Custis Lee to Marshall McDonald dated November 25, 1876, Leyburn Library, Special Collections, Washington and Lee University.

[190] Letter from George Washington Custis Lee to W. J. Walthall, dated April 20, 1877, Musuem of the Confederacy.

[191] Larner, ed. Columbia Historical Society, Vol. 31-32, 183-184.

[192] Ibid. 184.

[193] Larner, ed. Columbia Historical Society, Vol. 31-32, 185.

[194] Ibid.

[195] Larner, ed. Columbia Historical Society, Vol. 31-32, 186.

[196] Ibid.

[197] Letter from George Washington Custis Lee to J. J. White, dated September 13, 1877, Leyburn Library, Special Collections, Washington and Lee University.

[198] Letter from L. E. Hunt to George Washington Custis Lee dated October 10, 1877, Leyburn Library, Special Collections, Washington and Lee University.

[199] Letter from George Washington Custis Lee to Jefferson Davis, dated January 15, 1878, Museum of the Confederacy.

[200] Letter from George Washington Custis Lee to Jefferson Davis, dated February 26, 1878 Special Collections Department William R. Perkins Library, Duke University.

[201] Larner, ed. Columbia Historical Society, Vol. 31-32, 187-188.

[202] Ibid., 188-189.

[203] Letter from George Washington Custis Lee to Jefferson Davis, dated March 26, 1878 Special Collections Department William R. Perkins Library, Duke University.

[204] Letter from George Washington Custis Lee to W. T. Walthall, dated April 11,1878, Museum of the Confederacy.

[205] Letter from George Washington Custis Lee to J. J. White, dated May 6, 1878, Leyburn Library, Special Collections, Washington and Lee University.

[206] Crenshaw, 230.

[207] Letter from George Washington Custis Lee to J. J. White, dated October 8, 1878, Leyburn Library, Special Collections, Washington and Lee University.

[208] Letter from George Washington Custis Lee to Miss Tunstall, dated November 8,1878, Museum of the Confederacy.

[209] Letter from George Washington Custis Lee to Emily V. Mason, no dated Museum of the Confederacy.

[210] Reminiscences-19 of Henry T. Wickham, Hickory Hill, 1939, Leyburn Library, Special Collections, Washington and Lee University.

[211] Larner, ed. Columbia Historical Society, Vol. 31-32, 189-190.

[212] Ibid., 190.

[213] Larner, ed. Columbia Historical Society, Vol. 31-32, 190-191.

[214] Ibid., 191-192.

[215] Larner, ed. Columbia Historical Society, Vol. 31-32, 193.

[216] Private Collection.

[217] Ibid.

[218] Letter from George Washington Custis Lee to Jeremy F. Gilmer, dated January 30, 1880, Special Collections Department William R. Perkins Library, Duke University.

[219] Letter from George Washington Custis Lee to Marshall McDonald, dated January 30, 1880, Special Collections Department William R. Perkins Library, Duke University.

[220] Reminiscences of John M. Glenn, dated April 14, 1939 File R-14, W.& L.

[221] Letter from George Washington Custis Lee to Daniel Holt, dated April 20, 1881 Special Collections Department William R. Perkins Library, Duke University.

[222] Letter from George Washington Custis Lee to William Taylor Thom, dated August 6, 1881, Leyburn Library, Special Collections, Washington and Lee University.

[223] Washington and Lee University Annual President's Report for the Session of 1881-1882, submitted by George Washington Custis Lee, dated June 19, 1882, Leyburn Library, Special Collections, Washington and Lee University.

[224] Rockbridge Historical Society Miscellaneous, (No Folder Number), Leyburn Library, Special Collections, Washington and Lee University.

[225] Washington and Lee University Annual President's Report for the Session of 1881-1882, submitted by George Washington Custis Lee, dated June 19, 1882, Leyburn Library, Special Collections, Washington and Lee University.

[226] Ibid.

[227] Washington and Lee University Annual President's Report for the Session of 1881-1882, submitted by George Washington Custis Lee, dated June 19, 1882, Leyburn Library, Special Collections, Washington and Lee University.

[228] Rockbridge Historical Society Miscellaneous, (No Folder Number), Leyburn Library, Special Collections, Washington and Lee University.

[229] Letter from George Washington Custis Lee to Arthur Gilman dated June 10, 1882, The Houghton Library, Harvard University.

[230] Larner, ed. Columbia Historical Society, Vol. 31-32, 193-195.

[231] Ibid., 195.

[232] Larner, ed. Columbia Historical Society, Vol. 31-32, 195-196.

[233] Ibid., 196-197.

[234] Larner, ed. Columbia Historical Society, Vol. 31-32, 197.

[235] Ibid., 199.

[236] Larner, ed. Columbia Historical Society, Vol. 31-32, 200-201.

[237] Ibid., 202-203.

[238] Larner, ed. Columbia Historical Society, Vol. 31-32, 204-205.

[239] Ibid., 205.

[240] Larner, ed. Columbia Historical Society, Vol. 31-32, 205-206.

[241] Notice from George Washington Custis Lee to the students of Washington and Lee University, dated December 22, 1882, Leyburn Library, Special Collections, Washington and Lee University.

[242] Letter from George Washington Custis Lee to George W. Bagby, dated January 26, 1883, Virginia Historical Society.

[243] Larner, ed. Columbia Historical Society, Vol. 31-32, 206.

[244] Reminiscences of Leslie Lyle Campbell, dated January 17, 1939 File R-1a, Leyburn Library, Special Collections, Washington and Lee University.

[245] Letter from George Washington Custis Lee to George W. Bagby, dated June 12, 1883, Virginia Historical Society.

[246] Washington and Lee University Annual President's Report for the Session of 1882-1883, submitted by George Washington Custis Lee, dated June 25, 1883, Leyburn Library, Special Collections, Washington and Lee University.

[247] Crenshaw, 203.

[248] Ibid.

[249] Letter from George Washington Custis Lee to Isaac H. Carrington, February 12, 1884, Special Collections Department William R. Perkins Library, Duke University.

[250] Letter from George Washington Custis Lee to Isaac H. Carrington, May 7, 1884, Special Collections Department William R. Perkins Library, Duke University.

251 Faculty Minutes of Washington and Lee University, February 25, May 12, andJune 9, 1884, Leyburn Library, Special Collections, Washington and Lee University.

252 Letter from George Washington Custis Lee to Emily V. Mason, dated June 14, 1884, Museum of the Confederacy.

253 Washington and Lee University Annual President's Report for the Session of 1883-1884, submitted by George Washington Custis Lee, dated June 24, 1884, Leyburn Library, Special Collections, Washington andLee University.

254 Letter from George Washington Custis Lee to Emily V. Mason, dated July 1, 1884, Museum of the Confederacy.

255 Letter from George Washington Custis Lee to Marshall McDonald, dated July 1, 1884 Special Collections Department William R. Perkins Library, Duke University.

256 Letter from George Washington Custis Lee to Parke C. Bagby, dated July 5, 1884,Virginia Historical Society..

257 Letter from George Washington Custis Lee to Parke C. Bagby, dated September 11, 1884, Virginia Historical Society..

258 Reminiscences of Mary Quarles Turpin, dated June 20, 1939 File R-3a, Leyburn Library, Special Collections, Washington and Lee University.

259 Ibid.

260 Letter from George Washington Custis Lee to L. Q. C. Lamar, dated March 12, 1885, Museum of the Confederacy.

261 Letter from George Washington Custis Lee to Francis .H. Smith, dated June 10, 1885, Virginia Military Institute Archives.

262 Third Letter of Resignation from George Washington Custis Lee to the Board of Trustees of Washington and Lee University, dated June 16, 1885, W. & L.

263 Select Board of Trustee Minutes, dated June 1885, Folder 237, W.& L.

264 Letter from George Washington Custis Lee to Francis .H. Smith, dated June 25, 1885, Virginia Military Institute Archives.

265 Letter from J. M. Allen to Francis H. Smith, dated June 29, 1885, VMI.

266 Letter from George Washington Custis Lee to Isaac H. Carrington, January 25, 1886, Special Collections Department William R. Perkins Library, Duke University.

267 Letter from George Washington Custis Lee to Isaac H. Carrington, February 15, 1886, Special Collections Department William R. Perkins

Library, Duke University.

[268] Letter from George Washington Custis Lee to Isaac H. Carrington, March 4, 1886, Special Collections Department William R. Perkins Library, Duke University.

[269] Letter from George Washington Custis Lee to Francis H. Smith, dated May 4, 1886, Virginia Military Institute Archives.

[270] Letter from George Washington Custis Lee to Francis H. Smith, dated May 7, 1886, Virginia Military Institute Archives.

[271] Reminiscences of John V. McCall, dated February 9, 1939 File R-10, Leyburn Library, Special Collections, Washington and Lee University.

[272] W. J. Humphreys. Some Recollections of General G. W. C. Lee, no dated, no file number, Leyburn Library, Special Collections, Washington and Lee University.

[274] Letter from George Washington Custis Lee to Francis H. Smith, dated June 23, 1887, Virginia Military Institute Archives.

[275] Reminiscences of Wade H. Ellis, dated November 21, 1939 File R-16, W.& L.

[276] Letter from George Washington Custis Lee to Francis H. Smith, dated March 22, 1888, Virginia Military Institute Archives.

[277] Reminiscences of Wade H. Ellis, dated November 21, 1939 File R-16, W.& L.

[278] Letter from George Washington Custis Lee to Francis H. Smith, dated June 7, 1888, Virginia Military Institute Archives.

[279] Annual Report on Washington and Lee University from George Washington Custis Lee to the Board of Trustees, dated June 18, 1888, W & L.

[280] Letter from George Washington Custis Lee to Jean Yeatman, dated March 11, 1889, Special Collections Department William R. Perkins Library, Duke University.

[281] Letter from George Washington Custis Lee to Francis H. Smith, dated March 13, 1889, Virginia Military Institute Archives.

[282] Letter from W. H. Winfree to Francis H. Smith, dated May 31, 1889, VMI.

[283] Letter from George Washington Custis Lee to Scott Shipp, dated February 4, 1890, Virginia Military Institute Archives.

[284] Letter from George Washington Custis Lee to Scott Shipp, dated February 14, 1890, Virginia Military Institute Archives.

[285] Letter from George Washington Custis Lee to Scott Shipp, dated March 7, 1890, Virginia Military Institute Archives.

[286] Letter from George Washington Custis Lee to Scott Shipp, dated March 7, 1890, Virginia Military Institute Archives.

[287] Letter from George Washington Custis Lee to Emily V. Mason, dated May 5, 1890, Museum of the Confederacy.

[288] Reminiscences of George Bolling Lee, dated February 1, 1939 File R-20, W.& L.

[289] Letter from George Washington Custis Lee to Scott Shipp, dated June 26, 1890, Virginia Military Institute Archives.

[290] Letter from George Washington Custis Lee to Scott Shipp, dated October 13, 1890, Virginia Military Institute Archives.

[291] Reminiscences of an unknown student, dated February 9, 1939 File R-13, Leyburn Library, Special Collections, Washington and Lee University.

[292] Letter from George Washington Custis Lee to Scott Shipp, dated November 21, 1890, Virginia Military Institute Archives.

[293] Reminiscences of Harry B. Lewis, dated May 22, 1940 File R-21, Leyburn Library, Special Collections, Washington and Lee University.

[294] Letter from George Washington Custis Lee to Scott Shipp, dated April 29, 1891, Virginia Military Institute Archives.

[295] Letter from George Washington Custis Lee to Scott Shipp, dated June 10, 1891, Virginia Military Institute Archives.

[296] Executive Meeting Minutes of the Jackson Memorial Association, June 15, 1891 Special Collections Department William R. Perkins Library, Duke University.

[297] Letter from J. K. Edmonson to F. W. M. Holliday, June 17, 1891, Special Collections Department William R. Perkins Library, Duke University.

[298] Lyle and Simpson. *The Architecture of Historic Lexington*. 107.

[299] Letter from George Washington Custis Lee to Scott Shipp, dated February 9, 1892, Virginia Military Institute Archives.

[300] Letter from George Washington Custis Lee to Scott Shipp, dated March 21, 1892, Virginia Military Institute Archives.

[301] Letter from George Washington Custis Lee to Scott Shipp, dated April 22, 1892, Virginia Military Institute Archives.

[302] Letter from George Washington Custis Lee to Scott Shipp, dated June 6, 1892, Virginia Military Institute Archives.

[303] Washington and Lee University Annual President's Report for the Session of 1891-1892, submitted by George Washington Custis Lee, dated June 13, 1892, Leyburn Library, Special Collections, Washington and Lee University.

[304] Ibid.

[305] Letter from George Washington Custis Lee to Mrs. Parke C. Bagby, January 8, 1893, Virginia Historical Society..

[306] Letter from Robert E. Lee, Jr. to R. W. Hunter, dated February 19, 1893 File 064 Driver Folder (folder #99) Leyburn Library, Special Collections, Washington and Lee University.

[307] Letter from George Washington Custis Lee to R. W. Hunter, dated February 20, 1893 File 064 Driver Folder (folder #99) Leyburn Library, Special Collections, Washington and Lee University.

[308] Letter from George Washington Custis Lee to Scott Shipp, dated March 22, 1893, Virginia Military Institute Archives.

[309] Crenshaw, 180.

[310] Letter from George Washington Custis Lee to James A. Harrison dated August 31, 1893 File 064 L, R. E. Lee Family Letters (folder #17) Leyburn Library, Special Collections, Washington and Lee University.

[311] Letter from Thomas E. Marshall, Jr. to Edmund R. Cocke, dated September 4, 1893, Leyburn Library, Special Collections, Washington and Lee University.

[312] Letter from George Washington Custis Lee to Scott Shipp, dated November 9, 1893, [Folder X] Virginia Military Institute Archives.

[313] Letter from George Washington Custis Lee to Scott Shipp, dated November 9, 1893, [Folder Y] Virginia Military Institute Archives.

[314] Letter from George Washington Custis Lee to Scott Shipp, dated November 14, 1893, [Folder Y] Virginia Military Institute Archives.

[315] Letter from George Washington Custis Lee to Thomas T. Munford, December 7, 1893, Special Collections Department William R. Perkins Library, Duke University.

[316] Reminiscences of A. Fred White, dated November 7, 1938 File D-2, Leyburn Library, Special Collections, Washington and Lee University.

[317] Letter from George Washington Custis Lee to Scott Shipp, dated November 2, 1894, [Folder Z] Virginia Military Institute Archives.

[318] Letter from George Washington Custis Lee to Scott Shipp, dated February 9, 1895, [Folder A] Virginia Military Institute Archives.

[319] Letter from George Washington Custis Lee to Scott Shipp, dated May 16, 1895, [Folder B] Virginia Military Institute Archives.

[320] Letter from George Washington Custis Lee to Scott Shipp, dated May 18, 1895, [Folder B] Virginia Military Institute Archives.

[321] Letter from George Washington Custis Lee to Norvell Caskie Jones, dated August 20, 1895, [142 G.W.C.Lee papers, f.2] Leyburn Library, Special Collections, Washington and Lee University.

[322] Letter from George Washington Custis Lee to Bradley T. Johnson, dated September 20, 1895, Special Collections Department William R. Perkins Library, Duke University.

[323] Letter from George Washington Custis Lee to the Board of Trustees of Washington and Lee Univeristy, dated May 8, 1896, Leyburn Library, Special Collections, Washington and Lee University.

[324] Letter fromGeorge Washington Custis Lee to Scott Shipp dated July 27, 1896 [Folder C] Virginia Military Institute Archives.

[325] Reminiscences of Leslie L Campbell, dated 1896, File R-10, Leyburn Library, Special Collections, Washington and Lee University.

[326] Letter from George Washington Custis Lee to the Board of Trustees of Washington and Lee Unoversity, dated December 29, 1896, Leyburn Library, Special Collections, Washington and Lee University.

Chapter Five

Final Serenity

$\mathcal{E}$ ven though the Board of Trustees accepted Custis Lee resignation in December 1896, it was not effective until July 1,
1897. Only one member of the board voted against accepting his
resignation: Judge Edmondson. The letter from the Board of
Trustees accepting Lee's resignation was issued January 18, 1897:

> The Faculty of Washington and Lee University desire
> to express their deep regret that you have felt it necessary
> to resign the office of President of this University to take
> effect at the close of the present session. In twenty-six
> years of service as President you have drawn every
> member of the Faculty very close to you in friendship and
> admiration. Endowed most liberally by nature, by educa-
> tion, by public service in peace and war, and by extensive
> acquaintance with public men, you were eminently fitted
> for the honorable office left vacant by the death of your
> venerated father, and to which you were called by the
> unanimous vote of the Board of Trustees and welcomed
> by an admiring Faculty. In your long service you have

seen nearly all of your first Faculty pass away, some to other spheres of usefulness and honor and some to their final reward. Only two remain to attest with strongest feelings of friendship the many noble qualities of head and heart which have marked your public career. In these passing years you have seen many new and younger men added as members of your Faculty, and all unite in bearing witness to your uniform kindness and courtesy in all your intercourse with them.

While it is sad to realize that continued ill health has constrained you to give up the active duties of President, it is gratifying to know that as President Emeritus we may hope for your continued presence with us, and your counsel in the affairs of the University.

With sentiments of kindly interest in your comfort and happiness we are your friends and obedient servants The Faculty of Washington and Lee University.[1]

Lee acknowledged the above letter on February 1, 1897:

Your letter of the 18th ult. was duly received and gratefully appreciated.

It is just twenty-six years today, I think, since I entered upon my duties as President of this venerable institution of learning; and although I believe at the time, and have never since had reason to change the belief, that I was unfitted for the office for want of personal qualifications and previous training, I nevertheless undertook its duties, relying upon the kind assistance and forbearance of the Faculty, which have always been fully extended to me.

The severance of my official connection with W. & L. University was a hard step for me to take, but I thought it best to take advantage of the opportunity offered by the meeting of the Board of Trustees, the last of last year.

With every good wish for the Faculty, individually and collectively, I remain, Very sincerely Your friend and svt.[2]

But the matter of who would replace Lee was the paramount question in the minds of the Board of Trustees. Various professional people suggested several names but a final list of four were considered. Professor James A. Harrison of the University of Virginia, formerly a faculty member at Washington and Lee University, suggested Thomas Woodrow Wilson, a professor at Princeton University and a native of Staunton, Virginia and a Presbyterian.[3] Wilson was a brilliant writer and scholar, but the Trustees wanted to weigh all of their options.

The noted novelist and alumnus of Washington and Lee University, Thomas Nelson Page, suggested Colonel Thomas H. Carter, whose best qualification seemed to be his family connection to the Lees; he was the first cousin to Robert E. Lee's mother. The next gentleman to be considered was Colonel Thomas M. Jones, a graduate of the United States Military Academy whose experience as a military officer was concentrated mostly in the west teaching Native Americans. The ambitious Henry E. Shepherd of the College of Charleston was considered, due to the numerous recommendations given on his behalf.[4]

Trustee Clement D. Fishburne of Charlottesville offered the name of Professor William M. Thornton from the University of Virginia, but it was pointed out to Fishburne that Thornton's tenure at the University of Virginia was colored by criticism.

Finally, the name of William Lyne Wilson was proposed. Wilson was nationally known, due to his six-year term as a Congressman and his appointment as Postmaster General in the cabinet of President Stephen Grover Cleveland, 1895-1897. As a native Virginian [West Virginia], he rode with Major Generals Turner Ashby and James Ewell Brown Stuart and had the opportunity to be present when General Robert E. Lee surrendered at Appomattox. After the war, he returned to Columbian College, [George Washington University] where taught languages and studied law.

In 1871, he started his law practice in Charles Town, West Virginia. He served a short term as President of West Virginia University. It should be noted that as early the spring of 1896, Trustee Thomas D. Ranson inquired with Wilson if he would be open to a professorship at the Washington and Lee Law School. Their communication continued through January, 1897. By February 3, Wilson told his friend, Harry St. George Tucker, member of Congress and a trustee of the university, that he would accept the Presidency of Washington and Lee University if offered. The Trustees at last found their replacement for General Lee.[5] Void of any dissenting votes, William Lyne Wilson was elected President of Washington and Lee University on February 11, 1897. Tucker notified Wilson of the decision immediately.[6]

Wilson quickly moved into the transition period by visiting General Custis Lee on March 10, 1897. Wilson wrote in his diary about his visit to the President's House:

...Today at noon I called at Gen. Lee's, and was soon shown into the darkened bedroom where he lay. He told me his decision was irrevocable to vacate the house by July 1, spoke most despondingly of his health and even intimated that his physical ailments were so great that he would welcome a release by death. Among other things he said that he felt it necessary to leave Lexington for a while to escape the importunities and requests for money, which he was no longer able to respond to. We chatted pleasantly for half an hour—longer that I should have remained, if he had not kept up the conversation, when Miss Mildred came up and by Gen'l L's request showed me all over the house. I have seen a house more complete and substantial in its appointments, and conveniences all in perfect condition from attic to cellars, from parlor to stables, showing the sciences and skill of a great engineer. Miss M. is bright, and unusually clean, but I felt a pang in anticipating the occupancy of a house, endeared to her by so many sacred memories of parents, and now darkened by the ill health and despondency of her brother.[7]

Wilson departed Lexington with one major concern: the overwhelming spirit of "Lee worship." He thought it was evident in the tone and mood of not only the university population, but also in the townspeople. It was not far from the truth in believing this assumption. After all, he noted, the Board of Trustees offered Lee life right to the President's House and an annual salary of $2,000.00. Like his mother, Custis Lee refused such a proposal for the same reason: the house should be the residence of the next president. As far as the annual salary, Lee's refusal was more pragmatic. He knew all to well that the university needed all of its financial resources for the functioning of the facility.

Yet, the Board of Trustees wanted to thank him for his years of service in some manner in which he would accept. For the first time in the history of the university, the trustees bestowed the title of "President Emeritus" on him.[8] Lee accepted the new position with pleasure. Unlike past presidents of the university who departed under some cloud of discontent or alacrity, Lee perpetuated an amiable association with Washington and Lee University until his death.

At the board meeting of February 11 when the Trustees elected William Lyne Wilson, Lee's successor, they read Lee's letter in reference to their recent offers to him. Lee dictated the letter to Thomas E. Marshall, Jr., his private secretary:

> The President of this institution (G. W. C. Lee) who is not well enough to write, desires me to acknowledge the receipt of your kind answer to his application for relief for his official duties, and to thank you very sincerely for the generous provision you have been good enough to make for his comfort. He accepts with gratitude the office of Emeritus President of Washington and Lee University; but is unwilling to take any salary for the honorary position, and will try to make other arrangements.
>
> With regard to the house he respectfully suggests that as in the natural course of events he will have to give it up before very long it will probably be better to vacate it as soon as it may be needed, and when he can attend to the disposal of his personal effects.
>
> He submits this brief communication now in order that you may be able to make your arrangements for his successor without embarrassment on his account.
>
> With General Lee's best wishes for the Board of Trustees, individually and collectively...[9]

After the board received his last letter, a committee consisting of Trustees Edmondson, Preston and Ranson conferred with Lee verbally and insisted that he retain the house and the two thousand dollar stipend. In the end, Lee agreed to retain the salary of two thousand dollars per annum only.

Until he formally retired from the presidency, Lee remained relatively removed from society. His correspondence was conducted via a private secretary, Thomas E. Marshall, Jr. Two of his last notes as president was written to Captain H. E. Hyatt adjutant of the Virginia Military Institute: "The President of this institution (G. W. C. Lee) desires me to acknowledge the receipt of your communication of the 26th inst. and to thank General Shipp for the honor conferred in naming the Camp for him." [10] Then to his old friend, General Scott Shipp of the Virginia Military Institute: "Genl. G. W. C. Lee, who is not well, desires me to acknowledge with thanks the receipt of your kind invitation for Wednesday evening, and to express his regrets that he cannot take advantage of it on account of the state of his health."[11]

He did attend the last graduation as President of the University, as well as the end of year graduation activities. The remainder of the time he and Mildred sorted collections of items which had accumulated during the past thirty years in the residence. As written in the book, *The Lee Girls,* the author Mary P. Coulling stated, "Most trying of all was parting with intimate family items. Custis had sometimes teased her about her reluctance to give away household reminders that had belonged to their parents and grandparents. "It's as hard to get blood out of a beet, he used to say, "as to get anything out of Mildred." Now, however, she had no choice. She and Custis managed to distribute "nearly everything...in the way of mementos or relics."

Prior to his departure, Custis presented the University with many items of special interest to them. He presented over five hundred books to the library and purchased a grand piano. He established a scholarship fund and placed on permanent loan the beautiful family portraits from Mount Vernon of Generals Washington and Lafayette, painted from life by preeminent eighteenth century American artist Charles Willson Peale.

Mildred departed Lexington on July 29, 1897, while Custis lingered a few more days, finally departing on August 1, 1897 for Burke in Fairfax County, Virginia. Before Custis arrived at Ravensworth, Mildred had already departed for an extended tour of Europe meeting with Mary Custis Lee in France. Ultimately, Mildred settled with Rob at Romancoke for most of the remaining years of her life.[12]

Custis and Mildred were invited by Rooney's widow, Mrs. Mary Tabb Bolling Lee to make their permanent home at Ravensworth, the Fitzhugh family estate near Burke, Virginia.

The old familiar sight of the rambling oak park at the approach to the Ravensworth estate was an agreeable respite for Lee after his long years in Lexington. The huge wooden framed structure had massive pillars that was accentuated by a two-story veranda which extended the length of the house. Near the lower veranda was a impressive bay window looking over the wide expansive lawn. The abundance of flowers and blooming shrubs decorated the exterior of the mansion and provided an additional welcome in the summer.

Custis always felt at home here since he was a child. The structure was built in 1800 by William Fitzhugh on his 22,000 acres of land he inherited from his paternal great-grandfather. The mansion was akin to both the Fitzhugh and Lee families and finally the Custis family when William Fitzhugh's daughter Mary Lee Fitzhugh married George Washington Parke Custis in 1804.[13] The estate came full circle with the union of MaryAnna Randolph Custis and Robert Edward Lee in 1831. With Arlington lost forever, there was no other place that Custis wished to live out his days.

After the death of his brother Rooney, Tabb, as the family referred to Rooney's wife, invited her sister Miss Melville Bolling to reside with her at Ravensworth along with her two sons, Robert E. Lee III and George Bolling Lee. At the time of Custis' arrival, Tabb's younger son George Bolling Lee was living in New York City where he was a practicing gynecologist.

Ravensworth, Burke, Virginia
Virginia Historical Society

George Washington Custis Lee, 1912
Men of Mark Publishers

The mansion was built to accommodate many people. The rooms measured twenty-seven feet square and the walls were hung with the most impressive collection of early American portraits.

Custis was the very acquainted with the apartment he was to occupy within the house. From Lexington he brought his personal furniture, his presidential desk once housed in his office at Washington and Lee University and architectural or engineering drawing desk. A veracious reader, he brought many volumes of personal interest especially books on engineering and architecture. Custis slowly settled into his new home.

By this time it was late summer and the President emeritus received an invitation to attend the inauguration of William Lyne Wilson on September 15, 1897 at Washington and Lee University.[14] Lee declined the invitation due to his ill health.

Nevertheless, Wilson's induction as the new president was far more elaborate than the ceremonies for George Washington Custis Lee more than twenty-six year earlier. The ceremony in the Lee Chapel continued for more than three hours followed by a lavish banquet serving over three hundred and fifty people and then a formal evening reception. Many prominent people attended the festivities or sent congratulatory telegrams and letters.[15] For all of this pomp and magnificence, Wilson's tenure ended on October 17, 1900 with his death after seven months of illness.[16]

Custis was relieved not to be part of the Lexington social circle any longer. He was happy to be void of any responsibility but then he was elected to the Board of Trustees of Washington and Lee University. He promptly declined the honor, stating as always his health and the distance in which he would need to travel. His severe modesty prompted him to add that he had nothing to offer as a trustee.

Through the winter months, Lee communicated with John L. Campbell, Treasurer of Washington and Lee University, in reference to continuing university business:

> I have just received (2 P.M.) the enclosed letter from the Cashr. Bk. of Rockbridge, and the accompanying letter from W. H. L. Sellers to which reference is made. I

can not well send to the nearest telegraph office (some four miles from here) this afternoon; especially, as I do not see that there is anything to be gained by so doing. I venture therefore to request you to attend to this matter for me, that next time you go to the Bank. I am willing to endorse a new note for Mr. Sellers, if necessary, though is is about time for me to be relieved for matters of this kind. Manage the affair as you would if it were your own, and I shall be perfectly satisfied.

I trust that you, and the other members of your household, are well and comfortable, this winter—as comfortable as possible in the blizzard that we are now having here—and with every good wish for you and yours, I remain...[17]

Three days later Lee wrote again to Campbell on the same subject:

I send you another communication for the Bank of Rockbridge-just received (2 P.M.).

I am afraid that this matter of mine with the Bank will give you some trouble if so, please put it in the hands of a lawyer—on my account, of course. Last night, the self-registering thermometer her went down to 2 degrees Fah.; I suppose that you had something like it in Lexington.

With best wishes for yourself and household, I remain...[18]

The following week Lee wrote again to Campbell. This letter reflects business concerns at first and the lonely and isolated location of Ravensworth:

Your letter of the 7th inst. reached me on the afternoon of the 9th. I received at the same time a letter from Mr. Sellers (of the 4th inst.) enclosing the two Notes, which I endorsed and mailed to Mr McElevee yesterday. I am very much obliged to you for attending to the matter for me; I did not have Mr. Seller's address, and did not know what was best to be done.

I enclose check for $100.00 to take up the note of a student, whose name I have forgotten. [J. F. Rice] I endorsed his note (as I recollect) to enable him to be examined for his Degree, or Diploma of some kind. If you will let me know what the interest amounts to, I will send [a] check for the amount. I had forgotten all about this matter until Judge McLaughlin called attention to the note at one of the last meetings of the Ex. Committee that I attended.

It is pleasant to know that Mrs. Campbell is steadily regaining her strength; and I sincerely hope that she may be quite strong again in good time. I fear the skating is now over for the present for your boy.

My sister-in-law is in Richmond, but is expected home to-morrow. Her son, Rob, started for New Orleans yesterday in company with my sister Mildred. The later will probably stay there until the Spring; the former will only remain for ten days or two weeks.

I had heard of "Tom Leavell's" engagement, and wish him all the happiness possible in his marriage.

I see but few people here—especially at this time of year—and don't hear any news. My brother Bob has gone back to his place in King William Co., near West Point, which he thinks he prefers to Washington City.

With kind regards to all my friends in Lexington, and especially to the members of your household, I remain...[19]

Continuing his correspondence with Campbell, Lee wrote two more letters to him through early spring:

I enclose you an order for a register book, which is probably one of the set referred to in he accompanying letter. I wish to turn over the set of books in question to W. & L. U., unless the university is to have a set of its own; in which case an additional set may be in the way. When I hear from you on the subject, I will write to the

Supt. of Documents on the subject.

Your letter returning my check for $100.00 was duly received; I am somewhat better off in funds than I had supposed.[20]

Lee wrote to thank Senator J. W. Daniel in Washington, D. C. for being instrumental on his behalf toward obtaining the series of volumes entitled *Messages and Papers of the Presidents, 1789-1897*.

I have been notified by the Supt. of Documents, Govt. Printing Office, that I have been designated by you to receive a compilation entitled "Messages and Papers of the Presidents, 1789-1897"; and I have received the first three volumes of this valuable work.

Please accept my best thanks for your kind remembrance of me, and believe me to remain, with every good wish for your happiness.[21]

About two weeks later, Lee informed Campbell about this acquisition, yet on a more personal note, there is a hint of loneliness which prevails at the end of his note:

Your letter of the 26th ult., with enclosures, duly received. I shall be very glad for you to take my set of the "Messages and Papers of the Presidents, 1789-1897," for the working library of W. & L. U. as suggested.

If you can not otherwise arrange with the P. O., I can sign a general order for the purpose.

My nephew Rob has returned from New Orleans very much pleased with his visit; my sister Mildred will remain there some time longer-until the weather becomes too warm for her, I suppose.

My nephew is in Washington City for the day, as usual; and his mother is away on a visit. There is therefore no one here to join me in kind regards to your household and self.[22]

His nephew, George Bolling Lee recalled that his uncle led a quiet life somewhat secluded with comparatively few visitors to Ravensworth. Although he did not entertain the stream of visitors which occupied a great deal of his life in Lexington, he did receive many old friends and former colleagues from the Virginian Military Institute as well as Washington and Lee University.

He cultivated a close friendship with one of his Burke Station neighbors, Captain [actually Lieutenant from the United States-Mexican War] Upton H. Herbert of Bleak House Plantation, who lived about three miles from Ravensworth. Herbert was the first resident superintendent from 1859-1869 of Mount Vernon, the home of George Washington. His wife, the former Sarah Tracy of Troy, New York was employed as secretary to Ann Pamela Cunningham, the founder and first Regent of the Mount Vernon Ladies' Association. Miss Tracy and Herbert met during their tenure at Mount Vernon. [23] Mrs. Sarah Tracy Herbert died the year that Custis Lee retired to Ravensworth, while Herbert succumbed nine years later in 1906.

Custis Lee's daily routine was to rise at his usual hour, have breakfast, then stroll through the gardens and visit the stables and cow barn before retiring to the house. In the afternoon, he would read scientific and engineering books during inclement weather and in the fair weather, his afternoons were frequently spent horseback riding about the nearby vicinity, visiting only "Captain" Herbert.

He was very interested in maintaining the cisterns and sewers as well as other outer buildings. He spent many hours before his drafting table designing the needed dependencies which remained functional long after his death. His other drawings included stables, a dairy and a belfry for the Good Shepherd Episcopal Church where his nephew, Robert E. Lee III was superintendent of the Sunday School.[24]

Many afternoons were occupied by the visit of family friends and his siblings. Yet, many more afternoons he spent alone in the mansion.

Lee's nephew noted that his uncle departed Ravensworth monthly, leaving the Burke's Station at 11:00 A.M. and traveling into Washington to have his hair and beard trimmed. On these visits to the city, he would take on the role of president emeritus to browse the bookstores for any volumes he thought would be of interest or use to the Washington and Lee University Library. After his shopping excursion and visits with friends in their homes or at the Willard Hotel, he would return on the afternoon train to Burke's Station by 5:30 P.M.[25]

Through his position as president emeritus to Washington and Lee University, he continued to preserve a correspondence with John Campbell for many years after his retirement pertaining to topics of interest to the University:

> I believe you are not at home, but I wish to let some one in the office know that I have sent to W. & L. U. a box of books for the library, containing Confederate War history (12 vols.), and three or four other books that may be of some use to somebody.
>
> Hoping that Mrs. Campbell and yourself may return home in fine health, I remain Very sincerely yours..[26]

Shortly after this note was written to Campbell, Custis took his only extended absence from Ravensworth. He decided to visit Rob at his home "Romancoke", near West Point in King William County, Virginia. He departed from Burke's Station to Richmond where he stayed overnight in order to visit his old medical advisor and friend, Dr. Hunter H. McGuire. As he was leaving Dr. McGuire's office, by chance he met Mr. Dold of Lexington. Dold related the encounter with Lee to James L. Howe in a letter during the summer of 1941,

> Not a great time before General Custis death, [actually fourteen years would pass] I was en route from New York to Charlottesville, and stopped over in Richmond. Just outside of Dr. Hunter McGuire's office I chanced to meet General Lee and had a brief conversation with him, in the course of which he made a remark that fixed itself in my memory. It was to the effect that, rheumatoid affections had ever been a bete noire [a black beast, a person or object of fear] in the history of the Lee family. We parted gravely, and I never saw him again. He seemed to

lack entirely that keen sense of humor that characterized his father...[27]

From Richmond, Custis traveled onto "Romancoke" for a two-week visit with his brother, Rob and his family. In the recent book, *The Robert E. Lee Family Cooking and Housekeeping Book* by Anne Carter Ely Zimmer, great-granddaughter of Robert E. Lee, the author recalled her aunt remembering that Uncle Custis was "a whimsical, gentle man" who spent most of his time during visits playing with she and her sister. Mrs. Zimmer went onto state, "When the little girls got into mischief, he used to say, mock solemnly, "they *told* me to do it," to divert their punishment. The author also noted that "Uncle Custis" financed an addition at Romancoke house in order that his two nieces could have rooms of their own.[28] After his fortnight with Rob's family, he returned to Ravensworth and did not travel far beyond the Washington, D. C.-Burke area.

Custis continued his correspondence with many people especially John Campbell and his brother Rob. Shortly after the new year, Custis wrote to his brother:

> Dear Colonel:—Yours of the 31st came yesterday. I am glad that Anne [his neice] is better and hope that she will soon be quite herself again.
>
> Our self-registering thermometer, here, marked 0 (Fah.) last Saturday night; that was the lowest we have had. We have had two slight falls of snow, of about 2 inches each; and the ground is still well covered. Tabb's force began to cut ice on the accotine, near Andrew's house, on New Year's Day, and continue the cutting Tuesday; yesterday (Wednesday), they began hauling the ice to the ice-house, and are doing the same to-day. The ice is reported to be 6 in. thick, including some two inches of snow-ice. The pond does not hold water.
>
> With regard to the "Mount Vernon relics": When Presdt. Johnson ordered them returned to our Mother, Congress passed a joint resolution that they should not go back to the hands of Rebels, &c. I think there was a list of

them made and reported at that time. Some years after that, I gave my consent to the Mt. Vernon Regents to take the relics to Mt. Vernon if they could get the consent of the U.S. Govt. to do so. As the relics have not been taken to Mt. Vernon. I presume the consent of the Govt. could not be obtained. Some years after that (probably the last time our sister Mary was in this country), to stop her incessant nagging on the subject, I told her that she might have the Relics if she could get them, and gave her the necessary papers to that end—power of atty. &c. I believe she worked at the matter for two winters in Washington City without any result so far as I could learn. If the agitation of this matter is likely to hurt out claim for wood taken form Ravensworth, I think that is had better be let alone—for the present at least.

I have a letter from Mary of the 19th ult. written at Nice; it is principally on the subject of the war in South Africa. She is on the side of the Boars, and can't understand how any one in this country—especially in the South—can be otherwise. She sends some newspaper clippings, not complete, with the request that they be sent to you. I send them herewith as I received them. She reports herself pretty well, with the exception of occasional attacks of rheumatism; and seems at a loss about Mildred's condition, as the latter lives on the plan that whatever is agreeable to her is good for her health. I have a postal card from Mildred, written on Christmas Day at Rome. There is nothing in it but the good wishes of the season...I gave your messages to Miss Mebs [Melville Bolling] and Billerophan; Tabb is away.[29]

Several days later Lee wrote to his cousin Mrs. P. T. [Jean] Yeatman with a similar theme as the letter to his brother, Rob:

Your letter of the 11th inst. was duly received last week; thanks for the name of the birthplace of Hon. Charles Lee, which I have already sent to Mr. Bok, and for which he will doubtless be duly grateful.

If the weather of yesterday and to-day continue, you will not care to go further South; but there are other places in Florida besides Jacksonville, though they are all probably full of Yankees in the winter; there are also places in North and South Carolina, and Georgia.

I have a letter from Mary under date of 19th Dec., Nice, and one from Mildred of the 25th Dec., Rome. They do not speak of coming home.

Tabb has been confined to her room for more than a week with a bad cold, and "Robbie" is enjoying another carbuncle, and a sty on one of his eyes; Miss Mebs and I are having our usual rheumatic troubles. I hope to get to town, someday this week; but the roads are bad, though the skies are bright. The log (bridge) over the accotine is gone; it broke down, some time ago, under "Robbie" weight.

With love to Miss Minnie, and best wishes for you both, I remain...[30]

The winter quickly became spring. By mid-May, Lee received a letter from Mr. John Campbell in regards to Lee family portraits and a few personal comments:

I enclose a letter from Mr. W. W. Elsworth, which will explain itself. After consulting with Mr. Wilson [William Lyne, Lee's successor] I have given him permission to use the photograph of the Peale portrait of Washington; and have told him that I would write to you with regard to the others. If you have no objection to granting his request please let me know and I will inform Mr. Ellsworth and save you further trouble in the matter.

Mr. Herbert Welsh of Philadelphia has been with us for several days, and has cleaned and varnished the portraits of Washington and Lafayette, very much improving their appearance and bringing out many points which were before obscure; among other things, the name and date of the Lafayette portrait- (C. W. Peale Pinx. 1779).

I hope that your health is good; and I wish very much that you would pay as a visit to "Stono" whenever it may suit your convenience. Mrs. Campbell had a letter from Miss Mildred a few days ago promising that she would visit us sometime this summer. I am glad to say that Mrs. Campbell's health is better than it has been for years, and she is enjoying her life among the flowers and plants more than ever. Mr. Wilson returned early in May, somewhat improved in health, but his cough still troubles him a good deal. You will be sorry to learn that Mrs. Harry Tucker is in a very critical condition of health from an attack of appendicitis. The surgeons performed an operation yesterday, from which she has not yet satisfactorily rallied.

With kind regards and best wishes for your health and happiness, I am, as ever...[31]

A few days later Lee answered Campbell's letter:

I have just received your letter of the 24th inst. with enclosure, and have written to Mr. Ellsworth that his welcome to photographs of my pictures in Lexington, and that Mr. M. Miley can probably furnish them. I have no objection to anyone having copies of the pictures, except for the trouble it may give my friends in Lexington; I believe Mr. Miley has photographed most of them. I am glad that the portraits of Washington and Lafayette are so much improved by varnishing, &c. and that the name of "C. W. Peale" has been found on that of Lafayette; for, it has been disputed that it was painted by Peale.

I am more than glad to know that Mrs. Campbell's health is so good, and sincerely hope that it very never be worse, as for mine I am very lame and painful just now, but hope for improvement as the weather becomes more settled.

I was greatly distressed to see in the Washington Post of yesterday a notice of the death of Mrs. Harry Tucker; I had heard of her illness, but hoped to the last that she would recover. I have written to Harry Tucker, and have informed my sister Mildred of his wife's death and burial.

I do not know when the originals of the letters mentioned by Mr. Ellsworth can be found, even of they are in existence—which latter is doubtful.

Best thanks for your kind invitation to "Stono"; I am hardly in a condition to travel just now, but hope to get to Lexington some of these days. I must thank you also for the copy of the Law Catalogue and pictures, and for other favors that I have never acknowledged. With every good wish for yourself and household, I remain...[32]

Lee remained as active as he was physically able to be. In the November 30, 1900 issue of the Alexandria Gazette, the Treasurer of the Reunion [Confederate] Finance Committee published the names and donation of each person registered by the district in which they presently lived. The first name on the list under the Falls Church District was "Gen. G.W.C. Lee............10.00" a considerable amount of money at the time.

Shortly after the new year, Lee received a volume and letter of inquiry from Colonel Joseph Rubinfine of West Palm Beach, Florida. Rubinfine was seeking Lee's advice and comments on his book pertaining to the life of Robert E. Lee. Lee was prompt in responding to Rubinfine:

I received last week, your letter of the 31st ult. with enclosure. I am a very poor genealogist but I think that there is some error in your genealogy, as given in the first chapter of your Life of my father.Perhaps I am in error myself, and so not understand your narrative.

In the work entitled "Lee of Virginia" by Dr. Edmund J. Lee, the generations are given thus (the numbers refer to the generations):—

"Robert Edward 6, the fourth son of Henry Lee 5, (Henry 4, Henry 3, Richard 2, Richard 1) and Anne Hill Carter, his second wife, was born at Stratford, Westmoreland County, the 19th Jany., 1807, and died at his home in Lexington, the 12th Oct. 1870."

If you have not a copy of "Lee of Virginia," I shall be glad to send you one. It contains about all that is known of the genealogies of the Lee's of Maryland and Virginia, and tells also about other families.

As I understand my father's account of his family history, as given in the Memoirs of his father (Light-Horse Harry):-

We have Richard 1, the immigrant; his son, Richard 2, who married Miss Corbyn; the five sons of Richard 2 were—Richard 3, Philip. Francis, <u>Thomas</u> and <u>Henry</u>. <u>Henry Lee</u> of Leesylvania married <u>Lucy Grymes</u>, and their eldest son was <u>Henry</u> (Light-Horse Harry) <u>Lee</u>. The latter married (first) Matilda, daughter of <u>Philip Ludwell</u> and Elizabeth (Steptoe) Lee. This Philip Ludwell was, I believe, the eldest son of <u>Thomas</u>, mentioned above as the fourth son of Richard 2; but in all this I may be mistaken. I fear that can not furnish any facts connected with Genl. Lee's services in the Mexican War besides those which may be found in the pages of the several histories of that war. I was a school boy at the time and did not pay much attention to history I read, some years ago, Wilcox's History of the Mexican War; but do not recollect that it contained a great deal about my father's services. I left it with my other books in the library of W. & L. University, Lexington, Va. Genl. Long, in his "Memoir of R. E. Lee," had a good deal to say about my father's services in Mexico; you have doubtless seen this book. I had Genl. Scott's book. but left it in Lexington also, I think. I brought no books away with me, excepting a few works of general reference.

With best wishes for your health and happiness, I remain...[33]

Through the remaining years of his life, Lee kept up his steady correspondence with John L. Campbell of Washington and Lee University:

I have received the photograph that you have been kind enough to send me, and thank you for it very much. Bronze does not seem to make as good a picture, in a photography, as stone; I suppose that it is rather dark in color for the purpose.

My sister in law and her son, Rob, would I am sure, have kind messages for the members of your household, if they knew of this writing; her other son, Bo, is in New York City, as an M. D. as a general rule, Rob goes to Washington City every day except Sunday; and his Mother goes very often. With kindest regards to Mrs. Campbell, John Lyle, and other members of the family, I remain...[34]

In the Spring of 1902, President Emeritus Lee received a request for a letter of recommendation from a former student, Johnson Lee Blankson. In the first of two letters on this subject, Lee requests from Campbell any information available on the graduate:

I enclose a letter from an old student, whom I do not recollect. If you will send me, with the return of his letter, his official record, and anything you may be able to say in his favor, I will send him a testimonial.

With kind regards to all the members of your household, I remain...[25]

In this second letter, Lee informs Campbell that he has fulfilled the alumnus' request:

Your letter of the 23rd inst., enclosing memorandum for testimonial for Mr. Blankson, reached me yesterday evening. I have written the testimonial, and will forward it by the first mail.

I thank you very much for your kind invitation to Stono, and will not forget it when able to take the journey to Lexington. I should like, more than I can tell, to see all my friends there again; and hope to do so, some of these days.

I am glad to have such good accounts of all the members of your household; but hope that John may not equal my nephew in avoirdupois, as the latter must weigh 300 lbs. or more, I should think. This is rather too much weight for a comparatively young man. He is not here today; but he and his mother would, I am sure, have kind messages for Stono, if they knew of my writing.[36]

By mid-summer Lee continued exercising his role as president emeritus by reading and offering his opinion on the book, *The Confessions*: by Jean-Jacques Rousseau. The book was published posthumously in 1781 depicting the author's licentious and depraved life through the age of fifty-three. Among his debaucheries was the disposal of his five children born to the same woman, Therese Le Vasseur at a Foundling Hospital, stating, "This arrangement seemed so good and sensible and right to me that if I did not boast of it openly it was solely out of regard for their mother."[37]
President emeritus Lee was right in his appraisal of this book:

I have received the copy of the Calyx [the Washington and Lee University yearbook] for 1902, and thank you for it very much.

Not long ago, I subscribed for a limited edition of Rousseau's Confessions without knowing what an unexpurgated edition might amount to; in fact, I knew but little about the Confessions except the name. The work is not decent in places; and leaving the indecency out of the question, I do not consider it worth reading, taken as a whole. I had intended sending the book to the Library of W. & L. U.; but have hesitated between doing so and destroying the book (an expensive one).

It might answer for the part of the Library that is not circulating; but it is not fit for young people to read possibly not fit for anybody. If, after all this, you care to have the book for the Library, I will sent it to you— I could not send it to the Librarian.

With kind regards to all the members of your household, I remain...[38]

Lee's life maintained its usual physical routine and rounds of letter writing. Some months after his birthday in 1903, he finally was able to write to his cousin Jean Lloyd Yeatman in Alexandria, Virginia:

> The "Confederate Cup," that you and Miss Minnie were good enough to send me for my birthday gift, arrived the last of last week. It is very pretty, and I am very grateful for your kindness. You sent me (Miss Minnie and yourself, each) a birthday gift, some time ago, which I have not forgotten.
> We are all, here, much as usual, except myself, who am suffering from an attack of influenza, now generally termed the Grip; it is bad enough by any name. I trust you and my cousin Minnie are well, and have been enjoying the pleasant Autumn weather.
> I have not heard anything of Mary or Mildred lately.[39]

A few months later, in another letter to John L. Campbell, Lee informs him of his address change and an error in the publication *Dixieland* that mentions the Lee family's genealogy.

> The copy of "Dixieland" that you have been good enough to send me was duly received last week; and I thank you for it.
> The pictures are generally good, and altogether it seems to be a creditable production. I notice on page 25, middle column near the top, an error in genealogy. It should be, third line from top:- The son of her first marriage, John Parke Custis, married Eleanor Calvert; the only son of this marriage, G. W. P. Custis, married Mary Lee Fitzhugh; and their daughter, Mary Custis, was married to Robert E. Lee—
> Since my last letter to you the name of my Post office has been changed from "Burke's Station" to "Burke"; the

Ry. Station and Express Office retains the old name,
"Burke's Station."

With kind regards and good wishes for all the
members of your household, I remain...[40]

In the years since the War between the States, there had been
much controversy pertaining to the Arlington artifacts which were
pilfered from the property during the Federal army's occupation of
the house and grounds. On March 10, 1904, the *Richmond-Times
Dispatch* published an interview with Custis Lee in reference to the
Lee-Washington Bible and later the same article was published in
the *Philadelphia Bulletin*. Apparently, the reporter of the article
traveled to Ravensworth to interview Lee as the rightful owner of
the Bible only after the subsequent efforts of his sister Mary Custis
Lee to actively pursue the recovery of Bible was initiated. The
newspaper correspondent described the Ravensworth estate as
being, "In a secluded spot among the trees which cover the broad
lawns surrounding the house is the family burying ground of the
Fitzhughs...The interior of the house follows the colonial style of
the exterior, with its large rooms and lofty ceilings and broad hall-
ways, extending from the front to the rear door. The middle part is
taken up mostly by the dining-room, a spacious apartment with a
huge open fire-place and a large old-fashioned side-board, on which
reposes the silver plate of the Fitzhughs. On the walls are the
portraits of the Lees and the Custises and the Fitzhughs, nearly all
painted by famous artists, and constituting the most prized of the
family possessions."[41]

Through a series of newspaper articles published on the subject,
a public outcry arose urging George W. Kendrick, Jr. of
Philadelphia, the current possessor of the Lee family Bible to relin-
quish the artifact to the Lee family, but Kendrick preferred to give it
to some historical society for public display. Kendrick claimed that
he purchased the Bible in 1882 from a man named Stein whose
father unmistakably stole it from Arlington House after the Lees
had vacated the premises in 1861.

Custis Lee commented on Kendrick's position, as he sat in this
lovely dinning room half facing the blazing fireplace near the life-

size portrait of his famous father: "I shall make no formal request to
Mr. Kendrick for the Bible's return and shall for the present take no
legal action. I have decided to let Mr. Kendrick work out the matter
in his own mind and come to a decision as his conscience directs.
He knows my right to the book and I believe that he will ultimately
turn it over to me."[42]

The reporter observed that the room was decorated with many
portraits of Lee's relatives. As the interviewer started his inquiry,
the flickering embers gave a warm glow to the faces of Martha and
George Washington, as well as Lee's late brother, now deceased for
nearly thirteen years, William Henry Fitzhugh Lee. As to his
impressions of Lee himself, the correspondent described him in the
following manner:

> General Custis Lee is himself a worthy descendant of
> his ancestors. A brilliant soldier and a learned scholar, he
> combines the traits which have made the Lees so promi-
> nent in the affairs of the nation. Although seventy-two
> years old, he looks to be not a day over sixty, with his hair
> and closely cropped beard still retaining their brownish
> tinge. The erect military carriage developed in his youth at
> West Point has not left him, and the firm, assured poise of
> his well-shaped head, coupled with the steady glance of
> his eyes, betoken him a man accustomed to command.[43]

The reporter inquired as to why he thought the Lee family was
entitled to the return of the book, especially to Lee, himself: "I have
heard and read from the newspaper clippings sent to me that Mr.
Kendrick has declared that he has no way of telling whether one
descendant of Martha Custis is entitled to the Bible more than
another. It would take but a little investigation by him to clear this
question up in his mind."[44]

"Martha Custis had one son, John Custis, who became the
adopted son of General Washington. John Custis had a son, George
Washington Parke Custis, who was my mother's father. The Bible,
therefore came by direct descent to my mother.

There are three reasons for my claim to the book.

First, I am my mother's eldest son.

Secondly, I was appointed by the courts as executor of both my father's and my mother's estates.

Thirdly, my grandfather, George Washington Parke Custis, willed me Arlington house and all it contained."[45]

At this point in the interview Lee arose from his chair and left the room. He returned to the room in a few moments, at which time he produced a copy of his grandfather's will. He proceeded to read aloud the passages from the will which specifically related to his ownership of Arlington and the contents of the house. Aside from giving him clear title to the Arlington estate after the death of his mother, there was another paragraph which gave him clear title to the house's contents as well:

> Every article that I possess relating to Washington and that came from Mount Vernon is to remain with my daughter at Arlington House during her life, and at her death is to go to my eldest grandson, George Washington Custis Lee, and to descend from him entire and unchanged to my latest posterity.[46]

When he concluded reading the relevant passages, he said, "This will is the strongest proof that I have my title to the Bible. It seems to me that it would be grounds in itself for legal action, though the other two reasons for my claim to the Bible, aside from it, establish my right to it without a doubt.

I have thought several times since the discovery of the book that it is my duty as executor of my mother's estate to recover it, if not for my own sake, for that of my two sisters and my nephews, the sons of my dead brother. If I were sure that legal proceedings would recover it and would not be barred by the statue of limitations, I believe that I should place the matter in the hands of an attorney, but in the absence of such assurance, I have decided to leave the disposal of the Bible to Mr. Kendrick. I hear that he is giving the matter his careful deliberation, and I believe he will return the Bible to us of his own free will."[47]

The reporter questioned Lee as to the rumor that his mother had misplaced the Bible. But Lee unequivocally denied the suggestion. At this point in the interview, Lee described the events which lead to his family's departure from Arlington and their belief that their personal property would not be taken from the estate.

When my mother and my sisters left Arlington in April, 1861, it was in accordance with a request by the authorities at Washington, which gave no intimation that the place was to be confiscated. In fact, I do not think the Federal authorities themselves had this idea at that time.

My mother and sisters took nothing from the house but the paintings and the family plate. The paintings, some of which you see in this room, they took from the frames, leaving the latter hanging on the walls. All the servants were left at the house, just as though the family was going away on a trip. My mother believed that the war would still be averted and that they would soon return to our old home. The three women came here to Ravensworth, which was the home of her aunt, Mrs. William Henry Fitzhugh.

At this time my father was in Richmond and my brother and I were also not at Arlington. I was at Fort Washington, in the Engineer Corps of the United States Army, and, on the secession of Virginia, went at once to Washington and tendered my resignation. It was not accepted, however, and I was requested to finish some uncompleted work at Fort Washington before resigning. I acquiesced and returned to Fort Washington, stopping at Arlington on my way. My mother and sisters were still there.

A week later, however, when I stopped again, on my way to Washington, they had gone. The place was in good order, with no Union troops with miles of it, and I went to Washington where my resignation was at once accepted. The looting of our old home did not take place, as I understand it, until some time later, when the Northern troops took possession of it.

Another misapprehension in regard to the taking of the Washington and Custis heirlooms is that they were seized by Government authorities. The truth of the matter is that they were taken from the house by personal friends of our family in the army, who acted only in our interests. My father and my brothers and I had many intimate friends, some dating from West Point days, who, when our home was seized, realized the value to us of the Washington relics. They gathered then together and conveyed them to Washington for safe-keeping, fully intending, as I believe, to have them restored to us immediately at the settlement of the trouble between the North and South.

The Custis Bible was one of a number of Bibles in the house, and it was overlooked by them. It must have been picked up by a soldier, who saw the autographs in it and recognized its value.

At the close of the War the other relics, according to my recollection, were found to be in the Patent Office, whence they were later removed to the Smithsonian Institution. In President Johnson's administration a request was made to have them returned to us, and the President signed an order to that effect. Congress, however, forbade their removal from the Smithsonian Institution.

No further action was taken in the matter until President McKinley's second administration, when Senator Daniel, of Virginia, presented our claims to the relics, and they were returned to us. I gave them into the charge of my sister, Mary Lee, who still has most of them. Some she had donated to the Ladies of Mt. Vernon, among them the death bed of Washington.[48]

The interviewer asked him about Kendrick's determination that Fitzhugh Lee had the greatest claim to the Bible. Lee answered: "Fitzhugh Lee has no claim whatever to it. He is my cousin, a son of Sidney Smith Lee, who was a brother of my father. Neither he nor his wife was in anyway connected with Martha Custis. Sometime ago, I received a letter from a gentleman in Philadelphia, enclosing one from Fitzhugh Lee, in which he disclaimed all right to the Bible and expressed his desire that Mr. Kendrrick turn it over to me." Custis Lee added, "The old family Bible, which was so precious in my mother's eyes, is the only heirloom which is yet to be returned to us." The interviewer noted at this point in their conversation, Lee slipped "into a reverie, with his eyes fixed on the glowing embers in the fireplace, giving himself over for some moments to other memories of the troublous times of his early days."[49] This ended the interview with General G. W. C. Lee. Kendrick did not relenquish the Bible to Lee.

After traveling aboard for an extended period of time, Mildred Childe Lee returned to the United States. Her usual rounds of visits were comprised of spending the winters and springs with Rob at "Romancoke". In early December 1904, a column in the local newspaper entitled, "As Heard and Seen" written by August Henning noted in the section under the subtitle "Burke": "Mrs. W. H. F. Lee has gone to Richmond, and Miss Mildred Lee, who has been on a visit to her brother, Gen. G. W. C. Lee, at "Ravensworth," has gone to West Point [Virginia] to spend some time with Capt. R. E. Lee."[50]

Shortly after the new year, the Alexandria Gazette reported on January 20, 1905 in the column titled, "Local News Briefly Told" a one line paragraph, "Gen. G. W. C. Lee, we understand, is quite indisposed at "Ravensworth." Evidently, his old arthritis problems had flared up again during the cold of January. Nevertheless, he obviously recovered sufficiently enough to write a note to John L. Campbell:

> I acknowledge with thanks, the receipt of a copy of W. & L. U. catalogue for 1905; and am glad to note that it indicates prosperity, if appearances are not deceiving.
>
> I trust that all my friends are well and happy, especially the members of your household—and family in general. With kind regards to all, I remain...[51]

Within the next week, Mildred had departed her brother Robert's home for New Orleans to visit Mrs. William Preston Johnston. Mardi Gras was in full revelry on Shrove Tuesday, March

7 and Mildred loved every moment. She occupied herself visiting old friends, Confederate veterans and alumni from Washington and Lee University. Everyone enjoyed her company and were thrilled at the prospect that she may decide to live among them for the remainder of her life. But this was a short lived hope.

Suddenly, a few weeks later, Mrs. Johnston was concerned when she failed to join her for breakfast. When she knocked at Mildred's bedroom door, there was no response. Mrs. Johnston was shocked to find Mildred on the floor unconscious. Attempts to revive her were fruitless. Mildred Childe Lee died at nine in the morning on March 27, 1905 of an apparent massive cerebral hemorrhage. She was fifty-nine years old. Her funeral took place at the Robert E. Lee Memorial Episcopal Church a few days later.[52]

Mary Custis Lee was in Nice when she received notice of her sister's death. She remained abroad until the outbreak of World War I.

It is unclear whether Custis attended Mildred's funeral, as he wrote a note dated March 30th to General Scott Shipp from Burke, "Thanks for the invitation. Not able to go to Lexington."[53]

Undoubtedly, Custis felt he was not able to travel to Lexington. Yet, a few weeks later, he conferred with John L. Campbell by letter about the financial arrangements associated with his sister Mildred's funeral:

> Your letter of the 14th inst., with accounts requested, was received Saturday afternoon; and I thank you for them. Burke & Herbert, Bankers, Alexandria, Va., have offered, as I understand, to pay the bills connected with the burial of my sister Mildred. They have some funds to the credit of her account with them, I believe, and if they will settle the bills until an Executor or Administrator can be legally appointed, it will save trouble all-around.
>
> My sister [Lee is referring to Mary Tabb Bolling Lee] and her son, R. E. Lee are thinking of going to Lexington, early this week; and you may possibly see them before you receive this letter. If you can manage to let them have

the services of Willie Price [servant] for a little while, he may be of much assistance to them.

Thanking you again for all your kindness, and with kind regards to all the members of your household, I remain...[54]

Nearly a month to the day after losing Mildred, the Lees suffered yet another death in their family. On April 28th Fitzhugh Lee, the cavalryman who rode along side of Jeb Stuart, the one time Governor of Virginia, (1885-1889) as well as Consul General in Havana, Cuba, (1896-1898) and nephew to the illustrious General Robert E. Lee, died. A few days later Custis wrote to his father's former aide-de-camp, Colonel Walter H. Taylor:

Your kind letter of the 28th March was one of the first received after the death of my sister Mildred, and was gratefully appreciated. Looking upon you as a member of my father's family, I have taken the liberty of partaking writing to you until after the communications, more or less official, from Confederate Veteran association, Daughters of the Confederacy and strangers generally, had been acknowledged.

Last Monday, I went to the funeral service of my cousin, Fitz Lee, in Washington City; but did not feel able to go to Richmond for the internment of his remains to-day. My brother Robt. has informed me that he would be in Richmond to-day, and my nephew R. E. Lee, left yesterday, to attend the internment in Richmond to-day.

I infer from your writing that you are as well and active as ever, and I earnestly hope that you may long continue so.

With unfeigned thanks for your kind sympathy, and with kind regards and good wishes for all the members of your household, I remain, as ever...[26]

After a difficult spring, "General Custis'" life settled down to a more normal pace by mid-summer. He maintained his level of communication with his old friends at Washington and Lee University and the Virginia Military Institute. His interests in their varied activities never waned. In the following note Lee offers the Librarian of the Virginia Military Institute two of his personal books, "I have a copy of "The Centennial of the U. S. Mil. Academy., 1802-1902", which I shall be glad to give to your library, if you have not a copy of the work and care to have it. It is in two large 800 vols., bound."[56] The books were gratefully accepted by the V. M. I. librarian.

As usual, Lee did everything in his power to be useful to the University. When his portrait by Benjamin West Clinedinst was completed, he insisted on paying for it in order that it not become yet another financial burden for the University. In June, 1906, he wrote to John L. Campbell in reference to this matter:

> I have just received a letter from Mr. Humphreys, [David Carlisle Humphreys, Dean of the School of Applied Science, 1904-1921] who tells me, in accordance with my request, that the cost of my picture is $502.05, and that my check should be sent to you. The check is enclosed.
>
> I thank you for the copy of the *Rockbridge County News*, just received; we have no mail on Sunday.
>
> With kind regards to the members of your household, and other friends, I remain...[57]

He perpetuated his letter writing to Jean Lloyd Yeatman, although his traveling was limited to the Washington, D.C. area:

> I have just recieved your letter of the 18th inst., and am sincerely glad that you are comparatively so comfort-able; hope indeed that you may never be less confortable, but that you may be better off day by day. I trust your Dr. may be altogether right in his promises, and that a change of air, &c., may be of great benefit to you. There will probably be some of your acquaintances from Richmond and elsewhere at "The White Sulpher," and it is possible that my brother Rob. & family may be there, although it

had not been determined where they were to go when I last heard from him. He was then at Rozier Dulany's "Oakley", Fauquier County, near Upperville. I hope to be able to get to town, next week, if not before; and you must let me know if there is anything I can do for you, now or hereafter.

With love to Miss Minnie, I remain, Affectionately yrs...[58]

It is interesting to note that late in Lee's life he was still receiving requests for his autograph and those of other memebers of his family. Though always polite, when the request came from a Northerner, he response was short and curt:

My Dear Madame:—
I have just recieved your letter of the 26th inst., and enclose [the] autograph as requested.
Very sincerely...[59]

* * * *

Sir:
I have just recieved your letter of the 13th inst. and enclose the autograph as requested.
Very truly yrs...[60]

In the final years of Custis Lee's life, he wrote relatively few letters beyond the close circle he had cultivated during his retirement years. John L. Campbell prevailed at the top of his list to correspond with on a regular basis:

I acknowledge, with thanks, the receipt of a copy of the address delivered on the 19th inst., by the Hon. Charles Francis Adams; several Baltimore newspapers forwarded from Lexington; a copy of the Lexington Gazette of the 23rd inst., and a copy of the *Rockbridge County News* of the 24th inst.

I have been wishing for a long time to contribute something towards a fund for the preservation and improvement of the Chapel, and will give something to this object as soon as able to do so. My means are small, and I have a number of relatives and friends who are very poor.[61]

One of the people outside his regular circle of friends to whom he wrote was a lady by the name of Mrs. Howard. She wrote to Lee in the winter of 1907 inquiring about the portraits of Washington and Lafayette:

Your letter of the 30th inst, was recieved last week but I have not been able to answer it until today. Before leaving Lexington in the summer of 1897, I presented to Washington and Lee University my two portraits of historic interest, one of General Washington by the elder Peale and the other of General Lafayette by the same artist and have no further control over them. My other pictures retained to W. & L. Univeristy and a few other pictures owned jointly by my sister, brother, two nephews & myself are place with my own in the hallway of W. & L. University until claimed by my legal heirs— All the Mount Vernon Relics inherited from my grandfather (Custis) more given some years ago to my sister, Miss Mary C. Lee excepting a few articles that had previous been sent to Mt. Vernon. If the authories of W. & L. Univeristy are willing to loan my pictures (in their holding) to the Va. D. A. R. for the Jamestown Exposition, I give my consent-I enclose a list of the pictures in question; those marked with [a circle with a number one slashed] are my own- I have made some corrections on the list but have probably overlooked some errors. With kind regards and good wishes, I remain...[62]

Two months later, Lee wrote again to Campbell in reference to these painting requested for loan to the Virginia Daughters of the American Revolution for exhibition at the Jamestown Exposition:

I have just received your letter of the 3rd inst., with inclosures; and return the (clean) copy of the catalogue, marked as suggested. I think the four pictures, L.1, L.2, L.3 & L.6 will be enough to send, though I have no objection to sending L.21 & L.22, if you think it desirable to send more; in fact, I am willing to leave the whole matter to the authorities of W. & L. U., as the loan is theirs, with the understanding that I do not consent to the loan of the pictures that do not belong exclusively to me.

With regard to L.18, L.19 & L.20, one of them is probably George Lafayette, and the other two are probably G. W. P. Custis & his sister Nellie. As there is uncertainly about them, it may be best not to send them.

I can not refuse the daughter of Col. John A. Washington, of Mt. Vernon, anything not altogther unreasonable, although I should perfer the pictures to remain where they are.

Thanks for the Collegian and the pamphlet from the University of South Carolina.[63]

The paintings were placed on exhibit at the Jamestown Exposition. The historic display was attended by many people from all over the country, including President Theodore Roosevelt and Captain James Ewell Brown Stuart, Jr. The young Stuart had invited his father's old friend to visit him many times, but Lee was compeled to refuse once again:

Your letter of the 11th inst. with enclosure, received.

I thank you for the photo of the review of Presdt. Roosevelt of the ships in Hampton Roads on the 26th ult., and especially for your invitation to your house. I should like to take advantage of your kindness, but fear it will not be in my power to do so.

With kind regards to your household, I remain...[64]

As Lee's life wanned on he traveled less and less. His interest in local and state affairs continued and through this interest, he corresponded with a few former Confederate officers. In the early fall of 1907, Lee wrote to General Thomas T. Mumford of Lynchburg, Virginia in reference to data pertaining to the "Valley Campaign":

> Your kind letter of the 18th ult. and the accompanying pamphlet (Addresses, Confederate Veterns Association) were duly received, I beleive; but I have not been able to thank you for them before now, much to my regret.
>
> I am an old man, too; was 75 years old on the 16th inst., but do not feel the weight of years so much as the want of health.
>
> Some years ago when I was expecting to change my residence, I sent your paper on the Valley Campaign to Dr. Brock, Secty, Southern Historical Association, for safe keeping, with the request to hold it subject to your order; I did not know where to address you at that time.
>
> I have read your address on the Invasion of Maryland with much interest, and thank you for giving me the opportunity of so doing. I return the pamphlet, herewith, with many thanks, as you may not have another copy with your own notes.
>
> With best wishes for your happiness, I remain...[65]

During the last few years of Lee's life, he was happy and content, yet he was beginning to decrease his minimal activitity. This was in large part due to his increasing arthritic episodes. In a letter to his cousin Mary Lee Lloyd, he addresses his concern for his cousins, but notes his limitations:

> I thank you for your letter of the 19th inst., and wish you could have given a better account of "Sister." [Jean Lloyd Yeatman] What can be done for her? You would not hesitate, I am sure, to let me know if there is anything I could do for her.
>
> The weather has been very trying even to well people, but I hope we shall soon be comforted with more pleasant temperatures.

I had a letter from Mary [Mary Custis Lee] a few days ago; She was at Hamburg, and seemed to be enjoying herself; did not say anything of returning to this country.

We are all, here, about as usual; Miss Mebs. [Melville Bolling] walks a little without assistance, but is about the same in other respects. "Robbie" is not at home just now, but will probably be back next week.

I hope to be able to get to see you before very long; "the spirit is willing, but the flesh is weak."

With love to cousin Jean, I remain..[66]

Even though his body was failing more and more, his mind was sharp and alert to an issue that arose and was in his power to control or aid in the answer. Ever since the Lee Chapel was planned and constructed, there was a controversy as to who designed the structure. Some thought it was Robert E. Lee himself. Others were lead to believe it was Colonel Thomas Williamson, a Professor of Civil and Military Engineering at the Virginia Military Institute. This point took its reference from a letter Williamson wrote his daughter which in part said, "I have been thrown a good deal with Genl. Lee lately-The building Committee of College got me to design the New Chapel which they are erecting directly in front of the Central building in the lot on the south side of the college avenue and I have made all the working drawings and written out the specifications, all of which I had to confer with the Genl. and explain to him. He often stops at my lot and insists on coming over to help me."[67]

It is true that Williamson was responsible for completing early designs for the Lee Chapel, but the influence of two other engineers, Robert E. Lee and Custis Lee, soon became evident. All three men were conversant, not only in engineering but architecture as well. It was common in the nineteenth century for military engineering courses to be heavily laden in architecture. Nevertheless, the question remained where did the final design come from and why was it ultimately use? At last in the spring of 1909, the question was answered.

Around this time, the University was thinking about renovating the Lee Chapel. The trustees thought it proper to contact President

Emeritus Lee for his advice and opinion. The responsiblity for contacting Lee fell to Professor David C. Humphreys. In response to Humphreys' letter, Lee reveals where the design for the Chapel came from and why it was selected:

> I got the design for the Chapel out of book of Churches that I afterward gave, with some other books, to William G. McDowell, and which may possibly now be in Lexington. The design was selected because it was simple and comparatively inexpensive. The site of the Chapel had not then been decided upon, for the present site, a wider building with three aisles instead of two would have been better, I think. The spire, as well as I remember, was a simple Conical spire resting on the Present belfry (the roof being taken off). Possibly, something better can be devised. I don't see any way of enlarging the Chapel without taking down the to side walls and rebuilding them further apart; when this has to be done, it would probably be better to build a new Chapel altogether, as the present one has been patched enough already. Remember that the slope of the main building intersects the brick work of the tower of the spire too high up, cutting it in a recess (panel).
>
> There will be no objection, I am sure, on the part of any member of General Lee's family to anything the authorities may do to the Chapel.
>
> I neglected to mention in the proper place that the Chapel was originally designed to seat 500 students on the main floor, and that no plans were made for enlargement; the galleries were an addition afterwards, and somewhat spoil the auditorium.
>
> Your heating arrangements have doubtless continued to be successful and satisfatory, judging from the beginnings.[68]

The trustees decided not to enlarge the Chapel and it stands as it did when it was first constructed.

The date June 1, 1911 was selected for a Confederate Reunion in Fairfax County. The *Fairfax Herald* ran a short article in the Friday, April 28, 1911 issue to encourage contributions from the general public. Among the listed subscribers, including the amount of their contribution was S. R. Donohoe, owner of the *Fairfax Herald* and Gen. G. W. C. Lee, each donating $25.00, as well as the names and contributions of several other prominent citizens of Fairfax County. It is probable that Lee attended this function, since he did not have to travel a great distance or reside at accomodations away from Ravensworth.

It was in 1911 that he visited Arlington for the last time. Sending a photo postal card of Arlington from Washington, D. C. he noted to a friend, "We were here and toured the cemetery this afternoon. Then we went out to Carter's farm." It can be said with some certainty that his final visit to Arlington was bittersweet.

In mid-May, 1911, Lee received notice that Louis Hughes, a Lexington resident and employee of Washington and Lee University, died. Lee was compelled to respond to this notice from John L. Campbell within two letters. The first is a brief note: "Please make use of this check, or as much of it as may be necessary, for the relief of Lewis Hughes' widow; am sorry to add to your many troubles, but do not know what else to do in this case."[69] The second letter on the subject was dated June 9:

> Your letter of the 3rd inst. duly received.
>
> I thank you for kind attention to my request about Louisa Hughes; am sorry that her affairs are in such a bad condition. If my check can be of use for her, please expand it for her benefit in any way you may think best. I thank you, also, for the copy of the Treasurer's report, W. & L. U., for 1910-1911 am glad to note that the affairs of the Univesity are in such a satisfactory condition, and hope that they may become more so year by year.
>
> My nephew is in town for the day, as usual; and his mother is getting ready to go to Richmond, Va. If they knew of my writing, they would join me in kind regards to your and yours.[70]

His contribution to Mrs. Hughes was greatly appreciated. His act once again provided proof of his strong ties to the Lexington community.

For some time, Lee was contemplating a revisal of his last will and testament. He must have realized his life was waning. After the first of the new year, Lee contacted his attorney, R. R. Farr about this matter. His will was revised to read:

I, G. W. C. Lee, of Ravensworth, in the County of Fairfax, State of Virginia, being of sound and disposing mind, do hereby make, publish and declare this to be my last will and testament, hereby revoking all other wills by me at any time made:

FIRST: I give and bequeath to The Washington and Lee University, to be held by the Trustees thereof, the original portrait in oil of General George Washington by Charles Willson Peale, painted in 1772; the original portrait in oil of General LaFayette by the same artist, painted for General Washington in 1779; all my books and office furniture that I left in Lexington upon my departure there from in the summer of 1897, and all my interest in a certain claim against the United States Government on account of wood gotten from Ravensworth by representatives of the Government during the Civil War. By an agreement in writing, this claim was place in the hands of Mr. Charles Kerr, an attorney, for collection. I am advised that it has been allowed by the United States Court of Claims and will be paid as soon as the money is appropriated by Congress. I also give and bequeath to The Washington and Lee University, to be held by the Trustees therof, the sum of Five Thousand Dollars ($5,000.00), which sum is to be invested and the interest used in the preservation and improvement of the Lee Memorial Chapel. Should this bequest to the Chapel be helpd in violation of any rule of law, I give and bequeath the said sum of Five Thousand Dollars ($5,000.00) to said trustees absolutely.

SECOND: All by pictures and portraits, of every kind and description, except the two given to the The Washington and Lee University, are to be divided, as nearly as mey be, in three equal lots, considering number and vlue, both intrinsic and from the standpoint of sentiment; and I give and bequeath to my sister, Mary Custis Lee, one of said lots, to my bother, Robert Edward Lee, one of said lots, and to my two nephews, Robert Edward Lee, Jr. and George Bolling Lee, the remaining lot, to be equally divided between them.

I have heretofore given to my said sister, Mary Custis Lee, the "Mount Vernon Relics", and are further evidence of her title to them I now give and bequeath the same to her absolutely.

THIRD: I give and bequeath to my sister-in-law, Mary Tabb Lee, widow of my deceased brother William Henry Fitzhugh Lee, the sum of Five Thousand Dollars ($5,000.00) and all the furniture of which I may die possessed, except the office furniture given The Washington and Lee Univeristy.

FOURTH: I give and bequeath to my nephew, Robert E. Lee, Jr. the sum of Ten Thousand Dollars ($10,000.00) in cash, and a like sum to my nephew, George Bolling Lee.

FIFTH: I give and devise to my said nephews, Robert Edward Lee, Jr. and George Bolling Lee, in fee simple, all of the land in Fairfax County, Virginia, howsoever acquired, of which I may die seized, each of said nephews to have a one-half interest therein. I think said land will consist of between twenty-four and twenty-five hundred acres.

SIXTH: All the rest and residue of my estate, real, personal and mixed, wheresoever located, I give, devise and bequeath to my brother, Robert Edward Lee, absolutely and in fee simple.

SEVENTH:I hereby nominate and ppoint my nephew, Robert Edward Lee, Jr., executor of this my last will and testament, and having perfect confidence in his judgement and integrity, I direct that the said executor shall not be required to give security upon his executorial bond.

WITNESS my hand this 1st day of February, 1912.
SIGNED: G. W. C. Lee71

"His end came almost six weeks after a fall on a slippery staircase which caused a fractured hip. He never left his bed after this accident and finally succumbed to an attack of acute lobar pneumonia.[27] Dr. Fletcher of Fairfax was his physician," reported Lee's nephew as medical physician himself, George Bolling Lee. This would be the most accurrate diaganosis of Custis Lee's fatal condition; although in recent years it was suggested that he suffered from a tumor on his kidney which was speculated to be cancerious. This later report has not been substaniated in fact.

George Washington Custis Lee died on Tuesday morning, February 18, 1913 at ten o'clock at the age of eighty. Many newspapers carried the notice of his death. *The Evening Post: New York* published a lengthy account of his life and accomplishments on the day of his death, as did the Alexandria Gazette which stated he had "A Brillant Record" and "...blended with his nature all the traits which go to make the man of the highest type."

The following day the *Alexandria Gazette* did a follow-up story with the details of his life, as well as information as to his burial, "The interment will be in Lexington in the crypt beneath the Lee mausoleum in which the Valentine recumbent figure of his father, General Lee, his wife and several other members of the family are buried there."[73]

News of his death quickly spead to Lexington, where Henry Louis Smith, President of Washington and Lee University sent out the following notice on February 19, 1913:

The funeral of Gen. G. W. C. Lee, formerly Professor in the Virginia Military Institute and President of Washington and Lee University, will take place Friday morning in the Lee Memorial Episcopal Church at 10:30.

All the morning exercises of the University will be

intermitted on that day, and the two institutions will unite in the ceremonies of the occasion, a joint committee of students acting as pall-bearers, and the two faculties, with representatives of other organizations, as honorary pall-bearers.

As there is not room in the Church for the two bodies of students, they are requested to assemble by 11 o'clock and form two lines through which the casket will be borne from the Church to the Lee Mausoleum. The arrangement of the lines will be in charge of marshals appointed by the student-body Presidents, and it is hoped that all will be present in line when the procession leaves the Church.[74]

The *Alexandria Gazette* continued with articles daily about Custis Lee until Saturday, February 22, 1913. In the Saturday issue every detail of his funeral was noted. Aside from Captain and Mrs. Robert E. Lee, there was Miss Mary Custis Lee, Mrs. General W. H. F. Lee, Colonel Robert E. Lee III and Dr. George Bolling Lee of New York, as well as Colonel Walter H. Taylor of Norfolk, who was seated among the family. This was a great tribute to a man who sacrificed everything for his family and friends.

In the months that followed many accolades were postemostly given.

The *Southern Churchman* wrote their citation in the April 5, 1913 issue in which it states in part, "So, after a long and honorable life, in which he served his generation after the will of God, he fell on sleep, and passed to his eternal reward."

The *Lexington Gazette* set forth their tribute in the April 23, 1913 issue. The lengthy article described his life and contributions with the final paragraph: "That Washington and Lee University should have had such a man as president for twenty-six years and president emeritus for sixteen years longer is a sacred memory that will be cherished as a precious heritage so long as the world admires ability, service, self-sacrifice and delights to honor the altruistic."

Then finally the Board of Trustees of Washington and Lee University paid him a final plaudit by writing in their minutes a record of his life's work and their gratitude for his service. The mintues begin:

> Since the last meeting of this Board, the University has suffered, in the death of General George Washington Custis Lee, the loss of one whose name and person have been, for many years, a part of the life of this institution and now a part of its history.
>
> It is deemed fitting that the minutes of the Trustees shall preserve a record of the disinterested service to the cause of education rendered at this University by the distinguished son of him whose name, linked with that of Washington, gives to the University a heritage that carries with it the best traditions and loftiest ideals of our state and nation.[75]

Shortly after the fifth anniversery of Lee's death, the *Rockbridge County News* ran an article written by the Honorable Matthew W. Paxton and a former student of Lee and graduate of Washington and Lee Univeristy:

> His influence with the boys was due, in a large measure, to one fact—the wholesome dread of receiving the consure of a man like General Lee, and the desire to measure up to that standard which he so eminently illustrated in his own life. Indeed, it is simply marvelous to recall the universal respect and admiration which not only the students, but every inhabitant of the town, showed for General Custis Lee. His liberality, his benefactions, his thoughtfulness in sickness, his kindly interest in the children of the town, were the things that bound the people to him and created a respect and deference toward him that I have never witnessed toward another man. And it was of interest to note how the professors who had served under General Robert E. Lee admired and loved General Custis Lee as they did his father. The college, the town, the community with one accord were united in their love and devotion to him. These words describe General Lee more

aptly than all the other words in the English vocabulary, "the perfect gentleman."

George Washington Custis Lee, scholar, officer and gentleman, met his final serenity.

George Washington Custis Lee

Borne to the strains of the dead march,
Slowly the hero goes,
On to the tomb's deep quiet,
On to his last repose,
Proud of the cause he honored.
True to the South's great trust,
Loved when he lived among us,
Loved, now returned to dust.

Sired of the great war chieftain,
First at the front was he,
Brave at the South's reverses,
Calm in her victory,
Lovingly watch him lowered
To rest 'neath the spreading trees,
Pray do not spare in your tribute
To the last of the fighting Lees.

Lift high your head, Virginia,
Smile thro' your blinding tears,
Give, thanks to the Great Commander
For this life that has seen the years
Bring to the South redemption,
After the war cloud passed,
Honor, the grand old leader,
Faithful and true to the last.

The *Alexandria Gazetter*, Alexandria,
Virginia February 19, 1913.

Endnotes

[1] Howe, James Lewis. *Annals of Washington and Lee University during the Administration of General George Washington Custis Lee 1871-1896.* dated 1940. Leyburn Library, Special Collections, Washington and Lee University.

[2] Ibid.

[3] Crenshaw, 236.

[4] Ibid., 236-237.

[5] Crenshaw, 237-238,240.

[6] Ibid., 240.

[7] Diary of William Lyne Wilson, dated March 10, 1897, 029 folder 31, Leyburn Library, Special Collections, Washington and Lee University.

[8] Crenshaw, 180-181.

[9] Howe, James Lewis. *Annals of Washington and Lee University during the Administration of General George Washington Custis Lee 1871-1896.* dated 1940. Leyburn Library, Special Collections, Washington and Lee University.

[10] Letter from Thomas E. Marshall, Jr. to H.E. Hyatt, dated May 31, 1897, Virginia Military Institute Archives.

[11] Letter from Thomas E. Marshall, Jr. to Scott Shipp, dated June 22, 1897, Virginia Military Institute Archives.

[12] Coulling, 193.

[13] *Historical Society of Fairfax County, Virginia, Inc.* 48.

[14] Crenshaw, 243.

[15] Ibid.

[16] Crenshaw, 253.

[17] Letter from George Washington Custis Lee to John L. Campbell, dated February 1, 1898, Leyburn Library, Special Collections, Washington and Lee University.

[18] Letter from George Washington Custis Lee to John L. Campbell, dated February 4, 1898, Leyburn Library, Special Collections, Washington and Lee University.

[19] Letter from George Washington Custis Lee to John L. Campbell, dated February 11, 1898, Leyburn Library, Special Collections, Washington and Lee University.

[20] Letter from George Washington Custis Lee to John L. Campbell, dated February 23, 1898, Leyburn Library, Special Collections, Washington and Lee University.

[21] Letter from George Washington Custis Lee to J. W. Daniel, dated March 10, 1898. Special Collections Department William R. Perkins Library, Duke University.

[22] Letter from George Washington Custis Lee to John L. Campbell, dated March 10, 1898, Leyburn Library, Special Collections, Washington and Lee University.

[23] Muir, Dorothy Troth. *Mount Vernon The Civil War Years*. 24, 121.

[24] Letter from George Bolling Lee to James Lewis Howe, dated February 8, 1940 Leyburn Library, Special Collections, Washington and Lee University.

[27] Letter from W. E. Dold to James Lewis Howe, dated July 24, 1941 Special Collections, Leyburn Library of Washington and Lee University.

[28] Zimmer. *The Robert E. Lee Family Cooking and Housekeeping Book*. 61.

[29] Letter from George Washington Custis Lee to Robert E. Lee Jr. dated January 4, 1900, Leyburn Library, Special Collections, Washington and Lee University.

[30] Letter from George Washington Custis Lee to Mrs. P.T. [Jean] Yeatman, dated January 15, 1900, Special Collections Department William R. Perkins Library, Duke University..

[31] Letter from John L. Campbell to George Washington Custis Lee, dated May 24, 1900, Leyburn Library, Special Collections, Washington and Lee University.

[32] Letter from George Washington Custis Lee to John L. Campbell dated May 28, 1900, Leyburn Library, Special Collections, Washington and Lee University.

[33] Letter from George Washington Custis Lee to Joseph Rubinfine dated January 7, 1901, Leyburn Library, Special Collections, Washington and Lee University.

[34] Letter from George Washington Custis Lee to John L. Campbell dated July 17, 1901, Leyburn Library, Special Collections, Washington and Lee University.

[35] Letter from George Washington Custis Lee to John L. Campbell dated April 21, 1902, Leyburn Library, Special Collections, Washington and Lee University.

[36] Letter from George Washington Custis Lee to John L. Campbell dated April 25, 1902, Special Collections, Leyburn Library of Washington and Lee University.

[37] Rousseau, Jean-Jacques. The Confessions. Penguin Classics, 1953, 333.

[38] Letter from George Washington Custis Lee to John L. Campbell dated July 16, 1902, Leyburn Library, Special Collections, Washington and Lee University.

[39] Letter from George Washington Custis Lee to Mrs. P.T. [Jean] Yeatman, dated November 9, 1903 Special Collections Department William R. Perkins Library, Duke University..

[40] Letter from George Washington Custis Lee to John L. Campbell dated February 22, 1904, Leyburn Library, Special Collections, Washington and Lee University.

[41] Virginia Military Institute Archives, File G.

[42] Virginia Military Institute Archives, File H.

[43] Virginia Military Institute Archives, File I.

[44] Ibid.

[45] Virginia Military Institute Archives, Files I and J.

[46] Virginia Military Institute Archives, File J.

[47] Virginia Military Institute Archives, Files J and K.

[48] Virginia Military Institute Archives, Files K and L.

[49] Virginia Military Institute Archives, File L.

[50] Alexandria Gazette, December 2, 1904.

[51] Letter from George Washington Custis Lee to John L. Campbell dated February 20, 1905, Leyburn Library, Special Collections, Washington and Lee University.

[52] Coulling, 193-195.

[53] Letter from George Washington Custis Lee to Scott Shipp, dated March 30, 1905, Virginia Military Institute Archives.

[54] Letter from George Washington Custis Lee to John L. Campbell dated April 17, 1905, Leyburn Library, Special Collections, Washington and Lee University.

[55] Letter from George Washington Custis Lee to Walter H. Taylor, dated May 4, 1905 Stratford Hall Library and Archives.

[56] Letter from George Washington Custis Lee to the Librarian of the Virginia Military Institute, dated August 4, 1905, Virginia Military Institute Archives.

[57] Letter from George Washington Custis Lee to John L. Campbell dated June 25, 1906, Leyburn Library, Special Collections, Washington and Lee University.

[58] Letter from George Washington Custis Lee to Mrs. P.T. [Jean] Yeatman, dated July 19, 1906, Special Collections Department William R. Perkins Library, Duke University.

[59] Private Collection.

[60] Private Collection.

[61] Letter from George Washington Custis Lee to John L. Campbell dated January 28, 1907, Leyburn Library, Special Collections, Washington and Lee University.

[62] Letter from George Washington Custis Lee to Mrs. Howard dated February 7, 1907, Leyburn Library, Special Collections, Washington and Lee University.

[63] Letter from George Washington Custis Lee to John L. Campbell dated April 5, 1907, Leyburn Library, Special Collections, Washington and Lee University.

[64] Private Collection.

[65] Letter from George Washington Custis Lee to Thomas T. Munford, dated September 19, 1907, Special Collections Department William R. Perkins Library, Duke University.

[66] Private Collection.

[67] 080 Howe, James Lewis Folder, 189 Leyburn Library, Special Collections, Washington and Lee University.

[68] Letter from George Washington Custis Lee to David C. Humphreys dated April 16, 1909, Leyburn Library, Special Collections, Washington and Lee University

[69] Letter from George Washington Custis Lee to John L. Campbell dated May 29, 1911, Leyburn Library, Special Collections, Washington and Lee University.

[70] Letter from George Washington Custis Lee to John L. Campbell dated June 9, 1911, Leyburn Library, Special Collections, Washington and Lee University.

[71] Last Will and Testament of G.W.C. Lee, File 142, Leyburn Library, Special Collections, Washington and Lee University.

[72] Letter from George Bolling Lee to James Lewis Howe, dated February 8, 1940 Leyburn Library, Special Collections, Washington and Lee

University.

[73] *Alexandria Gazettte*, dated February 19, 1913.

[74] Notice from Henry Louis Smith, President of Washington and Lee University, dated February 19, 1913, Virginia Military Institute Archives.

[75] Trustees' Papers Folder 373, Leyburn Library, Special Collections, Washington and Lee University.

Bibliography

Books:

Arber, E. ed. *The Travels and Works of Captain John Smith.* N.p.n.p.n.d.

Bond, Christina. *Memories of General Robert E. Lee.* Baltimore: The Norman, Remington Co.,1926.

Brock, R.A. ed. *Gen. Robert Edward Lee Soldier, Citizen and Christian Patriot.* Richmond: Royal Publishing Co. 1897.

Chinard, Gilbert, ed. *Durand of Dauphine. A Huegenot in Exiled in Virginia: or Voyages of a Frenchman Exiled for his religion with a description of Virginia and Maryland.* New York: n.p. 1934.

Custis, John IV. *Letter book.[Commonplace Book]* Custis-Lee Family Papers [Chicago Historical Society] Library of Congress.

Conti, Robert S. *The History of the Greenbrier America's Resort.* Charleston, West Virginia: Pictorial Histories Publishing Co., 1989.

Corner, George W. ed. *The Autobiography of Benjamin Rush.* Princeton: Princeton University Press, 1948.

Coulling, Mary P. *The Lee Girls.* Winston-Salem,North Carolina: John F. Blair, Publisher,1987.

Couper, William. *One Hundred Years at V.M.I.* Four Volumes Garrett & Masie, 1939.

Crute, Joseph H. *Derwent: Robert E. Lee's Sanctuary.* Midlothian, Virginia: Derwent Books, 1995.

_____. *The Derwent Letters.* Midlothian, Virginia: Derwent

Books, 1985.

Custis, George Washington Parke. *Recollections and Private Memoirs of Washington*. Philadelphia: William Flint, 1857.

Davis, Richard Beale. *Intellectual Life in Jefferson's Virginia 1790-1830*. Knoxville: The University of Tennessee, 1972.

Davis, William. *Jefferson Davis The Man and His Hour*. Baton Rouge: Louisiana State University: 1991.

deButts, Mary Custis Lee. ed. *Growing up in the 1850's The Journal of Agnes Lee*. Chapel Hill: The University of North Carolina, 1984.

Douglas, Henry Kyd. *I Rode with Stonewall*. Chapel Hill: University of North Carolina Press, 1940.

Dowdey, Clifford. ed. *The Wartime Papers of Robert E. Lee*. New York: Da Capo Paperback: 1961.

Freeman, Douglas Southall. *R. E. Lee: A Biography*. Four Volumes. New York: Scribner, 1934-1936.

Freeman, Douglas Southall. *George Washington: A Biography*. Seven Volumes New York: Scribner, 1948-1957.

Fitzpatrick, John C. ed. *Writings of Washington from the Original Manuscripts Sources, 1745-1799*. 39 Volumes. Washington, D.C. n.p. 1940.

_____. *The Last Will and Testament of George Washington and Schedule of his Property to which is appended the Last Will and Testament of Martha Washington*. Mount Vernon: Mount Vernon Ladies' Association, 1982.

Harwell, Richard B. T*he Confederate Reader How the South Saw the War*. New York: Dover Publications,1989.

Howard, McHenry. *Recollections of a Maryland Confederate Soldier and Staff Officer under Johnston, Jackson and Lee*. Baltimore: Williams and Wilkins Company, 1914.

Jacobs, Lee. *Cry Heart*. Mechanicburg, Pennsylvania: White Mane Publishing Co., 2000.

Jones, John B. *A Rebel War Clerk's Diary at the Confederate States Capital*. Volumes I and II, Philadelphia: J.B.Lippencott & Co.: 1866.

Jones, J. William. *Life and Letters of Robert E. Lee Soldier and Man*. New York: Neale Publishing, Co. 1906.

_____. *Personal Reminiscences of General Robert E. Lee.* Baton Rouge: Louisiana State University Press, 1994.

Laner, John B., ed. *Records of the Columbia Historical Society*, Washington, D.C.: Columbia Historical Society, 1930.

Lee, Fitzhugh. *General Lee.* Wilmington, North Carolina: Broadfoot Publishing Company, 1989.

Lee, Robert E. [Biographer.] *Henry Lee: Memoirs of the War in the Southern Department of the United States.* New York: University Publishing Company, 1870.

Lee, Robert E. Jr. *Recollections and Letters of General Robert E. Lee.* New York: Doubleday, Page & Company, 1904.

Lomax, Elizabeth Lindsay. *Leaves form an Old Washington Diary*, 1854-1863. New York: E. P. Dutton and Company, Inc. 1943.

Lyle, Royster Jr. and Pamela Hemenway Simpson. *The Architecture of Historic Lexington.* Charlottesville: The University Press of Virginia, 1977.

Lynch. James. B. Jr. *The Custis Chronicles: The Years of Migration.* Camden, Maine: Picton Press, 1992.

_____. *The Custis Chronicles: The Virginia Generation.* Camden, Maine: Picton Press, 1997.

MacDonald, Rose Mortimer Ellzey. *Mrs. Robert E. Lee.* Boston: Ginn and Company, 1939.

Martini, John A. *Fort Point Sentry at the Golden Gate.* San Francisco: Golden Gate National Park Association, 1981.

McCarthy, Carlton. *Detailed Minutiae of Soldier Life in the Army of Northern Virginia, 1861-1865.* Richmond: 1882.

Miller, Helen Hill. *Colonel Parke of Virginia: "The Greatest Hector in the Town."*

Mitchell, Adele. ed. *The Letters of General J.E.B. Stuart.* Richmond: Stuart-Mosby Historical Society, 1990.

Muir, Dorothy Troth. *Mount Vernon The Civil War Years.* Mount Vernon: Mount Vernon Ladies' Association, 1993.

Munford, Beverley B. *Virginia's Attitude Toward Slavery and Secession.* Richmond: L. H. Jenkins, Inc. 1909.

Nagel, Paul C. *The Lees of Virginia.* New York: Oxford University Press, 1990.

Neville, Ameilia Ransome. *The Fantastic City.* Cambridge:

Cambridge University Press, 1932.

Ollinger, Crenshaw. *General Lee's College The Rise and Growth of Washington and Lee University.* New York: Random House, 1969.

Osgood, H. L. *The American Colonies in the Seventeenth Century.* Two Volumes. New York: Scribner, 1904-1907.

Ribblett, David L. *Nelly Custis Child of Mount Vernon.* Mount Vernon: Mount Vernon Ladies' Association, 1993.

Rousseau, Jean-Jacques. *The Confessions.* London: Penguin Classics, 1953.

Royster, Charles. *Light-Horse Harry Lee and the Legacy of the American Revolution.* Baton Rouge: Louisiana State University Press, 1981.

Schmitt, Patricia Brady. *Nelly Custis Lewis's Housekeeping Book.* New Orleans: The Historic New Orleans Collection: 1982.

Shepard, Herschel. *The Construction of Fort Clinch.* N.p. 1965.

Stampp, Kenneth M. ed. *The Peculiar Institution.* New York: Random House, 1959.

Tatum, George Lee. *Disloyalty in the Confederacy.* Lincoln: University of Nebraska Press, 2000.

Tidwell, William A. *Come Retribution.* New York: Barnes and Noble Books, 1988.

_____. *April '65 Confederate Covert Action in the American Civil War.* Kent, Ohio: Kent State University, 1995.

Von Borcke, Heros. *Memoirs of the Confederate War.* Reprint Number 85. Dayton, Ohio: Morningside House, Inc.,1985.

Williams, George W. *History of the Negro Race in America, 1618-1880.* Two Volumes. N.p. n.p. 1883.

Woodward, C. Vann. ed. *Mary Chesnut's Civil War.* New Haven: Yale University Press, 1981.

Zimmer, Anne Carter. *The Robert E. Lee Family Cooking and Housekeeping Book.* Chapel Hill: The University of North Carolina Press, 1997.

Documents, Dispatches and Periodicals:

Alexandria Gazette, Alexandria Virginia, December 2, 1904, February 19, 1913

"A Marriage Agreement, Original Draft of An Agreement on File at

Eastville, Northampton County, Virginia," Virginia Magazine of History and Biography, 896-1897.

Annual Religious Statistics of Washington and Lee University, 1871.

Annual Report of the Superintendent of the Virginia Military Institute, 1866, 1867, 1869, 1870, 1871.

Board of Trustees Minutes of Washington and Lee University, 1885, 1913.

Daily Alta California, San Francisco, California, June 21, 1858.

Dispatch from O. Latrobe to George Washington Custis Lee, December 17, 1864, #1, Virginia Historical Society.

Dispatch from O. Latrobe to George Washington Custis Lee, December 17, 1864, #2, Virginia Historical Society.

Executive Meeting Minutes of the Jackson Memorial Association, 1891, Duke University.

Faculty Minutes of Washington and Lee University, 1884.

Ford, Gerald. R. *Remarks upon signing a bill restoring rights of citizenship to General Robert E. Lee*, August 5, 1975.

G.W.C. Lee Papers. Washington and Lee University, 1940.

Harper's New Monthly Magazine, January, 1866.

Historical Research and Miscellaneous Notes of James Lewis Howe, Washington and Lee University, 1940.

Historical Society of Fairfax County, Inc.

Howe, James Lewis. *Annual of Washington and Lee University during the Administration of General George Washington Custis Lee 1871-1896, 1940*, Washington and Lee University.

Last Will and Testament of George Washington Custis Lee, 1912, Washington and Lee University.

Notice of Executor Settlement on the Estate of Mrs. W.H. Fitzhugh, 1875 Washington and Lee University.

Notice from George Washington Custis Lee to the Students of Washington and Lee University, 1882, Washington and Lee University.

Notice from Henry Louis Smith, President of Washington and Lee University, February 19, 1913, Virginia Military Institute Archives.

Official Register of Cadets of the United States Military Academy,

1850, 1853, United States Military Academy Archives.

Official Record, Series 1, Vol. 46, 51.

President's Annual Report on Washington and Lee University, 1871, 1876, 1882, 1883, 1884, 1888, 1892.

Quitt, Martin H. "Immigrant Origins of the Virginia Gentry: A Study of Cultural Transmission and Innovation." *William and Mary Quarterly*, #45, 1988.

Reminiscences of Leslie Lyle Campbell, Washington and Lee University, 1896.

Reminiscences of A. Fred White, Washington and Lee University, 1938.

Reminiscences of Robert F. Campbell, Henry T.Wickham, John M. Glenn, Mary Quarles Turpin, John V. McCall, W. J. Humphreys, Wade H. Ellis, George W. Bolling, Henry B. Lewis, Washington and Lee University, 1939.

Rockbridge Historical Society Miscellaneous, Washington and Lee University.

The Southern Collegian, Washington and Lee University, February 11, 1871.

University of Maryland Timeline, Website: www.inform.umd.edu.

Veterans Records, National Archives.

Virginia Military Institute Archives, Files G, H, I, J, K, L, Z.

Will Book No. 1, 7 Clerk's Office, Fairfax County Virginia.

Will Book No. 4, Clerk's Office, Alexandria County, Virginia.

Zappen, Jo. "John Custis of Williamsburg, 1678-1749," Virginia Magazine of History and Biography, 1982.

Letters:

Letter from Henry Lee to Patrick Henry, February 4, 1795 Huntington Library and Art Gallery, San Marina, California.

_____. to Henry Banks, October 19, 1798, Henry Banks Papers, Virginia Historical Society.

_____. to James Madison, 1808, Madison Papers, Library of Congress.

Letter from Robert E. Lee to MaryAnna Randolph Custis Lee, June 2, 1832, Virginia Historical Society.

Letter from Robert E. Lee to MaryAnna Randolph Custis Lee, n.d.

Virginia Historical Society.

Letter from Robert E. Lee to MaryAnna Randolph Custis Lee, March 19, 1833, Virginia Historical Society.

Letter from Robert E. Lee to MaryAnna Randolph Custis Lee, June 2, 1832, Virginia Historical Society.

Letter from Robert E. Lee to MaryAnna Randolph Custis Lee, November 28, 1833, Huntington Library and Art Gallery, San Marina, California.

Letter from MaryAnna Randolph Custis Lee to Mary Lee Fitzhugh Custis, April 11, 1834, Virginia Historical Society.

Letter from Robert E. Lee to Andrew Talcott, November 1, 1834, Virginia Historical Society.

Letter from Robert E. Lee to Andrew Talcott, June 29, 1837,Virginia Historical Society.

Letter from Robert E. Lee to MaryAnna Randolph Custis Lee, September 10, 1837, Virginia Historical Society.

Letter from Robert E. Lee to MaryAnna Randolph Custis Lee, October 16, 1837, Virginia Historical Society.

Letter from MaryAnna Randolph Custis Lee and Robert E. Lee to Mary Lee Fitzhugh Custis, March 24, 1838,Virginia Historical Society.

Letter from MaryAnna Randolph Custis Lee to Mary Lee Fitzhugh Custis, April 11, 1838.

Letter from Robert E. Lee to George Washington Custis Lee June 1, 1844, Virginia Historical Society.

Letter from MaryAnna Randolph Custis Lee to Mary Lee Fitzhugh Custis, July 10, 1844, Virginia Historical Society.

Letter from MaryAnna Randolph Custis Lee to Mary Lee Fitzhugh Custis, September 14, 1844, Virginia Historical Society.

Letter from MaryAnna Randolph Custis Lee to Mary Lee Fitzhugh Custis, October 27, 1844, Virginia Historical Society.

Letter from Robert E. Lee to George Washington Custis Lee November 30, 1845, Virginia Historical Society.

Letter from Robert E. Lee to George Washington Custis Lee December 18, 1845, Virginia Historical Society.

Letter from MaryAnna Randolph Custis Lee to Mary Lee Fitzhugh Custis, December 25, 1845, Virginia Historical Society.

Letter from Robert E. Lee to MaryAnna Randolph Custis Lee, January 21, 1846, Virginia Historical Society.

Letter from Robert E. Lee to MaryAnna Randolph Custis Lee, March 24, 1846, Virginia Historical Society.

Letter from MaryAnna Randolph Custis Lee and Robert E. Lee to Mary Lee Fitzhugh Custis, June 13, 1846,Virginia Historical Society.

Letter from Robert E. Lee to MaryAnna Randolph Custis Lee, September 4, 1846, Virginia Historical Society.

Letter from Robert E. Lee to William Henry Fitzhugh Lee, March 31,1846, Virginia Historical Society.

Letter from Robert E. Lee to MaryAnna Randolph Custis Lee, December 7, 1846, Virginia Historical Society.

Letter from Robert E. Lee to George Washington Custis Lee and William Henry Fitzhugh Lee, December 24, 1846,Virginia Historical Society.

Letter from Robert E. Lee to George Washington Custis Lee April 11, 1847, Virginia Historical Society.

Letter from Robert E. Lee to George Washington Custis Lee April 25, 1847, Virginia Historical Society.

Letter from Robert E. Lee to MaryAnna Randolph Custis Lee, March 15, 1848, Virginia Historical Society.

Letter from Robert E. Lee to MaryAnna Randolph Custis Lee, March 24, 1848, Virginia Historical Society.

Letter from Robert E. Lee to MaryAnna Randolph Custis Lee, February 13, 1849, Virginia Historical Society.

Letter from Robert E. Lee to MaryAnna Randolph Custis Lee, February 22, 1849, Virginia Historical Society.

Letter from Robert E. Lee to MaryAnna Randolph Custis Lee, March 8, 1849, Virginia Historical Society.

Letter from Robert E. Lee to Anna Maria Sarah Goldsborough Fitzhugh, March 30, 1850, Virginia Historical Society.

Letter from Robert E. Lee to Anna Maria Sarah Goldsborough Fitzhugh, May 11, 1850, Virginia Historical Society.

Letter from Robert E. Lee to MaryAnna Randolph Custis Lee, December 2, 1850, Virginia Historical Society.

Letter from Robert E. Lee to MaryAnna Randolph Custis Lee,

January 2, 1851, Virginia Historical Society.

Letter from Robert E. Lee to George Washington Custis Lee April 13, 1851, Virginia Historical Society.

Letter from Robert E. Lee to George Washington Custis Lee June 22, 1851, West Point, New York: United States Military Academy Archives.

Letter from Robert E. Lee to George Washington Custis Lee August 3, 1851, West Point, New York: United States Military Academy Archives.

Letter from Robert E. Lee to Caroline Peters, November 20, 1851,Lexington, Virginia: Leyburn Library, Special Collections, Washington and Lee University.

Letter from Robert E. Lee and MaryAnna Randolph Custis Lee to George Washington Custis Lee , February 2, 1852, Virginia Historical Society.

Letter from Robert E. Lee to George Washington Custis Lee April 5, 1852, West Point, New York: United States Military Academy Archives.

Letter from Robert E. Lee to William Henry Fitzhugh Lee, February 2, 1853, Lexington,Virginia: Leyburn Library, Special Collections, Washington and Lee University.

Letter from Robert E. Lee to Anne Carter Lee, February 25, 1853, Virginia Historical Society.

Letter from James Ewell Brown Stuart to Elizabeth Hairston August 17, and September 1, 1853, Chapel Hill: Southern Historical Collections, University of North Carolina.

Letter from George Washington Custis Lee to Mary Lee Fitzhugh Custis, March 19, 1853, Virginia Historical Society.

Letter from Robert E. Lee to MaryAnna Randolph Custis Lee, April 27, 1853, Virginia Historical Society.

Letter from Robert E. Lee to MaryAnna Randolph Custis Lee, May 2, 1853, Virginia Historical Society.

Letter from James Ewell Brown Stuart to Archibald Stuart, December 23, 1853, Virginia Historical Society.

Letter from Robert E. Lee to J. M. Bonaparte, February 28, 1855, Baltimore: Maryland Historical Society.

Letter from George Washington Custis Lee to MaryAnna Randolph

Custis Lee, May 27, 1855, Virginia Historical Society.

Letter from George Washington Custis Lee to MaryAnna Randolph Custis Lee, July 26, 1855, Virginia Historical Society.

Letter from Robert E. Lee to MaryAnna Randolph Custis Lee, August 5, 1855, Virginia Historical Society.

Letter from Eleanor Agnes Lee to Robert E. Lee, May 24, 1856, Virginia Historical Society.

Letter from Robert E. Lee to MaryAnna Randolph Custis Lee, September 1, 1856, Virginia Historical Society.

Letter from Robert E. Lee to MaryAnna Randolph Custis Lee, April 26, 1857, Virginia Historical Society.

Letter from Robert E. Lee to MaryAnna Randolph Custis Lee, June 1, 1857, Virginia Historical Society.

Letter from George Washington Custis Lee to MaryAnna Randolph Custis Lee, June 28, 1857, Virginia Historical Society.

Letter from MaryAnna Randolph Custis Lee to Robert E. Lee, July 7, 1857, Virginia Historical Society.

Letter from MaryAnna Randolph Custis Lee to Robert E. Lee, July 25, 1857, Virginia Historical Society.

Letter from Robert E. Lee to MaryAnna Randolph Custis Lee, July 27, 1857, Virginia Historical Society.

Letter from Anne Carter Lee to Robert E. Lee, July 30, 1857, Virginia Historical Society.

Letter from Robert E. Lee to MaryAnna Randolph Custis Lee, August 12, 1857, Virginia Historical Society.

Letter from George Washington Custis Lee to MaryAnna Randolph Custis Lee, September 3, 1857, Virginia Historical Society.

Letter from George Washington Custis Lee to MaryAnna Randolph Custis Lee, November 2, 1857, Virginia Historical Society.

Letter from George Washington Custis Lee to MaryAnna Randolph Custis Lee, February 16, 1858, Virginia Historical Society.

Letter from George Washington Custis Lee to Eleanor Agnes Lee, May 18, 1859, Leyburn Library, Special Collections, Washington and Lee University.

Letter from George Washington Custis Lee to Margaret Stewart, May 18, 1859, Leyburn Library, Special Collections, Washington and Lee University.

Letter from Robert E. Lee to Annette Carter, November 8, 1859, Leyburn Library, Special Collections, Washington and Lee University.

Letter from Robert E. Lee to MaryAnna Randolph Custis Lee, March 3, 1860, Virginia Historical Society.

Letter from Robert E. Lee to MaryAnna Randolph Custis Lee, April 25, 1860, Virginia Historical Society.

Letter from George Washington Custis Lee to William O. Winston, April 25, 1860, Virginia Historical Society.

Letter from George Washington Custis Lee to William O. Winston, June 2, 1860, Virginia Historical Society.

Letter from Robert E. Lee to MaryAnna Randolph Custis Lee, June 3, 1860, Virginia Historical Society.

Letter from Robert E. Lee to MaryAnna Randolph Custis Lee, June 18, 1860, Virginia Historical Society.

Letter from Robert E. Lee to MaryAnna Randolph Custis Lee, June 25, 1860, Virginia Historical Society.

Letter from MaryAnna Randolph Custis Lee to Eleanor Agnes Lee, no date, Virginia Historical Society.

Letter from Robert E. Lee to MaryAnna Randolph Custis Lee, July 1, 1860, Virginia Historical Society.

Letter from George Washington Custis Lee to William O. Winston, July 16, 1860, Virginia Historical Society.

Letter from Eleanor Agnes Lee to Anne Carter Lee, August 6, 1860, Virginia Historical Society.

Letter from MaryAnna Randolph Custis Lee to Anne Carter Lee, August 10 & 13, 1860, Virginia Historical Society.

Letter from MaryAnna Randolph Custis Lee to Mildred Childe Lee, September 8, 1860, Virginia Historical Society.

Letter from MaryAnna Randolph Custis Lee to Anne Carter Lee, October 21, 1860, Virginia Historical Society.

Letter from MaryAnna Randolph Custis Lee to Mildred Childe Lee, December 4, 1860, Virginia Historical Society.

Letter from MaryAnna Randolph Custis Lee to Mildred Childe Lee, January 17, 1861, Virginia Historical Society.

Letter from MaryAnna Randolph Custis Lee to Mildred Childe Lee, February 24, 1861, Virginia Historical Society.

Letter from Robert E. Lee to Mildred Childe Lee, March 15, 1861, Virginia Historical Society.

Letter from Robert E. Lee to MaryAnna Randolph Custis Lee, April 30, 1861, Virginia Historical Society.

Letter from Robert E. Lee to MaryAnna Randolph Custis Lee, May 2, 1861, Virginia Historical Society.

Letter from Eleanor Agnes Lee to Anne Carter Lee, May 6, 1861, Virginia Historical Society.

Letter from Robert E. Lee to MaryAnna Randolph Custis Lee, May 8, 1861, Virginia Historical Society.

Letter from MaryAnna Randolph Custis Lee to Robert E. Lee, May 9, 1861, Virginia Historical Society.

Letter from MaryAnna Randolph Custis Lee to Mildred Childe Lee, May 11, 1861, Virginia Historical Society.

Letter from Robert E. Lee to MaryAnna Randolph Custis Lee, May 11, 1861, Virginia Historical Society.

Letter from MaryAnna Randolph Custis Lee to Robert E. Lee, May 12, 1861, Virginia Historical Society.

Letter from Eleanor Agnes Lee to Mildred Childe Lee, May 23, 1861, Virginia Historical Society.

Letter from Robert E. Lee to MaryAnna Randolph Custis Lee, June 9, 1861, Virginia Historical Society.

Letter from Robert E. Lee to MaryAnna Randolph Custis Lee, June 24, 1861, Virginia Historical Society.

Letter from Robert E. Lee to MaryAnna Randolph Custis Lee, July 2, 1861, Virginia Historical Society.

Letter from Robert E. Lee to MaryAnna Randolph Custis Lee, July 8, 1861, Virginia Historical Society.

Letter from Robert E. Lee to Eleanor Agnes Lee and Anne Carter Lee , August 29, 1861, Virginia Historical Society.

Letter from Robert E. Lee to George Washington Custis Lee, September 3, 1861, Virginia Historical Society.

Letter from Robert E. Lee to MaryAnna Randolph Custis Lee, September 9, 1861, Virginia Historical Society.

Letter from Robert E. Lee to MaryAnna Randolph Custis Lee, November 5, 1861, Virginia Historical Society.

Letter from Robert E. Lee to Anne Carter Lee, December 8, 1861,

Virginia Historical Society.

Letter from George Washington Custis Lee to Anne Carter Lee, January 27, 1862, Leyburn Library, Special Collections, Washington and Lee University.

Letter from George Washington Custis Lee to MaryAnna Randolph Custis Lee , May 2, 1862, Leyburn Library, Special Collections, Washington and Lee University.

Letter from Robert E. Lee to Eleanor Agnes Lee, May 29, 1861, Virginia Historical Society.

Letter from William Henry Fitzhugh Lee to Charlotte Georgiana Wickham Lee, June 3, 1862, Virginia Historical Society.

Letter from Robert E. Lee to MaryAnna Randolph Custis Lee, June 9, 1862, Virginia Historical Society.

Letter from Robert E. Lee to Eleanor Agnes Lee, June 22, 1862, Virginia Historical Society.

Letter from MaryAnna Randolph Custis Lee to Anne Carter Lee and Mildred Childe Lee, June 29, 1862, Virginia Historical Society.

Letter from Robert E. Lee to MaryAnna Randolph Custis Lee, June, 1862, Virginia Historical Society.

Letter from Robert E. Lee to Anne Carter Lee, Eleanor Agnes Lee and Mildred Childe Lee, July, 1862, Virginia Historical Society.

Letter from Robert E. Lee to MaryAnna Randolph Custis Lee, July 28, 1862, Virginia Historical Society.

Letter from Robert E. Lee to Mildred Childe Lee, July 28, 1862, Virginia Historical Society.

Letter from Robert E. Lee to MaryAnna Randolph Custis Lee, August 5, 1862, Virginia Historical Society.

Letter from MaryAnna Randolph Custis Lee to Anne Carter Lee August 4 & 6, 1862, Virginia Historical Society.

Letter from Robert E. Lee to Anne Carter Lee and Eleanor Agnes Lee, August 9, 1862, Virginia Historical Society.

Letter from Varina Howell Davis to William Preston Johnston, August 13, 1862, New Orleans: Manuscript Department, Tulane University Libraries.

Letter from George Washington Custis Lee to Anne Carter Lee and Eleanor Agnes Lee, August 18, 1862, Leyburn Library, Special

Collections, Washington and Lee University.

Letter from George Washington Custis Lee to Jefferson Davis, September 25, 1862 Cambridge: The Houghton Library, Frederick Dearborn Collection Harvard University.

Letter from Robert E. Lee to MaryAnna Randolph Custis Lee, September 29, 1862, Virginia Historical Society.

Letter from Robert E. Lee to Anne Carter Lee and Eleanor Agnes Lee, September 30, 1862, Virginia Historical Society.

Letter from Robert E. Lee to MaryAnna Randolph Custis Lee, October, 1862, Virginia Historical Society.

Letter from Jeremy Gilmer to his wife, October 12, 1862, Chapel Hill: Southern Historical Society Collection of the University of North Carolina.

Letter from Robert E. Lee to MaryAnna Randolph Custis Lee, October 19, 1862, Virginia Historical Society.

Letter from James Ewell Brown Stuart to Samuel S. Cooper, October 24, 1862, Virginia Historical Society.

Letter from MaryAnna Randolph Custis Lee to Mildred Childe Lee, November 15, 1862, Virginia Historical Society.

Letter from James Ewell Brown Stuart to George Washington Custis Lee, December 18, 1862, Manuscript Collection, William R. Perkins Library, Duke University.

Letter from Robert E. Lee to Mildred Childe Lee, December 25, 1862, Virginia Historical Society.

Letter from George Washington Custis Lee to James Ewell Brown Stuart, February 5, 1863, Virginia Historical Society.

Letter from George Washington Custis Lee to R. D. Minor, June 28, 1863, Virginia Historical Society.

Letter from Robert E. Lee to MaryAnna Randolph Custis Lee, August 9, 1863, Virginia Historical Society.

Letter from Robert E. Lee to Eleanor Agnes Lee, September 13, 1863, Virginia Historical Society.

Letter from MaryAnna Randolph Custis Lee to Mildred Childe Lee September 27, 1863, Virginia Historical Society.

Letter from William Henry Fitzhugh Lee to George Washington Custis Lee, November 12, 1863, Virginia Historical Society.

Letter from George Washington Custis Lee to Jefferson Davis,

November 17, 1863, Richmond: Eleanor Brockenbrough Library, Museum of the Confederacy.

Letter from Robert E. Lee to MaryAnna Randolph Custis Lee, November 21, 1863, Virginia Historical Society.

Letter from George Washington Custis Lee to Jefferson Davis, November 17, 1863, William L. Clements Library, Schoff Civil War Collections: Jefferson Davis Papers, University of Michigan.

Letter from George Washington Custis Lee to Lucius Bellinger Northrup February 9, 1864, Cambridge: The Houghton Library, Frederick Dearborn Collection Harvard University.

Letter from Joseph E. Johnston to George Washington Custis Lee, February 11, 1864, Cambridge: The Houghton Library, Frederick Dearborn Collection Harvard University.

Letter from Jefferson Davis to George Washington Custis Lee, December 30, 1864, Leyburn Library, Special Collections, Washington and Lee University.

Letter from Robert E. Lee to Robert E. Lee, Jr. July 10, 1865, Virginia Historical Society.

Letter from George Washington Custis Lee to Francis H. Smith, July 17, 1865, Lexington, Virginia: Virginia Military Institute Archives.

Letter from Robert E. Lee to Robert E. Lee, Jr. July 22, 1865, Virginia Historical Society.

Letter from George Washington Custis Lee to Francis H. Smith, August 18, 1865, Lexington, Virginia: Virginia Military Institute Archives.

Letter from George Washington Custis Lee to Alfred Landon Rives, October 19, 1865, Leyburn Library, Special Collections, Washington and Lee University.

Letter from Francis H. Smith to Scott Shipp, September 1, 1865, Lexington, Virginia: Virginia Military Institute Archives.

Letter from Robert E. Lee to Fitz Lee, September 1, 1865, Virginia Historical Society.

Letter from George Washington Custis Lee to Francis H. Smith, October 2, 1865, Lexington, Virginia: Virginia Military Institute Archives.

Letter from Robert E. Lee to MaryAnna Randolph Custis Lee,

October 3, 1865, Virginia Historical Society.

Letter from Robert E. Lee to MaryAnna Randolph Custis Lee, October 15, 1865, Virginia Historical Society.

Letter from Robert E. Lee to MaryAnna Randolph Custis Lee, October 27, 1865, Virginia Historical Society.

Letter from Robert E. Lee to Mildred Childe Lee, October 29, 1865, Virginia Historical Society.

Letter from Robert E. Lee to MaryAnna Randolph Custis Lee, November 5, 1865, Virginia Historical Society.

Letter from George Washington Custis Lee to William Washington, November 30, 1865, Manuscript Collection, William R. Perkins Library, Duke University.

Letter from Robert E. Lee to Eleanor Agnes Lee, December 5, 1865, Virginia Historical Society.

Letter from George Washington Custis Lee to Alfred Landon Rives, January 25, 1866, Manuscript Collection, William R. Perkins Library, Duke University.

Letter from Robert E. Lee to William Parker Snow, February 13, 1866, Leyburn Library, Special Collections, Washington and Lee University.

Letter from Robert E. Lee to Annette Carter, May 19, 1866, Leyburn Library, Special Collections, Washington and Lee University.

Letter from George Washington Custis Lee to Alfred Landon Rives, June 2, 1866, Manuscript Collection, William R. Perkins Library, Duke University.

Letter from Robert E. Lee to Robert E. Lee, Jr. June 13, 1866, Virginia Historical Society.

Letter from Robert E. Lee to MaryAnna Randolph Custis Lee, August 2, 1866, Virginia Historical Society.

Letter from George Washington Custis Lee to Adam Badeau, August 18, 1866, Manuscript Collection, William R. Perkins Library, Duke University.

Letter from Robert E. Lee to Annette Carter, August 30, 1866, Leyburn Library, Special Collections, Washington and Lee University.

Letter from William Henry Fitzhugh Lee to Eleanor Agnes Lee,

September 26, 1866, Virginia Historical Society.

Letter from James T. Earle to Francis H. Smith, December 15, 1866, Lexington, Virginia: Virginia Military Institute Archives.

Letter from Francis H. Smith to James T. Earle, December 21, 1866, Lexington, Virginia: Virginia Military Institute Archives.

Letter from Robert E. Lee to Mildred Childe Lee, December 21, 1866, Virginia Historical Society.

Letter from George Washington Custis Lee to James T. Earle, January 14, 1867, Lexington, Virginia: Virginia Military Institute Archives.

Letter from George Washington Custis Lee to Francis H. Smith, January 14, 1867, Lexington, Virginia: Virginia Military Institute Archives.

Letter from George Washington Custis Lee to Alfred Landon Rives, February 19, 1867, Manuscript Collection, William R. Perkins Library, Duke University.

Letter from MaryAnna Randolph Custis Lee to Robert E. Lee, Jr. August 6, 1867, Virginia Historical Society.

Letter from Robert E. Lee to Robert E. Lee, Jr. October 26, 1867, Virginia Historical Society.

Letter from Robert E. Lee to Annette Carter, November 1, 1867, Leyburn Library, Special Collections, Washington and Lee University.

Letter from Robert E. Lee to Annette Carter, March 28, 1868, Leyburn Library, Special Collections, Washington and Lee University.

Letter from Robert E. Lee to William Henry Fitzhugh Lee, October 19, 1868, Virginia Historical Society.

Letter from Robert E. Lee to William N. Burwell, Jr. February 15, 1869, Virginia Historical Society.

Letter from Robert E. Lee to Robert E. Lee, Jr., February 27, 1869, Virginia Historical Society.

Letter from Robert E. Lee to Robert E. Lee, Jr. April 17, 1869, Virginia Historical Society.

Letter from Robert E. Lee to Charlotte Taylor Haxall Lee, July 9, 1869, Virginia Historical Society.

Letter from Robert E. Lee to William Henry Fitzhugh Lee,

December 9, 1869, Virginia Historical Society.

Letter from Robert E. Lee to MaryAnna Randolph Custis Lee, April 11, 1869, Virginia Historical Society.

Letter from Robert E. Lee to Annette Carter, May 20, 1870, Leyburn Library, Special Collections, Washington and Lee University.

Letter from Robert E. Lee to Margaret Hunter, June 8, 1870, Leyburn Library, Special Collections, Washington and Lee University.

Letter from Robert E. Lee to Fitzhugh Lee, September 9, 1870, Leyburn Library, Special Collections, Washington and Lee University.

Letter from George Washington Custis Lee to Charles Marshall, December 5, 1870, Leyburn Library, Special Collections, Washington and Lee University.

Letter from George Washington Custis Lee to Walter H. Taylor, December 6, 1870, Stratford, Virginia: Stratford Hall Library and Archives.

Letter from George Washington Custis Lee to Charles Marshall, March 1, 1871, Leyburn Library, Special Collections, Washington and Lee University.

Letter from George Washington Custis Lee to Thomas F. Balfe, May 10, 1871, Leyburn Library, Special Collections, Washington and Lee University.

Letter from William Preston Johnston to George Washington Custis Lee, June 17, 1871, Leyburn Library, Special Collections, Washington and Lee University.

Letter from W. Allen to George Washington Custis Lee, June 19, 1871, Leyburn Library, Special Collections, Washington and Lee University.

Letter from MaryAnna Randolph Custis Lee to Mildred Childe Lee, March 1, 1872, Virginia Historical Society.

Letter from George Washington Custis Lee to Charles C. Jones, May 6, 1872, Manuscript Collection, William R. Perkins Library, Duke University.

Letter from George Washington Custis Lee to Charles C. Jones, May 17, 1872, Manuscript Collection, William R. Perkins

Library, Duke University.

Letter from George Washington Custis Lee to S. W. Somerville, December 9, 1872, Leyburn Library, Special Collections, Washington and Lee University.

Letter from George Washington Custis Lee to M. R. Patrick, March 31, 1873, Leyburn Library, Special Collections, Washington and Lee University.

Letter from George Washington Custis Lee to Charles Marshall,August 4, 1873, Leyburn Library, Special Collections, Washington and Lee University.

Letter from George Washington Custis Lee to J. J. White, August 14, 1874, Leyburn Library, Special Collections, Washington and Lee University.

Letter from George Washington Custis Lee to Charles C. Jones, October 31, 1874, Manuscript Collection, William R. Perkins Library, Duke University.

Letter from William Henry Fitzhugh Lee to Mary Tabb Bolling Lee, November 17, 1874, Virginia Historical Society.

Letter from George Washington Custis Lee to J. William Jones, January 27, 1875, Museum of the Confederacy.

Letter from George Washington Custis Lee to J. J. White, July 26, 1875, Leyburn Library, Special Collections, Washington and Lee University.

Letter from George Washington Custis Lee to J. J. White, August 28, 1875, Leyburn Library, Special Collections, Washington and Lee University.

Letter from Henry A. Ward to George Washington Custis Lee, October 8, 1875, Leyburn Library, Special Collections, Washington and Lee University.

Letter from George Washington Custis Lee to George B. Purcell, October 25, 1875, Leyburn Library, Special Collections, Washington and Lee University.

Letter from George Washington Custis Lee to Henry A. Ward, November 17, 1875, Leyburn Library, Special Collections, Washington and Lee University.

Letter from Henry A. Ward to George Washington Custis Lee, November 28, 1875, Leyburn Library, Special Collections,

Washington and Lee University.

Letter from Henry A. Ward to George Washington Custis Lee, December 18, 1875, Leyburn Library, Special Collections, Washington and Lee University.

Letter from George Washington Custis Lee to J. William Jones, February 7, 1876, Museum of the Confederacy.

Letter from George Washington Custis Lee to J. William Jones, February 17, 1876, Museum of the Confederacy.

Letter from E. B. Kruttschnitt to George Washington Custis Lee, March 16, 1876, Leyburn Library, Special Collections, Washington and Lee University.

Letter from Henry A. Ward to George Washington Custis Lee, March 17, 1876, Leyburn Library, Special Collections, Washington and Lee University.

Telegram from Henry A. Ward to George Washington Custis Lee, April 14, 1876, Leyburn Library, Special Collections, Washington and Lee University.

Letter from George Washington Custis Lee to J. J. White, May 4, 1876, Leyburn Library, Special Collections, Washington and Lee University.

Letter from George Washington Custis Lee to Harry C. Hines, September 30, 1876, Leyburn Library, Special Collections, Washington and Lee University.

Letter from George Washington Custis Lee to Marshall MacDonald, November 25, 1876, Leyburn Library, Special Collections, Washington and Lee University.

Letter from George Washington Custis Lee to W. J. Walthall, April 20, 1877, Museum of the Confederacy.

Letter from George Washington Custis Lee to J. J. White, September 13, 1877, Leyburn Library, Special Collections, Washington and Lee University.

Letter from L. E. Hunt to George Washington Custis Lee, October 10, 1877, Leyburn Library, Special Collections, Washington and Lee University.

Letter from George Washington Custis Lee to Jefferson Davis, January 15, 1878, Museum of the Confederacy.

Letter from George Washington Custis Lee to Jefferson Davis,

February 26, 1878, Manuscript Collection, William R. Perkins Library, Duke University.

Letter from George Washington Custis Lee to Jefferson Davis, March 26, 1878, Manuscript Collection, William R. Perkins Library, Duke University.

Letter from George Washington Custis Lee to W. J. Walthall, April 11, 1878, Museum of the Confederacy.

Letter from George Washington Custis Lee to J. J. White, May 6, 1878, Leyburn Library, Special Collections, Washington and Lee University.

Letter from George Washington Custis Lee to J. J. White, October 8, 1878, Leyburn Library, Special Collections, Washington and Lee University.

Letter from George Washington Custis Lee to Miss Tunstall, November 8, 1878, Museum of the Confederacy.

Letter from George Washington Custis Lee to Emily V. Mason, n.d. Museum of the Confederacy.

Letter from George Washington Custis Lee to Jeremy F. Gilmer, January 30, 1880, Manuscript Collection, William R. Perkins Library, Duke University.

Letter from George Washington Custis Lee to Marshall MacDonald, January 30, 1880, Manuscript Collection, William R. Perkins Library, Duke University.

Letter from George Washington Custis Lee to Daniel Holt, April 20, 1881,

Manuscript Collection, William R. Perkins Library, Duke University.

Letter from George Washington Custis Lee to William Taylor Thom,August 6, 1881, Leyburn Library, Special Collections, Washington and Lee University.

Letter from George Washington Custis Lee to Arthur Gilman, June 10, 1882, Cambridge: The Houghton Library, Frederick Dearborn Collection Harvard University.

Letter from George Washington Custis Lee to George W. Bagby, January 26, 1883, Virginia Historical Society.

Letter from George Washington Custis Lee to George W. Bagby, January 26, 1883, Virginia Historical Society.

Letter from George Washington Custis Lee to George W. Bagby, June 12, 1883, Virginia Historical Society.

Letter from George Washington Custis Lee to Louisa Porter Gilmer Minis, December 11, 1883, Museum of the Confederacy.

Letter from George Washington Custis Lee to Isaac H. Carrington, February 12, 1884, Manuscript Collection, William R. Perkins Library, Duke University.

Letter from George Washington Custis Lee to Isaac H. Carrington, May 7, 1884, Manuscript Collection, William R. Perkins Library, Duke University.

Letter from George Washington Custis Lee to Emily V. Mason, June 14, 1884,Museum of the Confederacy.

Letter from George Washington Custis Lee to Emily V. Mason, July 1, 1884 Museum of the Confederacy.

Letter from George Washington Custis Lee to Marshall MacDonald, July 1, 1884, Manuscript Collection, William R. Perkins Library, Duke University.

Letter from George Washington Custis Lee to George W. Bagby, July 5, 1884, Virginia Historical Society.

Letter from George Washington Custis Lee to George W. Bagby, September 11, 1884, Virginia Historical Society.

Letter from George Washington Custis Lee to L. Q. C. Lamar, March 12, 1885 Museum of the Confederacy.

Letter from George Washington Custis Lee to Francis H. Smith, June 10, 1885, Virginia Military Institute Archives.

Letter from George Washington Custis Lee to Francis H. Smith, June 25, 1885, Virginia Military Institute Archives.

Letter from J. M. Allen to Francis H. Smith, June 29, 1885, Virginia Military Institute Archives.

Letter from George Washington Custis Lee to Isaac H. Carrington, January 25, 1886, Manuscript Collection, William R. Perkins Library, Duke University.

Letter from George Washington Custis Lee to Isaac H. Carrington, February 15, 1886, Manuscript Collection, William R. Perkins Library, Duke University.

Letter from George Washington Custis Lee to Isaac H. Carrington, March 4, 1886, Manuscript Collection, William R. Perkins

Library, Duke University.

Letter from George Washington Custis Lee to Francis H. Smith, May 4, 1886, Virginia Military Institute Archives.

Letter from George Washington Custis Lee to Francis H. Smith, May 7, 1887, Virginia Military Institute Archives.

Letter from George Washington Custis Lee to Marshall MacDonald, May 2, 1887, Manuscript Collection, William R. Perkins Library, Duke University.

Letter from George Washington Custis Lee to Francis H. Smith, June 23, 1887, Virginia Military Institute Archives.

Letter from George Washington Custis Lee to Francis H. Smith, March 22, 1888, Virginia Military Institute Archives.

Letter from George Washington Custis Lee to Francis H. Smith, June 7, 1888, Virginia Military Institute Archives.

Letter from George Washington Custis Lee to Jean Yeatman, March 11, 1889, Manuscript Collection, William R. Perkins Library, Duke University.

Letter from George Washington Custis Lee to Francis H. Smith, March 13, 1889, Virginia Military Institute Archives.

Letter from W. H. Winfree to Francis H. Smith, May 31, 1889, Virginia Military Institute Archives.

Letter from George Washington Custis Lee to Scott Shipp, February 4, 1890, Virginia Military Institute Archives.

Letter from George Washington Custis Lee to Scott Shipp, February 14, 1890, Virginia Military Institute Archives.

Letter from George Washington Custis Lee to Scott Shipp, March 7, 1890, Virginia Military Institute Archives.

Letter from George Washington Custis Lee to Emily V. Mason, May 5, 1890, Museum of the Confederacy.

Letter from George Washington Custis Lee to Scott Shipp, June 26, 1890, Virginia Military Institute Archives.

Letter from George Washington Custis Lee to Scott Shipp, October 13, 1890, Virginia Military Institute Archives.

Letter from George Washington Custis Lee to Scott Shipp, November 21, 1890, Virginia Military Institute Archives.

Letter from George Washington Custis Lee to Scott Shipp, April 29, 1891, Virginia Military Institute Archives.

Letter from George Washington Custis Lee to Scott Shipp, June 10, 1891, Virginia Military Institute Archives.

Letter from J. K. Edmonson to F. W. M. Holliday, June 19 1891, Manuscript Collection, William R. Perkins Library, Duke University.

Letter from George Washington Custis Lee to Scott Shipp, February 9, 1892, Virginia Military Institute Archives.

Letter from George Washington Custis Lee to Scott Shipp, March 21, 1892, Virginia Military Institute Archives.

Letter from George Washington Custis Lee to Scott Shipp, April 22, 1892, Virginia Military Institute Archives.

Letter from George Washington Custis Lee to Scott Shipp, June 6, 1892, Virginia Military Institute Archives.

Letter from George Washington Custis Lee to Mrs. Parke C. Bagby, January 8, 1893, Virginia Historical Society.

Letter from Robert E. Lee, Jr. to R.W. Hunter, February 19, 1893, Leyburn Library, Special Collections, Washington and Lee University.

Letter from George Washington Custis Lee to R.W. Hunter, February 20, 1893, Leyburn Library, Special Collections, Washington and Lee University.

Letter from George Washington Custis Lee to Scott Shipp, March 22, 1893, Virginia Military Institute Archives.

Letter from George Washington Custis Lee to James A. Harrison, August 31, 1893, Leyburn Library, Special Collections, Washington and Lee University.

Letter from Thomas E. Marshall, Jr. to Edmund R. Cocke, September 4, 1893, Leyburn Library, Special Collections, Washington and Lee University.

Letter from George Washington Custis Lee to Scott Shipp, November 9, 1893, [#1] Virginia Military Institute Archives.

Letter from George Washington Custis Lee to Scott Shipp, November 9, 1893, [#2] Virginia Military Institute Archives.

Letter from George Washington Custis Lee to Scott Shipp, November 14, 1893, Virginia Military Institute Archives.

Letter from George Washington Custis Lee to Thomas T. Munford, December 7, 1893, Manuscript Collection, William R. Perkins

Library, Duke University.

Letter from George Washington Custis Lee to Scott Shipp, November 2, 1894, Virginia Military Institute Archives.

Letter from George Washington Custis Lee to Scott Shipp, February 9, 1895, Virginia Military Institute Archives.

Letter from George Washington Custis Lee to Scott Shipp, May 16, 1895, Virginia Military Institute Archives.

Letter from George Washington Custis Lee to Scott Shipp, May 18, 1895, Virginia Military Institute Archives.

Letter from George Washington Custis Lee to Norvell Caskie Jones, August 29, 1895, Leyburn Library, Special Collections, Washington and Lee University.

Letter from George Washington Custis Lee to Bradley T. Johnson, September 20, 1895, Manuscript Collection, William R. Perkins Library, Duke University.

Letter from George Washington Custis Lee to the Board of Trustee of Washington and Lee University, May 6, 1896, Leyburn Library, Special Collections, Washington and Lee University.

Letter from George Washington Custis Lee to Scott Shipp, July 27, 1896, Virginia Military Institute Archives.

Letter from George Washington Custis Lee to the Board of Trustee of Washington and Lee University, December 29, 1896, Leyburn Library, Special Collections, Washington and Lee University.

Letter from Thomas E. Marshall, Jr. to H. E. Hyatt, May 31, 1897, Virginia Military Institute Archives.

Letter from Thomas E. Marshall, Jr. to Scott Shipp, June 22, 1897, Virginia Military Institute Archives.

Letter from George Washington Custis Lee to John L. Campbell, February 1, 1898, Leyburn Library, Special Collections, Washington and Lee University.

Letter from George Washington Custis Lee to John L. Campbell, February 11, 1898, Leyburn Library, Special Collections, Washington and Lee University.

Letter from George Washington Custis Lee to John L. Campbell, February 23, 1898, Leyburn Library, Special Collections, Washington and Lee University.

Letter from George Washington Custis Lee to J. W. Daniel, March

10, 1898, Manuscript Collection, William R. Perkins Library, Duke University.

Letter from George Washington Custis Lee to John L. Campbell, March 10, 1898, Leyburn Library, Special Collections, Washington and Lee University.

Letter from George Washington Custis Lee to John L. Campbell, July 21, 1899, Leyburn Library, Special Collections, Washington and Lee University.

Letter from George Washington Custis Lee to Robert E. Lee, Jr., January 4, 1900, Leyburn Library, Special Collections, Washington and Lee University.

Letter from George Washington Custis Lee to Mrs. P.T.[Jean] Yeatman, January 15, 1900, Manuscript Collection, William R. Perkins Library, Duke University.

Letter from John L. Campbell to George Washington Custis Lee, May 24, 1900, Leyburn Library, Special Collections, Washington and Lee University.

Letter from George Washington Custis Lee to John L. Campbell, May 28, 1900, Leyburn Library, Special Collections, Washington and Lee University.

Letter from George Washington Custis Lee to Joseph Rubinfine, January 7, 1901, Leyburn Library, Special Collections, Washington and Lee University.

Letter from George Washington Custis Lee to John L. Campbell, July 17, 1901, Leyburn Library, Special Collections, Washington and Lee University.

Letter from George Washington Custis Lee to John L. Campbell, April 21, 1902, Leyburn Library, Special Collections, Washington and Lee University.

Letter from George Washington Custis Lee to John L. Campbell, April 25, 1902, Leyburn Library, Special Collections, Washington and Lee University.

Letter from George Washington Custis Lee to John L. Campbell, July 16, 1902, Leyburn Library, Special Collections, Washington and Lee University.

Letter from George Washington Custis Lee to Mrs. P.T.[Jean] Yeatman, November 9, 1903, Manuscript Collection, William R.

Perkins Library, Duke University.

Letter from George Washington Custis Lee to John L. Campbell, February 22, 1904, Leyburn Library, Special Collections, Washington and Lee University.

Letter from George Washington Custis Lee to John L. Campbell, February 20, 1905, Leyburn Library, Special Collections, Washington and Lee University.

Letter from George Washington Custis Lee to Scott Shipp, March 30, 1905, Virginia Military Institute Archives.

Letter from George Washington Custis Lee to John L. Campbell, April 17, 1905, Leyburn Library, Special Collections, Washington and Lee University.

Letter from George Washington Custis Lee to Walter H. Taylor, May 4, 1905 Stratford, Virginia: Stratford Hall Library and Archives.

Letter from George Washington Custis Lee to the Librarian of the Virginia Military Institute, August 5, 1905, Virginia Military Institute Archives.

Letter from George Washington Custis Lee to John L. Campbell, June 25, 1906, Leyburn Library, Special Collections, Washington and Lee University.

Letter from George Washington Custis Lee to Mrs. P.T.[Jean] Yeatman, July 19,1906, Manuscript Collection, William R. Perkins Library, Duke University.

Letter from George Washington Custis Lee to John L. Campbell, January 28, 1907, Leyburn Library, Special Collections, Washington and Lee University.

Letter from George Washington Custis Lee to Mrs. Howard, February 7, 1907, Leyburn Library, Special Collections, Washington and Lee University.

Letter from George Washington Custis Lee to John L. Campbell, April 5, 1907, Leyburn Library, Special Collections, Washington and Lee University.

Letter from George Washington Custis Lee to Thomas T. Munford, September 19, 1907, Manuscript Collection, William R. Perkins Library, Duke University.

Letter from George Washington Custis Lee to David C. Humphreys

April 16, 1909, Leyburn Library, Special Collections, Washington and Lee University.

Letter from George Washington Custis Lee to John L. Campbell, May 29, 1911, Leyburn Library, Special Collections, Washington and Lee University.

Letter from George Washington Custis Lee to John L. Campbell, June 9, 1911, Leyburn Library, Special Collections, Washington and Lee University.

Letter from George Bolling Lee to James Lewis Howe, February 8, 1940, Leyburn Library, Special Collections, Washington and Lee University.

Letter from W.E. Dold to James Lewis Howe, April 24, 1941, Leyburn Library, Special Collections, Washington and Lee University.

Letter from W.E. Dold to James Lewis Howe, July 24, 1941, Leyburn Library, Special Collections, Washington and Lee University.

Index

CPSIA information can be obtained
at www.ICGtesting.com
Printed in the USA
BVHW03s1622310818
526170BV00013B/7/P